sendmail 8.13 Companion

Bryan Costales
with Gregory Neil Shapiro and Claus Aßmann
Edited by George Jansen

O'REILLY®
Beijing • Cambridge • Farnham • Köln • Paris • Sebastopol • Taipei • Tokyo

sendmail 8.13 Companion

by Bryan Costales with Gregory Neil Shapiro and Claus Aßmann

Printed in the United States of America.

Published by O'Reilly Media, Inc., 1005 Gravenstein Highway North, Sebastopol, CA 95472.

O'Reilly books may be purchased for educational, business, or sales promotional use. Online editions are also available for most titles (*safari.oreilly.com*). For more information, contact our corporate/institutional sales department: (800) 998-9938 or *corporate@oreilly.com*.

Editor: Tatiana Apandi Diaz

Technical Editor: George Jansen

Production Editor: Mary Brady

Cover Designer: Ellie Volckhausen

Interior Designer: David Futato

Printing History:

September 2004: First Edition.

ISBN: 0-596-00845-7
[M]

This book is dedicated to

The Make Believe Sailors

A San Francisco Bay Area Writing Group

Table of Contents

Preface

Why This Companion Book

A separate book, containing mostly tables, proved a valuable companion to the second edition of *sendmail* (O'Reilly). It facilitated the easy lookup of options, macros, and other features, and aided in the day-to-day management of the *sendmail* program. Just as that companion book proved a valuable enhancement of the second edition, so, too, will this book prove an enhancement of the third.

This book also documents the improvements that have been added to the new V8.13 *sendmail*. Thus, all tables in this book include items from both the third edition and V8.13 *sendmail*. We hope that this combination will prove more valuable by synergy than would either in a standalone volume.

Why V8.13 sendmail

V8.12 *sendmail* contained the germ of many possible future enhancements (_FFR sections), which, in practice, proved very useful. In order to make those enhancements available for use, many of the _FFR sections have been converted into release code and have been folded into the new, officially supported release of V8.13. During that process, new spam techniques were detected, and support for rejecting that spam was also added.

Organization

We've divided this book into twenty-five chapters that parallel the chapters in the third edition of *sendmail* (O'Reilly). That way, if you are interested in the options introduced in V8.13, for example, you can simply turn to Chapter 24—the chapter that covers options in both books.

Audience and Assumptions

This book is primarily intended for users of the third edition of the *sendmail* book who are upgrading to V8.13 and need information about that new release. But the tables in this book will prove useful even to those users who don't intend to upgrade right away.

Unix and sendmail Versions

For the most part, we illustrate *sendmail* under BSD Unix and its variants (such as FreeBSD). But where AT&T System V (SysV) differs (such as Sun's Solaris 2.*x*), we illustrate those differences.

Although, our primary focus throughout this companion book is on V8.13 *sendmail*, we also discuss V8.12 and earlier versions when necessary.

Conventions Used in This Handbook

The following typographic conventions are used in this book:

Italic
: Used for names, including pathnames, filenames, program and command names, usernames, hostnames, machine names, and mailing-list names, as well as for mail addresses. Italics are also used to indicate that part of a program's output is not specific. For example, "`error:` *number or file*" indicates that the error will be shown either as a number or as a filename. In addition, italics are used to emphasize new terms and concepts when they are introduced.

`Constant Width`
: Used in examples to show the contents of files or the output from commands. This includes examples from the configuration file, or other files, such as message files, shell scripts, or C-language program source. Constant-width text is quoted only when it is necessary to show enclosed space; such as, the five-character "`From `" header.

: Single characters, symbolic expressions, and command-line switches are always shown in constant-width font. For instance, the `o` option illustrates a single character, the rule `$-` illustrates a symbolic expression, and `-d` illustrates a command-line switch.

`Constant Width Italic`
: Used in examples and text to show variables for which a context-specific substitution should be made. (The variable *`filename`*, for example, would be replaced by some actual filename.)

`Constant Bold`

Used in examples to show commands or other text that is to be typed literally by the user. For example, the phrase **`cat /var/run/sendmail.pid`** means the user should type "cat /var/run/sendmail.pid" exactly as it appears in the text or example.

[V8.13] and [3ed] symbols

Placed with section cross references to indicate whether the cross reference is referring to the *sendmail 8.13 Companion* ([V8.13]) or *sendmail*, Third Edition ([3ed]).

Using Code Examples

This book is here to help you get your job done. In general, you may use the code in this book in your programs and documentation. You do not need to contact us for permission unless you're reproducing a significant portion of the code. For example, writing a program that uses several chunks of code from this book does not require permission. Selling or distributing a CD-ROM of examples from O'Reilly books does require permission. Answering a question by citing this book and quoting example code does not require permission. Incorporating a significant amount of example code from this book into your product's documentation does require permission.

We appreciate, but do not require, attribution. An attribution usually includes the title, author, publisher, and ISBN. For example: "*sendmail 8.13 Companion*, by Bryan Costales with Claus Aßmann and Gregory Neil Shapiro, Copyright 2004 O'Reilly Media, Inc., 0-596-00845-7."

If you feel your use of code examples falls outside fair use or the permission given above, feel free to contact us at *permissions@oreilly.com*.

How to Contact Us

Please address comments and questions concerning this book to the publisher:

O'Reilly Media, Inc.
1005 Gravenstein Highway North
Sebastopol, CA 95472
(800) 998-9938 (in the United States or Canada)
(707) 829-0515 (international or local)
(707) 829-0104 (fax)

We have a web page for this book, where we list errata, examples, and any additional information. You can access this page at:

http://www.oreilly.com/catalog/sendmailcomp

To comment or ask technical questions about this book, send email to:

bookquestions@oreilly.com

For more information about our books, conferences, Resource Centers, and the O'Reilly Network, see our web site at:

http://www.oreilly.com

Safari Enabled

When you see the Safari® Enabled icon on the back cover of your favorite technology book, that means the book is available online through the O'Reilly Network Safari Bookshelf.

Safari offers a solution that's better than e-books. It's a virtual library that lets you easily search thousands of top technology books, cut and paste code samples, download chapters, and find quick answers when you need the most accurate, current information.

Try it for free at *http://safari.oreilly.com*.

Acknowledgments

Special thanks must go to George Jansen, that superbly nitpicky editor who helped mold this book into its final, and so-well-written form.

Thanks to Tatiana Apandi Diaz, our editor at O'Reilly; David Chu, our editorial assistant; Mary Brady, our production editor; Sarah Sherman, who worked on the proofread; and Johnna Van Hoose Dinse, who wrote the index.

CHAPTER 1

Release Notes

Each release of *sendmail* is packaged with a file called *RELEASE_NOTES*, located in the top level of the source distribution. The *RELEASE_NOTES* file itemizes new features that have been added to each particular version of *sendmail* since Version 8.1 (released in 1993). This file is very complete but, on the downside, can be difficult to parse.

In this chapter, we first show you the parts of a *RELEASE_NOTES* file, then we provide the code for a short program that makes reading the *RELEASE_NOTES* file easier.

1.1 Parts of RELEASE_NOTES

Basically, the *RELEASE_NOTES* file is divided into sections, each of which deals with a separate release of *sendmail*. These sections are left-justified in the file. Each begins with a single line that contains the version number of the *sendmail* release, followed by a slash, followed by the version number of the configuration file release, followed by the date of the release. For example:

```
8.13.0/8.13.0   2004/06/20
```

Here, the first release of the V8.13 series (8.13.0) is indicated. The release of *sendmail* and its configuration file are the same. The date of the release is in the form year (first), month, and day.

Each such release section is then followed by indented sections that document a change in the *sendmail* binary. Some indented sections are prefixed with a keyword and colon. For the most part, those keyword sections describe a change in something other than the binary* and can look like this, for example:

```
SECURITY: Some security matter was fixed, and the description of
        that fix will appear here.
```

* But the SECURITY keyword can, and generally does, describe the binary too.

```
This item describes a change made to the sendmail binary.
LIBMILTER: This documents a change made to one of the files in the
        libmilter directory.
```

The keywords and the meaning of each is shown in Table 1-1.

Table 1-1. RELEASE_NOTES file keywords

Keyword	Description
`SECURITY:`	This type of information is usually very important. You should read it first, as it contains information about a security matter and may involve some vital action.
`NOTICE:`	This documents something you need to be aware of, usually an important change that might otherwise be overlooked.
none	This item documents the *sendmail* binary.
`CONFIG:`	A change in the configuration file (located in the *cf* directory).
`CONTRIB:`	A change in one of the user-contributed programs (located in the *contrib* directory).
`DEVTOOLS:`	A change in how things are built (located in the *devtools* directory).
`LIBMILTER:`	A change in the Milter library (located in the *libmilter* directory).
`LIBSM:`	A change in the *sendmail* library (located in the *libsm* directory).
`LIBSMDB:`	A change in the database library (located in the *libsmdb* directory).
`LIBSMUTIL:`	A change in the *sendmail* utilities library (located in the *libsmutil* directory).
`DOC:`	These documents are updated each release, so there is normally no need to indicate changes here. (See the *doc* directory.)
`EDITMAP:`	A change in the *editmap*(8) program or its manual (located in the *editmap* directory).
`MAIL.LOCAL:`	A change in the *mail.local*(8) program or its manual (located in the *mail.local* directory).
`MAILSTATS:`	A change in the *mailstats*(8) program or its manual (located in the *mailstats* directory).
`MAKEMAP:`	A change in the *makemap*(8) program or its manual (located in the *makemap* directory).
`PRALIASES:`	A change in the *praliases*(8) program or its manual (located in the *praliases* directory).
`RMAIL:`	A change in the *rmail*(8) program or its manual (located in the *rmail* directory).
`SMRSH:`	A change in the *smrsh*(8) program or its manual (located in the *smrsh* directory).
`VACATION:`	A change in the *vacation*(1) program or its manual (located in the *vacation* directory).
`New Files:`	The path to brand new files.
`Renamed Files:`	The old and new names for renamed files.
`Copied Files:`	A new file has been added by copying an existing file.
`Deleted Files:`	Obsolete files that have been removed.
`Changed Files:`	Files whose attributes have changed (such as file permissions).

1.2 A Useful Program

The *rnote* program is a simple way to keep track of which version did what. Just compile it and run:

```
% rnote RELEASE_NOTES | more
```

The program itself is written in C and should compile on most systems. The numbers along the left are for descriptive purposes and are not a part of the code.

```
 1  # include <stdio.h>
 2  # include <ctype.h>
 3  # include <stdlib.h>
 4  # include <strings.h>
 5  # include <errno.h>
 6
 7  int
 8  main(int argc, char **argv)
 9  {
10          char *c, *cp, *prefix = NULL;
11          FILE *fp;
12          char buf[BUFSIZ];
13
14          if (argc != 2)
15          {
16                  (void) printf("Usage: rnote RELEASE_NOTES\n");
17                  exit(EINVAL);
18          }
19
20          if ((fp = fopen(argv[1], "r")) == NULL)
21          {
22                  (void) fprintf(stderr, "rnote: %s: %s\n",
23                          argv[1], strerror(errno));
24                  (void) exit(errno);
25          }
26
27          while ((cp = fgets(buf, BUFSIZ, fp)) != NULL)
28          {
29                  if (isdigit((int)*cp))
30                  {
31                          if ((c = strchr(cp, '/')) != NULL)
32                          {
33                                  *c = '\0';
34                                  if (prefix != NULL)
35                                          (void) free(prefix);
36                                  prefix = strdup(cp);
37                                  continue;
38                          }
39                  }
40                  if (prefix == NULL)
41                          continue;
42
43                  (void) printf("%-7.7s%s", prefix, cp);
44          }
45          if (ferror(fp))
46          {
47                  (void) fprintf(stderr, "rnote: %s: %s\n",
48                          argv[1], strerror(errno));
49                  (void) exit(errno);
50          }
51          return 0;
52  }
```

After opening the *RELEASE_NOTES* file (*line 20*), it is read in a loop, one line at a time (*line 27*). If a line of the file begins with a digit (*line 29*), it is presumed to be a release number (such as `8.12.11`). Everything following the first slash character is removed (*line 33*), and the result becomes the new prefix (*line 36*) for all following file lines. Each line of the file is then prefixed with the release that created it and printed (*line 43*).

By piping the output of this program through a program such as *more*(1) or *less*(1), you may search for such things as new macros or changes to *libmilter*. We leave as an exercise to the reader the option to create improvements in, or additions to, this program.

CHAPTER 2

Build and Install sendmail

2.1 What's New As of V8.13

V8.12.6 *sendmail* introduced one new *Build* m4-macro that arrived too late for inclusion in the third edition of the *sendmail* book: the `confMSP_STFILE` *Build* m4-macro (§2.1.1[V8.13]).

2.1.1 confMSP_STFILE Build m4-macro

Beginning with V8.12.6 *sendmail*, the `confMSP_STFILE` *Build* macro may be used to define a new name under which the statistics file (§24.9.106[3ed]) used by the MSP (§2.6.2.4[3ed]) invocation of *sendmail* can be installed. It is used like this:

```
define(`confMSP_STFILE´, `mspstats´)
```

Here, a statistics file with the new name `mspstats` will be installed in the default directory */var/spool/clientmqueue* (unless you redefine the default directory using the `confMSP_QUEUE_DIR` (§2.8.37[3ed]) *Build* macro). The default name for this statistics file is *sm-client.st*.

Note that if you rename this MSP statistics file, you will also have to redefine the `StatusFile` option (§24.9.106[3ed]) in the *submit.cf* file (§2.6.2.4[3ed]) to reflect the new name. The proper way to modify that file is to first edit the *cf/cf/submit.mc* file in the source distribution and then to regenerate a new *submit.cf* file, like this:

```
# cd cf/cf
... edit the submit.mc file here
# make install-submit-cf
... the submit.cf file is recreated and installed
```

Or, run `make submit.cf` rather than `make install-submit-cf` if you want to check the result before installation.

See also the *mailstats* program and its `-c` command-line switch (§5.4.4.1[3ed]), which is used to print the contents of this statistics file.

2.2 Useful Tables

This section contains two tables of information that are useful for building and installing *sendmail*:

- Table 2-1 (§2.2.1[V8.13]) shows the directories and files that will populate the source directory after you extract the *sendmail* source.
- Table 2-2 (§2.2.2[V8.13]) shows the *m4* directives that determine how the *sendmail* program (and its companion programs) will be built.

2.2.1 The sendmail Source Directory

The files and directories that appear after you unpack *sendmail* into its source directory are listed in Table 2-1. They are described in detail in the sections indicated.

Table 2-1. Files and directories in the distribution directory

File/Directory	sendmail text reference	Description
Build	§2.2.1.1[3ed]	A top-level *Build* script
CACerts	[V8.13]	A list of CA certificates used by members of the sendmail consortium
cf	§4.2[3ed]	Top of the tree for building a configuration file
contrib	§2.2.1.2[3ed]	Unsupported, user-contributed software
devtools	§2.2.1.3[3ed]	Top of the tree for *Build* support tools
doc	§2.2.1.4[3ed]	Current and background documentation
editmap	§5.2[3ed]	Edit database file entries
FAQ		See *http://www.sendmail.org/faq/*
include	§2.2.1.5[3ed]	Header files common to all programs
INSTALL	§2.2.1.6[3ed]	An overview of how to build and install *sendmail*
KNOWNBUGS	§2.2.1.7[3ed]	Tough problems that remain unfixed
libmilter	§2.2.1.8[3ed]	Library used to create a multithreaded filter
libsm	§2.2.1.9[3ed]	Library routines used to build *sendmail* and its companion programs
libsmdb	§2.2.1.10[3ed]	Database library used by some programs
libsmutil	§2.2.1.11[3ed]	A library of utilities used by all programs
LICENSE	§2.2.1.12[3ed]	Terms for using the source and programs
mail.local	§5.3[3ed]	Source tree for the *mail.local* program
mailstats	§5.4[3ed]	Source tree for the *mailstats* program
Makefile	§2.2.1.13[3ed]	A top-level way to build everything
makemap	§5.5[3ed]	Source tree for the *makemap* program
PGPKEYS	§2.2.1.14[3ed]	Keys to validate the *sendmail* source distribution
praliases	§5.6[3ed]	Source tree for the *praliases* program

Table 2-1. Files and directories in the distribution directory (continued)

File/Directory	sendmail text reference	Description
README	§2.2.1.15[3ed]	The top-level guide to what is where
RELEASE_NOTES	§2.2.1.16[3ed]	A comprehensive history of *sendmail* changes
rmail	§5.7[3ed]	Source tree for the *rmail* program
sendmail	§2.2[3ed]	Source tree for the *sendmail* program
smrsh	§5.8[3ed]	Source tree for the *smrsh* program
test	§2.2.1.17[3ed]	Source tree for some security checks
vacation	§5.9[3ed]	Source tree for the *vacation* program

2.2.2 Build m4 Directives

The *Build* program builds using the directives that are shown in Table 2-2 and described in the sections indicated. These directives are placed into a *Build*-input file, the name of which is specified by the -f switch to *Build*. One part of such a *Build*-input file might look like this:

```
define(`confENVDEF´, `-DMATCHGECOS=0´)
APPENDDEF(`confMAPDEF´, `-DNIS´)
```

Note that most macros are defined with the define *m4* directive (as in the first line of the example above), while a few others are standalone. Those that stand alone (as in the second line of the example above) are indicated in the table with trailing parentheses.

If an argument to define or APPENDDEF contains a comma, you must double the half-quotes surrounding it—for example:

```
define(`confDAEMON_OPTIONS´, ``Name=MTA-v4, Family=inet´´)
```

Here, the second argument to define contains a comma, so the entire second argument must begin with two left half-quotes and end with two right half-quotes.

Table 2-2. Build m4 directives

Directive	sendmail text reference	Description
APPENDDEF()	§2.8.1[3ed]	Append to an existing definition
confBEFORE	§2.8.2[3ed]	Establish files before compiling
confBLDVARIANT	§2.8.3[3ed]	Controls variations on objects
confBUILDBIN	§2.8.4[3ed]	Location of *devtools/bin*
confCC	§2.8.5[3ed]	The compiler with which to build *sendmail*
confCCOPTS	§2.8.6[3ed]	Command-line switches to pass to the compiler
confCOPY	§2.8.8[3ed]	The copy command to use
confDEPEND_TYPE	§2.8.9[3ed]	How to build *Makefile* dependencies

Table 2-2. Build m4 directives (continued)

Directive	sendmail text reference	Description
confDEPLIBS	§2.8.10[3ed]	Shared object dependencies
confDONT_INSTALL_CATMAN	§2.8.11[3ed]	Don't install preformatted manual pages
confEBINDIR	§2.8.12[3ed]	Bin directory for *mail.local* and *smrsh*
confENVDEF	§2.8.13[3ed]	Pass -D switches during compilation
conf_prog_ENVDEF	§2.8.13[3ed]	Pass -D switches during compilation (Program specific)
confFORCE_RMAIL	§2.8.14[3ed]	Install the *rmail* program no matter what
confGBIN...	§2.8.15[3ed]	The set-group-id settings
confHFDIR	§2.8.16[3ed]	Where to install the *sendmail* help file
confHFFILE	§2.8.17[3ed]	The name of the *sendmail* help file
confINCDIRS	§2.8.18[3ed]	Compiler -I switches
confINC...	§2.8.19[3ed]	Permissions and locations for installed `#include` files
confINSTALL	§2.8.20[3ed]	Program to install programs and files
confINSTALL_RAWMAN	§2.8.21[3ed]	Install unformatted manuals
confLD	§2.8.22[3ed]	The linker to use
confLDOPTS	§2.8.23[3ed]	Linker options
confLIB...	§2.8.25[3ed]	Location and modes for installed library files
confLIBDIRS	§2.8.26[3ed]	Linker -L switches
confLIBS	§2.8.27[3ed]	Linker -l libraries
conf_prog_LIBS	§2.8.27[3ed]	Linker -l libraries
confLIBSEARCH	§2.8.28[3ed]	Automatic library search
confLIBSEARCHPATH	§2.8.29[3ed]	Paths to search for libraries
confLINKS	§2.8.32[3ed]	What to link to *sendmail*
confLN	§2.8.30[3ed]	Program to link files
confLNOPTS	§2.8.31[3ed]	Switches for the program to link files
confMAN...	§2.8.33[3ed]	How to install manual pages
confMAPDEF	§2.8.34[3ed]	Which database libraries to use
confMBIN...	§2.8.35[3ed]	Where and how to install *sendmail*
confMSPQOWN	§2.8.36[3ed]	Owner of the MSP queue
confMSP_QUEUE_DIR	§2.8.37[3ed]	Location of the MSP queue
confMSP_STFILE	§2.1.1[V8.13]	Location of the MSP statistics file
confNO_HELPFILE_INSTALL	§2.8.40[3ed]	Prevent installation of the *helpfile*
confNO_MAN_BUILD	§2.8.41[3ed]	Prevent formatting of manuals
confNO_MAN_INSTALL	§2.8.42[3ed]	Prevent installation of manuals
confNO_STATISTICS_INSTALL	§2.8.43[3ed]	Prevent installation of the *statistics* file
confNROFF	§2.8.33.5[3ed]	Program to format the manual pages

Table 2-2. Build m4 directives (continued)

Directive	sendmail text reference	Description
confOBJADD	§2.8.44[3ed]	Extra *.o* files to be linked in all programs
confOPTIMIZE	§2.8.45[3ed]	How to optimize the compile
confRANLIB	§2.8.46[3ed]	The *ranlib* program for library archive files
confRANLIBOPTS	§2.8.47[3ed]	Arguments to give the *ranlib* program
confREQUIRE_LIBSM	§2.8.48[3ed]	Define if *libsm* is required
confSBINDIR	§2.8.49[3ed]	Root-oriented program directory
confSBINGRP	§2.8.50[3ed]	Group for set-user-id programs
confSBINMODE	§2.8.51[3ed]	Permissions for set-user-id programs
confSBINOWN	§2.8.52[3ed]	Owner for set-user-id programs
confSHAREDLIB...	§2.8.53[3ed]	Shared library definitions
confSHELL	§2.8.54[3ed]	`SHELL=` for Makefile
confSM_OS_HEADER	§2.8.55[3ed]	Platform-specific `#include` file
confSMOBJADD	§2.8.56[3ed]	Extra *.o* files to be linked in *sendmail*
confSMSRCADD	§2.8.57[3ed]	Source *.c* files corresponding to `confSMOBJADD`
confSONAME	§2.8.58[3ed]	Shared object ID flag
conf_prog_SRCADD	§2.8.60[3ed]	Extra *.o* files to be linked per program
conf_prog_OBJADD	§2.8.59[3ed]	*.c* files corresponding to `conf_prog_OBJADD`
confSRCADD	§2.8.60[3ed]	Source for `confOBJADD` files
confSRCDIR	§2.8.61[3ed]	Location of *sendmail* source
confSTDIOTYPE	§2.8.62[3ed]	Use `torek` for buffered file I/O (V8.10 and earlier)
confSTDIR	§2.8.63[3ed]	Location of the *statistics* file
confSTFILE	§2.8.64[3ed]	Name of the *statistics* file
confSTMODE	§2.8.64[3ed]	Name of the *statistics* file
confSTRIP	§2.8.65[3ed]	Name of the program to strip the binary
confSTRIPOPTS	§2.8.66[3ed]	Command-line arguments for the strip program
confUBINDIR	§2.8.67[3ed]	Location of user executables
confUBINGRP	§2.8.68[3ed]	Group for user executables
confUBINMODE	§2.8.69[3ed]	Permissions for user executables
confUBINOWN	§2.8.70[3ed]	Ownership of user executables
PREPENDDEF( )	§2.8.71[3ed]	Prepend to an existing definition

CHAPTER 3

Tune sendmail with Compile-Time Macros

For most users, the default *sendmail* that is produced by running *Build* is perfectly suitable. For others, however, support for certain desirable features—such as hesiod, LDAP, or NIS—will have to be added. The open source distribution of *sendmail* has many such support items that you can include or exclude from your compiled binary using compile-time macros.

3.1 What's New with V8.13

V8.13 has introduced six new compile-time macros:

- The new SOCKETMAP compile-time macro enables use of the new socket database-map type (§3.1.1[V8.13]).
- The new SM_CONF_LDAP_INITIALIZE compile-time macro (§3.1.2[V8.13]) if set, declares that the ldap_initialize(3) routine exists in your LDAP library.
- The new NEEDINTERRNO compile-time macro, if set, says that errno is not declared in your system's *errno.h* file.
- The new SM_CONF_POLL compile-time macro causes poll(2) to be used instead of select(2) in the Milter library.
- The new HASCLOSEFROM compile-time macro may be defined if your system has the closefrom(3) C-library function.
- The new HASFDWALK compile-time macro may be defined if your system has the fdwalk(3) C-library function.

3.1.1 The SOCKETMAP Compile-Time Macro

The SOCKETMAP compile-time macro enables use of the new socket database-map type (§23.1.5[V8.13]). Define SOCKETMAP inside your *Build m4* file with a line like this:

```
APPENDDEF(`confMAPDEF', `-DSOCKETMAP')
```

If you use a vendor supplied *sendmail* program, you may check to see whether it includes SOCKETMAP support by running a command like the following:

```
% /usr/sbin/sendmail -bt -d0.4 < /dev/null | grep SOCKETMAP
```

If a line of text is printed containing SOCKETMAP, you indeed have support for it. If not, you will either need to contact your vendor or download and build open source *sendmail*.

3.1.2 The SM_CONF_LDAP_INITIALIZE Compile-Time Macro

When *sendmail* is built with LDAPMAP defined (§3.4.19[3ed]), LDAP database-maps are available for use. If the LDAP library contains an `ldap_initialize()` routine, and if this SM_CONF_LDAP_INITIALIZE macro is defined, `ldap_initialize()` is called if your LDAP server supports direct use of URIs.

Note that LDAP URIs can still be used even if SM_CONF_LDAP_INITIALIZE is not set, but the `scheme://` in (`scheme://host:port/...`) is ignored. Therefore, if SM_CONF_LDAP_INITIALIZE is not available, the scheme `ldap://` is always used, but the schemes `ldaps://` and `ldapi://`, if used, may result in an error.

For most LDAP libraries, SM_CONF_LDAP_INITIALIZE will be set properly for you.* But in the event it is improperly set, you may define it with the following and then rebuild *sendmail*:

```
APPENDDEF(`conf_libsm_ENVDEF', `-DSM_CONF_LDAP_INITIALIZE')
```

3.2 A Useful Table

In Table 3-1, we list all the compile-time macros that are available as of V8.13 *sendmail*. See Table 3-2[3ed] in §3.2[3ed] for a full description of each, including how each is used to port, tune, or debug *sendmail*.

Table 3-1. Define macros for compiling sendmail

Compile-time macro	sendmail text reference	Description
ARBPTR_T	§3.4.68[3ed]	How to cast an arbitrary pointer
AUTO_NIS_ALIASES	§3.4.1[3ed]	Add fallback alias techniques
BROKEN_RES_SEARCH	§3.4.17[3ed]	Broken resolver fix (e.g., Ultrix)
BSD4_3	§3.4.2[3ed]	BSD 4.3–style signal handling
BSD4_4	§3.4.3[3ed]	Compile for BSD 4.4 Unix

* It is automatically defined if LDAP_OPT_URI is defined by the LDAP include files, which is how OpenLDAP implements `ldap_initialize()`.

Table 3-1. Define macros for compiling sendmail (continued)

Compile-time macro	sendmail text reference	Description
DATA_PROGRESS_TIMEOUT	§3.4.4[3ed]	Timeout inbound DATA phase
DNSMAP	§3.4.5[3ed]	Enable use of dns databases
DSN	§3.4.6[3ed]	Support DSN
EGD	§3.4.7[3ed]	Enable use of EGD
ERRLIST_PREDEFINED	§3.4.8[3ed]	Correct sys_errlist types
FAST_PID_RECYCLE	§3.4.9[3ed]	Quick reuse of pids
FFR...	§3.4.10[3ed]	Try using future features
FORK	§3.4.11[3ed]	The type of fork(5) to use
GIDSET_T	§3.4.68[3ed]	Second argument to getgroups(2)
HAS...	§3.4.12[3ed]	Has specific system call support
HESIOD	§3.4.13[3ed]	Support hesiod database-maps
HES_GETMAILHOST	§3.4.14[3ed]	Use hesiod hes_getmailhost(3)
IDENTPROTO	§3.4.15[3ed]	See Timeout.ident (§24.9.109.13)
IP_SRCROUTE	§3.4.16[3ed]	Add IP source routing to $_
...IS_BROKEN	§3.4.17[3ed]	Things that can be broken
LA_TYPE	§3.4.18[3ed]	Define load-average support
LDAPMAP	§3.4.19[3ed]	Enable use of LDAP databases
LOG	§3.4.20[3ed]	Perform logging
MAP_NSD	§3.4.28[3ed]	Support Irix nsd maps
MAP_REGEX	§3.4.29[3ed]	Support regular expression maps
MATCHGECOS	§3.4.21[3ed]	Support fuzzy name matching
MAX...	§3.4.22[3ed]	Redefine maximums
MEMCHUNKSIZE	§3.4.23[3ed]	Specify memory malloc size
MILTER	§3.4.24[3ed]	Enable the X config command
MIME7TO8	§3.4.25[3ed]	Support MIME 7- to 8-bit
MIME8TO7	§3.4.26[3ed]	Support MIME 8- to 7-bit
NAMED_BIND	§3.4.27[3ed]	Support DNS
NDBM	§3.4.30[3ed]	Support Unix ndbm(3) maps
NEED...	§3.4.31[3ed]	Something amiss with your OS?
NET...	§3.4.32[3ed]	Select network type
NETINFO	§3.4.33[3ed]	Support NeXT netinfo(3) maps
NEWDB	§3.4.34[3ed]	Support Berkeley db(3) maps
NIS	§3.4.35[3ed]	Support NIS maps
NISPLUS	§3.4.36[3ed]	Support NISPLUS maps
NOFTRUNCATE	§3.4.37[3ed]	Lack ftruncate(2) support

Table 3-1. Define macros for compiling sendmail (continued)

Compile-time macro	sendmail text reference	Description
NO_GROUP_SET	§3.4.38[3ed]	Prevent multigroup file access
NOTUNIX	§3.4.39[3ed]	Exclude "From" line support
_PATH...	§3.4.40[3ed]	Hardcode paths inside *sendmail*
PH_MAP	§3.4.41[3ed]	Support for PH maps
PICKY_HELO_CHECK	§3.4.42[3ed]	Become picky about HELO
PIPELINING	§3.4.43[3ed]	Enable PIPELINING extension
PSBUFSIZ	§3.4.44[3ed]	Size of `prescan()` buffer
QUEUE	§3.4.45[3ed]	Enable queueing (prior to V8.12)
QUEUESEGSIZE	§3.4.46[3ed]	Amount to grow queue work list
REQUIRES_DIR_FSYNC	§3.4.47[3ed]	`fsync(2)` for directory updates
SAFENFSPATHCONF	§3.4.17[3ed]	`pathconf(2)` is broken
SASL	§3.4.48[3ed]	Support AUTH (V8.10 and above)
SCANF	§3.4.49[3ed]	Support `scanf(3)` with `F` command
SECUREWARE	§3.4.50[3ed]	Support SecureWare C2 security
SFS_TYPE	§3.4.51[3ed]	How to determine free disk space
SHARE_V1	§3.4.52[3ed]	Support for the fair share scheduler
SIOCGIFCONF_IS_BROKEN	§3.4.17[3ed]	SIOCGIFCONF `ioctl(2)` is broken
SIOCGIFNUM_IS_BROKEN	§3.4.17[3ed]	SIOCGIFNUM `ioctl(2)` is broken
SLEEP_T	§3.4.68[3ed]	Type of return value for `sleep(2)`
SM_...	§3.4.53[3ed]	*sendmail* porting settings (V8.12 and above)
SM_HEAP_CHECK	§3.4.54[3ed]	Memory-leak detection (V8.12 and above)
SM_CONF_SHM	§3.4.55[3ed]	Use shared memory (V8.12 and above)
SM_CONF_LDAP_INITIALIZE	§3.1.2[V8.13]	The `ldap_initialize(3)` routine is available in the LDAP library (V8.13 and above)
SMTP	§3.4.56[3ed]	Enable SMTP (prior to V8.12)
SMTPDEBUG	§3.4.57[3ed]	Enable remote debugging
SMTPLINELIM	§3.4.58[3ed]	Default for obsolete `F=L` flag
SOCKADDR_LEN_T	§3.4.68[3ed]	`accept(2)`'s 3rd argument type
SOCKOPT_LEN_T	§3.4.68[3ed]	`getsockopt(2)`'s 5th arg type
SPT_TYPE	§3.4.59[3ed]	Process title support
STARTTLS	§3.4.60[3ed]	Enable TLS (V8.11 and above)
SUID_ROOT_FILES_OK	§3.4.61[3ed]	Allow root delivery to files
SYSLOG_BUFSIZE	§3.4.62[3ed]	Limit `syslog(3)` buffer size
SYSTEM5	§3.4.63[3ed]	Support SysV-derived machines
SYS5SIGNALS	§3.4.63[3ed]	Use SysV-style signals
TCPWRAPPERS	§3.4.64[3ed]	Use *libwrap.a* (V8.8 and above)

Table 3-1. Define macros for compiling sendmail (continued)

Compile-time macro	sendmail text reference	Description
TLS_NO_RSA	§3.4.65[3ed]	Turn off RSA (V8.12 and above)
TOBUFSIZE	§3.4.66[3ed]	Set buffer for recipient list
TTYNAME	§3.4.67[3ed]	Set $y to tty name (obsolete)
...T	§3.4.68[3ed]	The types returned by functions
UDB_DEFAULT_SPEC	§3.4.69[3ed]	Default User Database location
USE_DOUBLE_FORK	§3.4.70[3ed]	Fork twice (V8.12 and above)
USE_ENVIRON	§3.4.71[3ed]	Use environ (V8.12 and above)
USING_NETSCAPE_LDAP	§3.4.72[3ed]	Netscape LDAP (V8.10 and above)
USERDB	§3.4.73[3ed]	Support the User Database
USESETEUID	§3.4.74[3ed]	Support seteuid(2) changes
WILDCARD_SHELL	§3.4.75[3ed]	Redefine wild card shell
XDEBUG	§3.4.76[3ed]	Support sanity checks

CHAPTER 4

Configure sendmail.cf with m4

In the *cf* subdirectory of the V8 *sendmail* source distribution, you will find the file *README*. It contains easy-to-understand, step-by-step instructions that will allow you to create a custom configuration file for your site. This chapter supplements that file.

4.1 What's New with V8.13

Three new *mc* configuration macros have been introduced (which correspond to three new *sendmail* configuration file options):

- The new `confREJECT_LOG_INTERVAL` *mc* macro (§4.1.1[V8.13]) sets the new `RejectLogInterval` option (§24.1.11[V8.13]). It specifies how often a message advising that connections are still being refused should be logged.
- The new `confREQUIRES_DIR_FSYNC` *mc* macro (§4.1.2[V8.13]) sets the new `RequiresDirfsync` option (§24.1.12[V8.13]). It causes *sendmail* to change the effect if the compile-time flag `REQUIRES_DIR_FSYNC` (§3.4.47[3ed]) at runtime.
- The new `confCONNECTION_RATE_WINDOW_SIZE` *mc* macro (§4.1.3[V8.13]) sets the new `ConnectionRateWindowSize` option (§24.1.13[V8.13]). It defines the window of time over which a count of the number of connections is maintained in order to enable connection rate-control.

Two existing options have been given new extensions that require two new *mc* configuration macros:

- The new `confTO_QUEUERETURN_DSN` *mc* macro (§4.1.4[V8.13]) adds a new timeout to the `Timeout.queuereturn` option (§24.9.109.18[3ed]). This affects only normal DSN messages.
- The new `confTO_QUEUEWARN_DSN` *mc* macro (§4.1.5[V8.13]) adds a new timeout to the `Timeout.queuewarn` option (§24.9.109.19[3ed]). This affects only normal DSN messages.

One feature has been eliminated:

- The nodns feature (§4.8.29[3ed]) has been removed. It was present prior to V8.13, but has done nothing since V8.9. If you wish to disable DNS, use your service-switch file (§24.9.100[3ed]).

Two features have been changed in small, but significant, ways. If you use either of them, you should note these changes:

- The local_lmtp feature (§4.8.19[3ed]) has added a third optional argument (§4.1.6[V8.13]), which you may use to define additional or new command-line arguments for the *mail.local* program and other LMTP-enabled delivery agents (§5.3[3ed]).
- The dnsbl feature (§7.2.1[3ed]) no longer uses the host database-map type to look up addresses. Instead, it uses the dns database-map type (§9.1.1[V8.13]). The DNSBL_MAP_OPT *mc* macro (§9.1.1[V8.13]) has been added to help tune the use of the dns database-map type with the dnsbl feature.

Three new features that control connections have been added:

- The ratecontrol feature (§4.1.7[V8.13]) limits the incoming connection rate for specified hosts or networks.
- The conncontrol feature (§4.1.8[V8.13]) limits the number of simultaneous connections from specified hosts or networks.
- The greet_pause feature allows protection from SMTP slamming (§7.1.3[V8.13]).

One new experimental feature has been added:

- The (experimental) mtamark feature implements MTA marking by looking up TXT records in the in-addr.arpa domain (§7.1.4[V8.13]).

A *mc* new macro has been added to enhance the use of the uucp delivery agents:

- The LOCAL_UUCP *mc* macro (§4.1.9[V8.13]) allows you to add new rules and rule sets to the uucp delivery agents.

4.1.1 confREJECT_LOG_INTERVAL

The confREJECT_LOG_INTERVAL *mc* configuration macro defines the logging interval used by the RejectLogInterval option. See §24.1.11[V8.13] for a description of this option and the nature of the warning message that is logged.

4.1.2 confREQUIRES_DIR_FSYNC

The confREQUIRES_DIR_FSYNC *mc* configuration macro defines the RequiresDirfsync option and causes *sendmail* to change the effect of the compile-time flag REQUIRES_DIR_FSYNC (§3.4.47[3ed]) at runtime. See §24.1.12[V8.13] for a description of this new option and how it may be used.

4.1.3 confCONNECTION_RATE_WINDOW_SIZE

The new `confCONNECTION_RATE_WINDOW_SIZE` *mc* configuration macro defines the `ConnectionRateWindowSize` option as well as the window of time over which a count of the number of connections is maintained. See §24.1.13[V8.13] for a description of this new option and how it may be used.

4.1.4 confTO_QUEUERETURN_DSN

Prior to V8.13, there were only three ways to modify the timeouts for the `Timeout.queuereturn` option (§24.9.109.18[3ed]):

```
define(`confTO_QUEUERETURN_URGENT',`timeout')           ← V8.7 and later
define(`confTO_QUEUERETURN_NORMAL',`timeout')           ← V8.7 and later
define(`confTO_QUEUERETURN_NONURGENT',`timeout')        ← V8.7 and later
```

V8.13 has added a fourth way to modify that same option. If the precedence (§25.10[3ed]) for the message is `normal`, and if the message is a DSN return message, the new `Timeout.queuereturn.dsn` timeout will be used:

```
define(`confTO_QUEUERETURN_DSN',`timeout')  ← V8.13 and later
```

See §24.1.15[V8.13] for a description of this addition to an existing option and how it may be used.

4.1.5 confTO_QUEUEWARN_DSN

Prior to V8.13, there were only three ways to modify the timeouts for the `Timeout.queuewarn` option (§24.9.109.19[3ed]):

```
define(`confTO_QUEUEWARN_URGENT',`timeout')           ← V8.7 and later
define(`confTO_QUEUEWARN_NORMAL',`timeout')           ← V8.7 and later
define(`confTO_QUEUEWARN_NONURGENT',`timeout')        ← V8.7 and later
```

V8.13 has added a fourth way to modify that same option. If the precedence (§25.10[3ed]) for the message is `normal`, and if the message is a DSN return message, the new `Timeout.queuewarn.dsn` timeout will be used:

```
define(`confTO_QUEUEWARN_DSN',`timeout')  ← V8.13 and later
```

See §24.1.16[V8.13] for a description of this addition to an existing option and how it may be used.

4.1.6 Feature local_lmtp Additional Argument

The *Local Mail Transfer Protocol (LMTP)* can be used to transfer mail from *sendmail* to the program that delivers mail to the local user. Historically, that has been a program such as */bin/mail* that simply gathered a message on its standard input and wrote that message to the end of the file that the user reads. Beginning with V8.9, *sendmail* can speak LMTP to local delivery programs. The *mail.local* program (§5.3[3ed]), supplied in source form with the *sendmail* open source distribution, is one such program, and *procmail*(1) is another.

The `local_lmtp` feature (§4.8.19[3ed]) is used to enable the *mail.local* program. Prior to V8.13, that feature could only take one or, optionally, two arguments:

```
FEATURE(`local_lmtp´)
FEATURE(`local_lmtp´, `/usr/sbin/mail.local´)
```

Here, the first line both enables the use of the *mail.local* program and defines the location of that program by default, as the path */usr/libexec/mail.local*. The second line supplies a second argument to the feature, which defines a different location for the program */usr/sbin/mail.local*. Essentially, the second argument is supplied as the value to the `P=` equate (§20.5.11[3ed]) for the local delivery agent.

V8.13 allows you to add a third, optional argument that supplies the command-line arguments for the *mail.local* program (as well as for any other program that uses LMTP, such as *procmail*). Essentially, the third argument is supplied as the value to the `A=` equate (§20.5.2[3ed]). For example, the following supplies the `-7` command-line switch for the *mail.local* program (don't advertise 8-bit MIME support):

```
FEATURE(`local_lmtp´, , `mail.local -l -7´)
```

And the following enables *procmail*(1) to be used for LMTP delivery:

```
FEATURE(`local_lmtp´, `/mail/bin/procmail´, `procmail -Y -a $h -z´)
```

Note that the second argument, if unused, must be present and empty if you wish to specify a third argument. Also note that you should manually append new command-line switches to the default switches, rather than replace them.

4.1.7 The New ratecontrol Feature

The `ratecontrol` feature allows you to use the *access* database to control the rate at which other machines can connect to your server. The rate is based on the setting of the `ConnectionRateWindowSize` option (§24.1.13[V8.13]), which defaults to 60 seconds. So, for example, it you want to reject more than 10 connections per minute (60 seconds) from the IP address `192.168.23.45`, you would put the following into your *access* database source file:

```
ClientRate:192.168.23.45        10
```

Here, if the host with the IP address `192.168.23.45` connects to your server more than 10 times in a given 60 seconds (the default window of time), the eleventh and subsequent connections during that interval will be rejected.

You enable the `ratecontrol` feature like this:

```
FEATURE(`ratecontrol´)
```

But note, if you have not already declared the *access* database (§7.5[3ed]), you must do so before declaring this new feature, or you will get the following error when building your new configuration file:

```
*** ERROR: FEATURE(ratecontrol) requires FEATURE(access_db)
```

Once you have successfully enabled this ratecontrol feature, you may use it to control the connection rate by the IP addresses of hosts or networks or to set the default limit:

```
ClientRate:192.168.23.45                2
ClientRate:127.0.0.1                    0
ClientRate:                             10
ClientRate:10.5.2                       2
ClientRate:IPv6:2002:c0a8:51d2::23f4    5
```

Here, the first line (as you have seen) limits the number of connections from the IP address 123.45.67.89 to no more than two connections per minute (where the ConnectionRateWindowSize option, §24.1.13[V8.13], is set to 60 seconds or one minute).

The second line specifies a limit of zero, which means there is no limit imposed on the rate. This is suitable for the loopback interface address (127.0.0.1), because that is where the local submission version of *sendmail* delivers its mail.

The third line omits the IP address entirely, thereby setting a default limit for all other IP (unspecified) addresses. Without this default setting, any unspecified address would be unlimited.

The fourth line shows how network addresses may also be limited. However, note that this does not apply to the entire network (only to individual hosts inside the network) because the values are not cumulative for a network.

The last line shows that IPV6 addresses can be specified merely by prefixing each with a literal IPv6:.

Note that the rates we show here are just examples, not recommendations. The rates you choose as limits will depend on your particular circumstances.

4.1.7.1 ratecontrol and delay checks

If you also declare the delay_checks feature (§7.5.6[3ed]), rate-control checks will be delayed until after the first envelope recipient has been received. Clearly, this makes this rate-control check less useful than it should be. If you use delay_checks, you may add an additional argument to this ratecontrol feature to get it to run as early as possible despite the use of that delaying feature:

```
FEATURE(`ratecontrol´, `nodelay´)
```

Here, the nodelay is literal and prevents the delay_checks feature from having any effect on connection rate-controls. Note that if you declare both the delay_checks and ratecontrol features, the delay_checks feature must appear first in your *mc* file.

4.1.7.2 Terminate connections with 421

Normally, the ratecontrol feature rejects connections with a temporary error:

```
452 Connection rate limit exceeded
```

If the connecting client terminates the connection by sending an SMTP QUIT, ratecontrol terminates as you would expect. But if the client chooses to ignore that return value, the client will be given 4yz replies to all commands it sends until it sends an SMTP QUIT command. Clearly, this may not be acceptable at your site. If you want the excess connection rates terminated without regard to the connecting client's other behavior, you may do so by adding a second argument to this ratecontrol feature:

```
FEATURE(`ratecontrol´, `nodelay´, `terminate´)
FEATURE(`ratecontrol´, , `terminate´)
```

Here, the terminate is literal and, when present, causes all rejected connections to be rejected with a 421 return code. Note that 421 is special, because it allows *sendmail* to terminate the connection without waiting for the client to send a QUIT. If you omit the nodelay first argument, you must use two commas (as in the second line of the example above) to make terminate the second argument.

4.1.8 The New conncontrol Feature

The conncontrol feature allows you to use the *access* database to control the number of simultaneous connections another machine may have to your server. The number of simultaneous connections allowed each interval is based on the setting of the ConnectionRateWindowSize option (§24.1.13[V8.13]), which defaults to 60 seconds. So, for example, if you want to reject a host that has more than 10 simultaneous connections to your server (sometime in the last 60 seconds), where that host has the IP address 192.168.23.45, you would put the following into your *access* database source file:

```
ClientConn:192.168.23.45        10
```

Here, if the host with the IP address 192.168.23.45 tries to set up an eleventh simultaneous connection to your server, that connection will be denied.

Enable the conncontrol feature like this:

```
FEATURE(`conncontrol´)
```

But note, if you have not already declared the *access* database (§7.5[3ed]), you must do so before declaring this new feature, or you will get the following error when building your new configuration file:

```
*** ERROR: FEATURE(conncontrol) requires FEATURE(access_db)
```

Once you have successfully enabled this conncontrol feature, you may use it to control the number of simultaneous connections, based on IP addresses of hosts or networks, or to set the default limit:

```
ClientConn:192.168.23.45                2
ClientConn:127.0.0.1                    0
ClientConn:                             10
ClientConn:10.5.2                       2
ClientConn:IPv6:2002:c0a8:51d2::23f4    5
```

Here, the first line (as you have seen) limits the number of simultaneous connections from the IP address 1192.168.23.45 to two.

The second line specifies a limit of zero, which means that there is no limit imposed on the number of simultaneous connections. This is suitable for the loopback interface address (127.0.0.1), because that is where the local submission version of *sendmail* delivers its mail.

The third line omits the IP address entirely, thereby setting the default limit for all other IP (unspecified) addresses.

The fourth line shows how network addresses may also be limited.

The last line shows that IPV6 addresses may be specified merely by prefixing each with a literal IPv6:.

Note that the limits we show here are just examples, not recommendations. The limits you choose will depend on your particular circumstances.

4.1.8.1 conncontrol and delay checks

If you also declare the delay_checks feature (§7.5.6[3ed]), connection-control checks will be delayed until after the first envelope recipient has been received. Clearly, this makes this connection check less useful than it should be. If you use delay_checks, you may add an additional argument to this conncontrol feature to get it to run as early as possible despite the use of that delaying feature:

```
FEATURE(`conncontrol´, `nodelay´)
```

Here, the nodelay is literal and prevents the delay_checks feature from having any effect on connection-controls. Note that if you declare both the delay_checks and conncontrol features, the delay_checks feature must appear first in your *mc* file.

4.1.8.2 Terminate connections with 421

Normally, the conncontrol feature rejects connections with a temporary error:

```
452 Too many open connections
```

If the connecting client terminates the connection by sending an SMTP QUIT, connection-control terminates as you would expect. But if the client chooses to ignore that return value, the client will be given 4yz replies to all commands it sends until it sends an SMTP QUIT command. Clearly, this may not be acceptable at your site. If you want the connection terminated without regard to the connecting client's behavior, you may do so by adding a second argument to this conncontrol feature:

```
FEATURE(`conncontrol´, `nodelay´, `terminate´)
FEATURE(`conncontrol´,  ,`terminate´)
```

Here, the terminate is literal and, when present, causes all rejected connections to be rejected with a 421 return code. Note that 421 is special, because it allows *sendmail* to terminate the connection without waiting for the client to send a QUIT. If you omit the nodelay first argument, you must use two commas (as in the second line of the example above) to make terminate the second argument.

4.1.9 The LOCAL_UUCP mc Macro

Use of UUCP is enabled by declaring the uucp delivery agent (§20.4.15[3ed]):

```
MAILER(`uucp´)
```

This *mc* file declaration causes delivery agents, rules, and rule sets to be added to your configuration file so that UUCP mail may be handled.

Inside the parse rule set 0, rules are added that select UUCP delivery agents. First, locally connected UUCP addresses are detected and the appropriate UUCP delivery agent is selected based on each such address found. Addresses in the class $=Z select the uucp-uudom delivery agent. Addresses in the class $=Y select the uucp-new delivery agent. And addresses in the class $=U select the uucp-old delivery agent.

Next, rules are included (which will be added to your *sendmail* configuration file) that detect remotely connected UUCP addresses.

But if you need to add rules between these two phases (between the detection of local UUCP addresses and remote UUCP addresses), you may do so by utilizing this new LOCAL_UUCP *mc* macro. For example, the following *mc* file entry:

```
LOCAL_UUCP
R$* < @ $={ServerUUCP} . UUCP. > $*          $#uucp-uudom $@ $2 $: $1 < @ $2 .UUCP.> $3
```

causes the above new rule to be added to the parse rule set 0 in the location shown here:

```
# resolve locally connected UUCP links
...
                                        ← New rules added here.
# resolve remotely connected UUCP links (if any)
```

Note that the LOCAL_UUCP *mc* macro is not intended for casual use. It should only be used to solve special UUCP needs that cannot be solved using more conventional means.

4.2 A Useful Table

The *m4* method of creating a configuration file using an *mc* configuration file is covered in Chapter 4[3ed]. In Table 4-1, we list nearly all of the macros available to use when creating your configuration file.

Note that most of these *mc* macros are defined with the `define` method. For example:

```
define(`ALIAS_FILE´, `/etc/mail/aliases´)
```

In the table, these are shown without trailing parentheses.

Others macros are self-defining. For example:

```
CANONIFY_DOMAIN_FILE(`/etc/mail/canonify-domains´)
```

In Table 4-1, these are shown with trailing parentheses. For example:

```
ALIAS_FILE                    ← use with define()
CANONIFY_DOMAIN_FILE( )       ← use by itself
```

Table 4-1. mc configuration macros and directives

Item	sendmail text reference	Description
`ALIAS_FILE`	§24.9.1[3ed]	Define the location of the *aliases* files
`BITNET_RELAY`	§21.9.11[3ed]	Define the BITNET relay host
`CANONIFY_DOMAIN( )`	§4.8.28[3ed]	Add a value to the `$={Canonify}` class
`CANONIFY_DOMAIN_FILE( )`	§4.8.28[3ed]	Add values to the `$={Canonify}` class from a file
`CLIENT_OPTIONS( )`	§24.9.17[3ed]	Define client port option settings
`confALIAS_WAIT`	§24.9.2[3ed]	Wait for an *aliases* rebuild to complete
`confALLOW_BOGUS_HELO`	§24.9.3[3ed]	Allow HELO or EHLO sans host
`confAUTH_MAX_BITS`	§24.9.4[3ed]	Limit max encryption strength for SASL
`confAUTH_MECHANISMS`	§24.9.5[3ed]	List the AUTH mechanisms
`confAUTH_OPTIONS`	§24.9.6[3ed]	Tune authentication parameters
`confAUTO_REBUILD`	§24.9.7[3ed]	Rebuild *aliases* automatically (deprecated)
`confBAD_RCPT_THROTTLE`	§24.9.8[3ed]	Slow excess bad SMTP RCPT commands
`confBIND_OPTS`	§24.9.91[3ed]	Set DNS resolver options
`confBLANK_SUB`	§24.9.9[3ed]	Define the blank-substitution character in rewriting
`confCACERT`	§24.9.10[3ed]	File containing certificate for certificate authorities
`confCACERT_PATH`	§24.9.11[3ed]	Directory with certificates of certificate authorities
`confCF_VERSION`	§21.9.100[3ed]	The version of the *mc* configuration
`confCHECKPOINT_INTERVAL`	§24.9.13[3ed]	How often to checkpoint the *qf* file
`confCHECK_ALIASES`	§24.9.12[3ed]	Check the righthand side of aliases
`confCLIENT_CERT`	§10.10.5[3ed]	Location of the client (outbound) digital certificate

Table 4-1. mc configuration macros and directives (continued)

Item	sendmail text reference	Description
confCLIENT_KEY	§10.10.5[3ed]	Location of the key file for the client (outbound) digital certificate
confCLIENT_OPTIONS	§24.9.17[3ed]	Define client port option settings (deprecated)
confCOLON_OK_IN_ADDR	§24.9.18[3ed]	Allow colons in addresses
confCONNECTION_RATE_THROTTLE	§24.9.21[3ed]	When to throttle the incoming SMTP connection rate
confCONNECT_ONLY_TO	§24.9.22[3ed]	Send only to this host
confCONTROL_SOCKET_NAME	§24.9.23[3ed]	Define the path of the control socket
confCON_EXPENSIVE	§24.9.50[3ed]	Queue when using expensive delivery agents
confCOPY_ERRORS_TO	§24.9.79[3ed]	Extra copies of bounce messages
confCR_FILE	§22.6.12[3ed]	File to read for hosts for whom to relay
confCT_FILE	§4.8.47[3ed]	File to read for a list of trusted users
confCW_FILE	§4.8.48[3ed]	File to read for a list of alternative names for the local host
confDAEMON_OPTIONS	§24.9.24[3ed]	Set options for the listening daemon (deprecated)
confDEAD_LETTER_DROP	§24.9.26[3ed]	Define *dead.letter* file location
confDEF_AUTH_INFO	§24.9.27[3ed]	Source of AUTH information (deprecated)
confDEF_CHAR_SET	§24.9.28[3ed]	Define the default `Content-Type:` header character set
confDEF_GROUP_ID	§24.9.29[3ed]	Define the default user's group (deprecated)
confDEF_USER_ID	§24.9.29[3ed]	Define the default user
confDELAY_LA	§24.9.30[3ed]	Add a one-second SMTP sleep on high load
confDELIVERY_MODE	§24.9.32[3ed]	Set *sendmail*'s delivery mode
confDELIVER_BY_MIN	§24.9.31[3ed]	Set DELIVERBY minimum
confDEQUOTE_OPTS	§23.7.5[3ed]	Add `dequote` database-map switches
confDF_BUFFER_SIZE	§24.9.25[3ed]	Set the buffered-I/O *df* limit
confDH_PARAMETERS	§24.9.33[3ed]	Define the parameters for DSA/DH cipher suite
confDIAL_DELAY	§24.9.34[3ed]	Set the connect failure retry time
confDIRECT_SUBMISSION_MODIFIERS	§24.9.35[3ed]	Define daemon flags for command-line submission
confDOMAIN_NAME	§21.9.56[3ed]	The official canonical name
confDONT_BLAME_SENDMAIL	§24.9.36[3ed]	Prevent file security checks
confDONT_EXPAND_CNAMES	§24.9.37[3ed]	Prevent CNAME expansion
confDONT_INIT_GROUPS	§24.9.38[3ed]	Don't use `initgroups(3)`
confDONT_PROBE_INTERFACES	§24.9.39[3ed]	Don't probe interfaces for `$=w`
confDONT_PRUNE_ROUTES	§24.9.40[3ed]	Don't prune route addresses
confDOUBLE_BOUNCE_ADDRESS	§24.9.41[3ed]	Where to send errors about bounce delivery errors
confEIGHT_BIT_HANDLING	§24.9.42[3ed]	How to convert 8-bit input

Table 4-1. mc configuration macros and directives (continued)

Item	sendmail text reference	Description
confERROR_MESSAGE	§24.9.43[3ed]	Set error message header
confERROR_MODE	§24.9.44[3ed]	Specify mode of error handling
confFALLBACK_MX	§24.9.45[3ed]	Specify Fallback MX host
confFAST_SPLIT	§24.9.46[3ed]	Suppress MX lookups on initial submission
confFORWARD_PATH	§24.9.48[3ed]	Set the forward file search path
confFROM_HEADER	§25.7[3ed]	Define the format for the `From:` header
confFROM_LINE	§24.9.114[3ed]	Define the five-character "`From `" format
confHOSTS_FILE	§24.9.51[3ed]	Specify an alternative */etc/hosts* file
confHOST_STATUS_DIRECTORY	§24.9.52[3ed]	Specify the location of persistent host status
confIGNORE_DOTS	§24.9.53[3ed]	Ignore leading dots in messages
confINPUT_MAIL_FILTERS	§24.9.54[3ed]	Define the order of input filters
confLDAP_CLUSTER	§21.9.82[3ed]	Specify which LDAP cluster to use in queries
confLDAP_DEFAULT_SPEC	§24.9.55[3ed]	Specify the default LDAP database-map switches
confLOG_LEVEL	§24.9.56[3ed]	Set the logging level
confMAILBOX_DATABASE	§24.9.57[3ed]	Choose the type of mailbox database
confMAILER_NAME	§21.9.68[3ed]	Set the error message sender
confMATCH_GECOS	§24.9.58[3ed]	Match recipient in GECOS field
confMAX_ALIAS_RECURSION	§24.9.59[3ed]	Limit maximum recursion of *aliases*
confMAX_DAEMON_CHILDREN	§24.9.60[3ed]	Maximum forked daemon children
confMAX_HEADERS_LENGTH	§24.9.61[3ed]	Set the maximum header length
confMAX_HOP	§24.9.62[3ed]	Set the maximum hop count
confMAX_MESSAGE_SIZE	§24.9.63[3ed]	Maximum incoming message size
confMAX_MIME_HEADER_LENGTH	§24.9.64[3ed]	Maximum MIME header length
confMAX_QUEUE_CHILDREN	§24.9.65[3ed]	Limit total concurrent queue processors
confMAX_QUEUE_RUN_SIZE	§24.9.66[3ed]	Maximum queue messages processed per queue run
confMAX_RCPTS_PER_MESSAGE	§24.9.67[3ed]	Maximum recipients per envelope
confMAX_RUNNERS_PER_QUEUE	§24.9.68[3ed]	Limit concurrent queue processors per queue group
confMCI_CACHE_SIZE	§24.9.19[3ed]	Set the SMTP connection cache size
confMCI_CACHE_TIMEOUT	§24.9.20[3ed]	Set the SMTP connection cache timeout
confMESSAGE_TIMEOUT	§24.9.87[3ed]	Limit life of a message in the queue (deprecated)
confMESSAGEID_HEADER	§25.1.2[V8.13]	Define a new value for the `Message-Id:` header
confME_TOO	§24.9.69[3ed]	Send to me too (deprecated)
confMILTER_LOG_LEVEL	§24.9.70[3ed]	Set the log level for the MILTER interface
confMILTER_MACROS_CONNECT	§24.9.70[3ed]	Specify the macros to send the MILTER filters following the initial connection

Table 4-1. mc configuration macros and directives (continued)

Item	sendmail text reference	Description
confMILTER_MACROS_ENVFROM	§24.9.70[3ed]	Specify the macros to send the MILTER filters following MAIL FROM:
confMILTER_MACROS_ENVRCPT	§24.9.70[3ed]	Specify the macros to send the MILTER filters following RCPT TO:
confMILTER_MACROS_HELO	§24.9.70[3ed]	Specify the macros to send the MILTER filters following HELO or EHLO
confMIME_FORMAT_ERRORS	§24.9.97[3ed]	Return MIME-format errors
confMIN_FREE_BLOCKS	§24.9.71[3ed]	Define minimum free disk blocks
confMIN_QUEUE_AGE	§24.9.72[3ed]	Skip queue file if too young
confMUST_QUOTE_CHARS	§24.9.73[3ed]	Quote nonaddress characters
confNICE_QUEUE_RUN	§24.9.74[3ed]	Default `nice`(3) setting for queue processors
confNO_RCPT_ACTION	§24.9.75[3ed]	How to handle no recipients in header
confOLD_STYLE_HEADERS	§24.9.76[3ed]	Allow spaces in recipient lists
confOPERATORS	§24.9.77[3ed]	Set token separation operators
confPID_FILE	§24.9.78[3ed]	Location of the *sendmail* process ID file
confPRIVACY_FLAGS	§24.9.80[3ed]	Increase privacy of *sendmail*
confPROCESS_TITLE_PREFIX	§24.9.81[3ed]	Set the process listing prefix
confQUEUE_FACTOR	§24.9.83[3ed]	Set the factor for high-load queuing
confQUEUE_FILE_MODE	§24.9.84[3ed]	Set the default permissions for queue files
confQUEUE_LA	§24.9.85[3ed]	On high load, queue only
confQUEUE_SORT_ORDER	§24.9.86[3ed]	How to presort the queue
confRAND_FILE	§24.9.88[3ed]	Location of the random file for use with STARTTLS
confREAD_TIMEOUT	§24.9.109[3ed]	Set assorted timeouts (deprecated)
confRECEIVED_HEADER	§25.7[3ed]	Define the format for the `Received:` header
confREFUSE_LA	§24.9.90[3ed]	Refuse connections on high load
confREJECT_LOG_INTERVAL	§4.1.1[V8.13]	Logging interval for connections that are still being rejected
confREJECT_MSG	§7.5.4[3ed]	Customize a rejection message for the *access* database `REJECT` keyword
confRELAY_MAILER	§20.3.1.4[3ed]	The name of the delivery agent used to relay mail
confRELAY_MSG	§7.4.2[3ed]	The message used to reject relaying
confREQUIRES_DIR_FSYNC	§4.1.2[V8.13]	Disable directory `fsync`(2)
confRRT_IMPLIES_DSN	§24.9.93[3ed]	`Return-Receipt-To:` requests success DSN
confRUN_AS_USER	§24.9.94[3ed]	Run as a user other than *root*
confSAFE_FILE_ENV	§24.2.1[3ed]	Directory for safe file writes
confSAFE_QUEUE	§24.9.107[3ed]	Queue everything just in case
confSAVE_FROM_LINES	§24.9.96[3ed]	Save Unix-style From lines

Table 4-1. mc configuration macros and directives (continued)

Item	sendmail text reference	Description
confSEPARATE_PROC	§24.9.47[3ed]	Process queue files with separate processes
confSERVER_CERT	§24.9.98[3ed]	Location of the server (inbound) digital certificate
confSERVER_KEY	§24.9.99[3ed]	Location of the key file for the server (inbound) digital certificate
confSERVICE_SWITCH_FILE	§24.9.100[3ed]	Specify file for switched services
confSEVEN_BIT_INPUT	§24.9.101[3ed]	Force 7-bit input
confSHARED_MEMORY_KEY	§24.9.102[3ed]	Enable shared memory by setting the key
confSINGLE_LINE_FROM_HEADER	§24.9.103[3ed]	Strip newlines from `From:` headers
confSINGLE_THREAD_DELIVERY	§24.9.104[3ed]	Set single-threaded delivery
confSMTP_LOGIN_MSG	§24.9.105[3ed]	Set the SMTP greeting message
confSMTP_MAILER	§20.2.1[3ed]	Define the SMTP delivery agent
confTEMP_FILE_MODE	§24.9.108[3ed]	Permissions for temporary files
confTIME_ZONE	§24.9.110[3ed]	Set the time zone
confTLS_SRV_OPTIONS	§24.9.111[3ed]	Tune the server TLS settings
confTO_ACONNECT	§24.9.109.1[3ed]	Overall timeout for all connect attempts
confTO_AUTH	§24.9.109.2[3ed]	Timeout for the client's response to the AUTH command
confTO_COMMAND	§24.9.109.3[3ed]	Timeout for the next SMTP command
confTO_CONNECT	§24.9.109.4[3ed]	Timeout for the connection to be established
confTO_DATABLOCK	§24.9.109.6[3ed]	Overall timeout for the SMTP DATA phase
confTO_DATAFINAL	§24.9.109.7[3ed]	Timeout waiting for acknowledgment of the SMTP DATA dot
confTO_DATAINIT	§24.9.109.8[3ed]	Timeout waiting for acknowledgment of the SMTP DATA command
confTO_FILEOPEN	§24.9.109.9[3ed]	Timeout waiting for a file to be opened
confTO_HELO	§24.9.109.10[3ed]	Timeout waiting for the other side to acknowledge the HELO or EHLO SMTP command
confTO_HOSTSTATUS	§24.9.109.11[3ed]	Define how long host information will be considered valid
confTO_ICONNECT	§24.9.109.12[3ed]	Timeout the very first connection attempt
confTO_IDENT	§24.9.109.13[3ed]	Timeout the wait for an *ident* lookup
confTO_INITIAL	§24.9.109.14[3ed]	How long to wait for the initial 220 line following the connection
confTO_LHLO	§24.9.109.15[3ed]	Timeout waiting for the reply to the LHLO LMTP command
confTO_MAIL	§24.9.109.16[3ed]	How long to wait for the reply to the SMTP MAIL FROM: command
confTO_MISC	§24.9.109.17[3ed]	How long to wait for the reply to miscellaneous SMTP commands

Table 4-1. mc configuration macros and directives (continued)

Item	sendmail text reference	Description
confTO_QUEUERETURN	§24.9.109.18[3ed]	How long to leave a message queued before bouncing it
confTO_QUEUERETURN_DSN	§4.1.4[V8.13]	How long to leave a DSN message queued before bouncing it
confTO_QUEUERETURN_NONURGENT	§24.9.109.18[3ed]	How long to leave a nonurgent message queued before bouncing it
confTO_QUEUERETURN_NORMAL	§24.9.109.18[3ed]	How long to leave a normal message queued before bouncing it
confTO_QUEUERETURN_URGENT	§24.9.109.18[3ed]	How long to leave an urgent message queued before bouncing it
confTO_QUEUEWARN	§24.9.109.19[3ed]	How long to leave a message queued before announcing it has not yet been sent
confTO_QUEUEWARN_DSN	§4.1.5[V8.13]	How long to leave a DSN message queued before announcing it has not yet been sent
confTO_QUEUEWARN_NONURGENT	§24.9.109.19[3ed]	How long to leave a nonurgent message queued before announcing it has not yet been sent
confTO_QUEUEWARN_NORMAL	§24.9.109.19[3ed]	How long to leave a normal message queued before announcing it has not yet been sent
confTO_QUEUEWARN_URGENT	§24.9.109.19[3ed]	How long to leave an urgent message queued before announcing it has not yet been sent
confTO_QUIT	§24.9.109.20[3ed]	How long to wait for the reply to the QUIT SMTP command
confTO_RCPT	§24.9.109.21[3ed]	How long to wait for the reply to the RCPT TO: SMTP command
confTO_RESOLVER_RETRANS	§24.9.109.22[3ed]	The amount of time to wait between retries before a retransmission
confTO_RESOLVER_RETRANS_FIRST	§24.9.109.22[3ed]	The amount of time to wait between retries before a retransmission on the first connection attempt
confTO_RESOLVER_RETRANS_NORMAL	§24.9.109.22[3ed]	The amount of time to wait between retries before a retransmission on all subsequent connection attempts
confTO_RESOLVER_RETRY	§24.9.109.22[3ed]	The number of retries allowed before giving up
confTO_RESOLVER_RETRY_FIRST	§24.9.109.22[3ed]	The number of retries allowed before giving up for the first connection attempt
confTO_RESOLVER_RETRY_NORMAL	§24.9.109.22[3ed]	The number of retries allowed before giving up for all subsequent connection attempts
confTO_RSET	§24.9.109.23[3ed]	The amount of time to wait for the reply to the RSET SMTP command
confTO_STARTTLS	§24.9.109.24[3ed]	The amount of time to wait for the other side to begin the STARTTLS negotiation
confTRUSTED_USER	§24.9.112[3ed]	Alternative to *root* administration
confTRUSTED_USERS	§4.8.47[3ed]	Define who can rebuild the *aliases* database

Table 4-1. mc configuration macros and directives (continued)

Item	sendmail text reference	Description
confTRY_NULL_MX_LIST	§24.9.113[3ed]	Use A or AAAA if no best MX record
confUNSAFE_GROUP_WRITES	§24.9.115[3ed]	Check unsafe group permissions (deprecated)
confUSERDB_SPEC	§24.9.118[3ed]	Specify the user database
confUSE_ERRORS_TO	§24.9.116[3ed]	Use `Errors-To:` header for errors
confUSE_MSP	§24.9.117[3ed]	Run as a mail submission program
confUUCP_MAILER	§20.3.1.2[3ed]	Specify your preference for the delivery agent that will handle outbound UUCP mail
confWORK_CLASS_FACTOR	§24.9.14[3ed]	Multiplier for priority increments
confWORK_RECIPIENT_FACTOR	§24.9.89[3ed]	Penalize large recipient lists
confWORK_TIME_FACTOR	§24.9.92[3ed]	Increment per job priority
confXF_BUFFER_SIZE	§24.9.120[3ed]	Set *xf* file buffered I/O limit
CYRUS_BB_MAILER_ARGS	§20.4.1[3ed]	Define the A= arguments for the `cyrusbb` delivery agent
CYRUS_BB_MAILER_FLAGS	§20.4.1[3ed]	Define the F= flags for the `cyrusbb` delivery agent
CYRUS_MAILER_ARGS	§20.4.1[3ed]	Define the A= arguments for the `cyrus` delivery agent
CYRUS_MAILER_FLAGS	§20.4.1[3ed]	Define the F= flags for the `cyrus` delivery agent
CYRUS_MAILER_MAX	§20.4.1[3ed]	Define the M= limit for the `cyrus` delivery agent
CYRUS_MAILER_PATH	§20.4.1[3ed]	Define the P= path for the `cyrus` delivery agent
CYRUS_MAILER_USER	§20.4.1[3ed]	Define the U= *user:group* identity for the `cyrus` delivery agent
CYRUS_MAILER_QGRP	§20.4.1[3ed]	Define the Q= queue group for the `cyrus` delivery agent
CYRUSV2_MAILER_ARGS	§20.4.2[3ed]	Define the A= arguments for the `cyrusv2` delivery agent
CYRUSV2_MAILER_CHARSET	§20.4.2[3ed]	Define the C= character set for the `cyrusv2` delivery agent
CYRUSV2_MAILER_FLAGS	§20.4.2[3ed]	Define the F= flags for the `cyrusv2` delivery agent
CYRUSV2_MAILER_MAXMSGS	§20.4.2[3ed]	Define the m= limit for the `cyrusv2` delivery agent
CYRUSV2_MAILER_MAXRCPTS	§20.4.2[3ed]	Define the r= limit for the `cyrusv2` delivery agent
CYRUSV2_MAILER_QGRP	§20.4.2[3ed]	Define the Q= queue group for the `cyrusv2` delivery agent
DAEMON_OPTIONS( )	§24.9.24[3ed]	Set options for the listening daemon
DATABASE_MAP_TYPE	§23.5.1[3ed]	Set a default database type for features
DECNET_RELAY	§4.5.2[3ed]	The DECnet relay
DNSBL_MAP_OPT	§23.7.6[3ed]	Change the K configuration command switches for the `dns` type database-map used by the `dnsbl` feature
DOL( )	§4.1.4[3ed]	Insert literal $ character into *m4*'s output
DOMAIN( )	§4.2.2.3[3ed]	Specify common domain-wide information

Table 4-1. mc configuration macros and directives (continued)

Item	sendmail text reference	Description
DNSBL_MAP	§4.1.6[V8.13]	Redefine -R A for dnsbl feature
DNSBL_MAP_OPT	§4.1.6[V8.13]	Add database-map switches for dnsbl feature
DSMTP_MAILER_ARGS	§20.4.13[3ed]	Define the A= arguments for the dsmtp delivery agent
DSMTP_MAILER_QGRP	§20.4.13[3ed]	Define the Q= queue group for the dsmtp delivery agent
EDNSBL_TO	§23.7.6[3ed]	Change the K configuration command's -r switch for the dns type database-map used by the enhdnsbl feature to set resolver's retries
ESMTP_MAILER_ARGS	§20.4.13[3ed]	Define the A= arguments for the esmtp delivery agent
ESMTP_MAILER_QGRP	§20.4.13[3ed]	Define the Q= queue group for the esmtp delivery agent
EXPOSED_USER( )	§4.4.1[3ed]	Add users individually to the exposed-user class
EXPOSED_USER_FILE( )	§4.4.1[3ed]	File of users to add individually to the exposed-user class
FAX_MAILER_ARGS	§20.4.5[3ed]	Define the A= arguments for the fax delivery agent
FAX_MAILER_MAX	§20.4.5[3ed]	Define the M= size limit for the fax delivery agent
FAX_MAILER_PATH	§20.4.5[3ed]	Define the P= path for the fax delivery agent
FAX_MAILER_QGRP	§20.4.5[3ed]	Define the Q= queue group for the fax delivery agent
FAX_RELAY	§4.5.3[3ed]	Define the FAX relay host
FEATURE(accept_unqualified_senders)	§7.4.11[3ed]	Accept MAIL FROM: addresses that lack a domain part
FEATURE(accept_unresolvable_domains)	§7.4.10[3ed]	Accept MAIL FROM: addresses for which the domain cannot be found
FEATURE(access_db)	§7.5[3ed]	Enable use of the *access* database
FEATURE(allmasquerade)	§4.8.4[3ed]	Masquerade the recipient too
FEATURE(always_add_domain)	§4.8.5[3ed]	Add the local domain even on local mail
FEATURE(authinfo)	§10.9.3[3ed]	Use a separate database for outbound authentication information
FEATURE(bestmx_is_local)	§4.8.7[3ed]	Accept best MX record as local if in $=w
FEATURE(bitdomain)	§4.8.8[3ed]	Convert BITNET addresses into Internet addresses
FEATURE(blacklist_recipients)	§7.5.5[3ed]	Selectively reject envelope-recipient addresses
FEATURE(compat_check)	§7.5.7[3ed]	Screen sender/recipient pairs
FEATURE(conncontrol)	§4.1.8[V8.13]	Limit the number of simultaneous connections to your server by other hosts and networks
FEATURE(delay_checks)	§7.5.6[3ed]	Check envelope recipient first
FEATURE(dnsbl)	§7.2.1[3ed] and §4.1.6[V8.13]	Reject based on various DNSBL lists
FEATURE(domaintable)	§4.8.13[3ed]	Accept old as equivalent to new domain
FEATURE(enhdnsbl)	§7.2.2[3ed]	Enhanced DNSBL rejection
FEATURE(genericstable)	§4.8.16[3ed]	Transform sender addresses

Table 4-1. mc configuration macros and directives (continued)

Item	sendmail text reference	Description
FEATURE(generics_entire_domain)	§4.8.15[3ed]	Match subdomains in generics table
FEATURE(greet_pause)	§7.1.3[V8.13]	Control SMTP slamming
FEATURE(ldap_routing)	§23.7.11.17[3ed]	Reroute recipients based on LDAP queries
FEATURE(limited_masquerade)	§4.8.18[3ed]	Masquerade a subset of the hosts in $=w
FEATURE(local_lmtp)	§4.8.19[3ed] and §4.1.6[V8.13]	Deliver locally with LMTP and *mail.local*
FEATURE(local_no_masquerade)	§4.8.20[3ed]	Don't masquerade local mail
FEATURE(local_procmail)	§4.8.21[3ed]	Use *procmail*(1) as local delivery agent
FEATURE(lookupdotdomain)	§4.8.22[3ed]	Enable V8.13 domain secondary access database lookups
FEATURE(loose_relay_check)	§7.4.2[3ed]	Allow %-hack relaying
FEATURE(mailertable)	§4.8.24[3ed]	Database selects new delivery agents
FEATURE(masquerade_entire_domain)	§4.8.25[3ed]	Masquerade all hosts in a domain
FEATURE(masquerade_envelope)	§4.8.26[3ed]	Masquerade the envelope too
FEATURE(msp)	§2.6.2[3ed]	Create a mail submission *cf* file
FEATURE(mtamark)	§7.1.4[V8.13]	Experimental feature for detecting MTA marking
FEATURE(nocanonify)	§4.8.28[3ed]	Don't canonify with $[and $]
FEATURE(nodns)	§4.8.29[3ed]	Removed as of V8.13
FEATURE(notsticky)	§4.8.31[3ed]	Don't differ *user* from *user@local.host* (deprecated)
FEATURE(nouucp)	§4.8.32[3ed]	Eliminate all UUCP support
FEATURE(no_default_msa)	§4.8.30[3ed]	Disable the automatic listening on the MSA port 587
FEATURE(nullclient)	§4.8.33[3ed]	Relay all mail through a mail host
FEATURE(preserve_local_plus_detail)	§4.8.35[3ed]	Retain plussed addresses for local delivery
FEATURE(preserve_luser_host)	§4.8.36[3ed]	Preserve recipient host with LUSER_RELAY
FEATURE(promiscuous_relay)	§7.4.3[3ed]	Allow unbridled relaying
FEATURE(queuegroup)	§11.4.4[3ed]	Select queue groups via the *access* database
FEATURE(ratecontrol)	§4.1.7[V8.13]	Limit the rate at which other hosts may connect to your server
FEATURE(rbl)	§4.8.38[3ed]	Reject hosts based on *rbl.maps.vix.com* (deprecated)
FEATURE(redirect)	§4.8.39[3ed]	Add support for address.REDIRECT
FEATURE(relay_based_on_MX)	§7.4.4[3ed]	Relay based on MX records
FEATURE(relay_entire_domain)	§7.4.5[3ed]	Relay based on $=m and the *access* database
FEATURE(relay_hosts_only)	§7.4.6[3ed]	Relay individual hosts, not domains
FEATURE(relay_local_from)	§7.4.7[3ed]	Relay based on MAIL FROM: address
FEATURE(relay_mail_from)	§7.4.8[3ed]	Relay based MAIL FROM: and on RELAY in access_db

Table 4-1. mc configuration macros and directives (continued)

Item	sendmail text reference	Description
FEATURE(smrsh)	§5.8[3ed]	Use *smrsh* (*sendmail* restricted shell)
FEATURE(stickyhost)	§4.8.46[3ed]	Differ user from *user@local.host*
FEATURE(use_ct_file)	§4.8.47[3ed]	Use */etc/mail/trusted-users*, or the file defined by confCT_FILE, for a list of trusted users
FEATURE(use_cw_file)	§4.8.48[3ed]	Use */etc/mail/local-host-names* for a list of local identities
FEATURE(uucpdomain)	§4.8.49[3ed]	Convert UUCP hosts via a database
FEATURE(virtusertable)	§4.8.51[3ed]	Enable support for virtual domains
FEATURE(virtuser_entire_domain)	§4.8.50[3ed]	Match subdomains in the virtual user table
GENERICS_DOMAIN( )	§4.8.16.1[3ed]	Add domains to genericstable class
GENERICS_DOMAIN_FILE( )	§4.8.16.2[3ed]	Add domains to genericstable class from file
HACK( )	§4.2.3.2[3ed]	Include a special, but temporary, customization
HELP_FILE	§24.9.49[3ed]	Alternate location or name for */etc/mail/helpfile*
INPUT_MAIL_FILTER( )	§24.9.54[3ed]	Define input mail filters and their order
LDAPROUTE_DOMAIN( )	§23.7.11.18[3ed]	Add domains to the $={LDAPRoute} class
LDAPROUTE_DOMAIN_FILE( )	§23.7.11.18[3ed]	Add domains to the $={LDAPRoute} class from a file
LDAPROUTE_EQUIVALENT( )	§23.7.11.18[3ed]	Additional domains to look up for LDAP routing
LDAPROUTE_EQUIVALENT_FILE( )	§23.7.11.18[3ed]	Additional domains to look up for LDAP routing in a file
LOCAL_CONFIG	§4.3.3.1[3ed]	Add general information, such as database and header declarations
LOCAL_DOMAIN( )	§22.6.16[3ed]	Add domains to $=w
LOCAL_MAILER_ARGS	§20.4.7.1[3ed]	Define the A= arguments for the local delivery agent
LOCAL_MAILER_CHARSET	§20.4.7.1[3ed]	Define the C= character set for the local delivery agent
LOCAL_MAILER_DSN_DIAGNOSTIC_CODE	§20.4.7.1[3ed]	Define the T= DSN diagnostic code for the local delivery agent
LOCAL_MAILER_EOL	§20.4.7.1[3ed]	Define the E= end-of-line characters for the local delivery agent
LOCAL_MAILER_FLAGS	§20.4.7.1[3ed]	Define the F= flags for the local delivery agent
LOCAL_MAILER_MAX	§20.4.7.1[3ed]	Define the M= size limit for the local and prog delivery agents
LOCAL_MAILER_MAXMSGS	§20.4.7.1[3ed]	Define the m= messages limit for the local delivery agent
LOCAL_MAILER_MAXRCPTS	§20.4.7.1[3ed]	Define the r= recipients limit for the local delivery agent
LOCAL_MAILER_PATH	§20.4.7.1[3ed]	Define the P= path for the local delivery agent
LOCAL_MAILER_QGRP	§20.4.7.1[3ed]	Define the Q= queue group for the local delivery agent
LOCAL_NET_CONFIG	§4.3.3.7[3ed]	Add rules for SMART_HOST

Table 4-1. mc configuration macros and directives (continued)

Item	sendmail text reference	Description
LOCAL_PROG_QGRP	§20.4.7.2[3ed]	Specify the Q= queue group for the prog delivery agent
LOCAL_RELAY	§4.5.4[3ed]	Relay for unqualified users
LOCAL_RULESETS	§4.3.3.5[3ed]	Group local rules with others
LOCAL_RULE_0	§4.3.3.2[3ed]	Add rules to parse rule set 0
LOCAL_RULE_1	§4.3.3.3[3ed]	Add rules to rule set 1
LOCAL_RULE_2	§4.3.3.3[3ed]	Add rules to rule set 2
LOCAL_RULE_3	§4.3.3.4[3ed]	Add rules to the canonify rule set 3
LOCAL_SHELL_ARGS	§20.4.7.2[3ed]	Define the A= arguments for the prog delivery agent
LOCAL_SHELL_FLAGS	§20.4.7.2[3ed]	Define the F= flags for the prog delivery agent
LOCAL_SHELL_DIR	§20.4.7.2[3ed]	Define the D= directory list for the prog delivery agent
LOCAL_SHELL_PATH	§20.4.7.2[3ed]	Define the P= path for the prog delivery agent
LOCAL_SRV_FEATURES	§19.9.4[3ed]	Add or create rules for the srv_features rule set
LOCAL_TLS_CLIENT	§10.10.8.2[3ed]	Add your own rules to the tls_client rule set
LOCAL_TLS_RCPT	§10.10.8.3[3ed]	Add your own rules to the tls_rcpt rule set
LOCAL_TLS_SERVER	§10.10.8.2[3ed]	Add your own rules to the tls_server rule set
LOCAL_TRY_TLS	§10.10.8.4[3ed]	Add your own rules to the try_tls rule set
LOCAL_USER( )	§4.5.5[3ed]	Users that must be delivered locally
LOCAL_USER_FILE( )	§4.5.5[3ed]	Users that must be delivered locally listed in a file
LUSER_RELAY	§4.5.6[3ed]	Relay for unknown local users
MAIL11_MAILER_ARGS	§20.4.8[3ed]	Specify the A= arguments for the mail11 delivery agent
MAIL11_MAILER_FLAGS	§20.4.8[3ed]	Specify the F= flags for the mail11 delivery agent
MAIL11_MAILER_PATH	§20.4.8[3ed]	Specify the P= path for the mail11 delivery agent
MAIL11_MAILER_QGRP	§20.4.8[3ed]	Specify the Q= queue group for the mail11 delivery agent
MAILER( )	§4.2.2.2[3ed]	Define your necessary delivery agents
MAILER_DEFINITIONS	§20.3.3.1[3ed]	Define custom delivery agents
MAIL_FILTER( )	§7.6.2[3ed]	Define mail input filters
MAIL_HUB	§4.5.7[3ed]	Specify that all local delivery be on a central server
MASQUERADE_AS( )	§4.4.2[3ed]	Masquerade as the host specified
MASQUERADE_DOMAIN( )	§4.4.3[3ed]	Masquerade additional domains as the host specified
MASQUERADE_DOMAIN_FILE( )	§4.4.4[3ed]	File containing a list of domains to masquerade as the host specified
MASQUERADE_EXCEPTION( )	§4.4.5[3ed]	Hosts to not masquerade
MASQUERADE_EXCEPTION_FILE( )	§4.4.5[3ed]	A file containing a list of hosts to not masquerade
MODIFY_MAILER_FLAGS( )	§20.5.6.1[3ed]	Modify a delivery agent's F= equate's values

Table 4-1. mc configuration macros and directives (continued)

Item	sendmail text reference	Description
MSP_QUEUE_DIR( )	§2.8.37[3ed]	Specify the location for the MSP queue
OSTYPE( )	§4.2.2.1[3ed]	Include necessary support for your operating system
PH_MAILER_ARGS	§20.4.9[3ed]	Define the A= arguments for the ph delivery agent
PH_MAILER_FLAGS	§20.4.9[3ed]	Define the F= flags for the ph delivery agent
PH_MAILER_PATH	§20.4.9[3ed]	Define the P= path for the ph delivery agent
PH_MAILER_QGRP	§20.4.9[3ed]	Define the Q= queue group for the ph delivery agent
POP_MAILER_ARGS	§20.4.10[3ed]	Define the A= arguments for the pop delivery agent
POP_MAILER_FLAGS	§20.4.10[3ed]	Define the F= flags for the pop delivery agent
POP_MAILER_PATH	§20.4.10[3ed]	Define the P= path for the pop delivery agent
POP_MAILER_QGRP	§20.4.10[3ed]	Define the Q= queue group for the pop delivery agent
PROCMAIL_MAILER_ARGS	§20.4.11[3ed]	Define the A= arguments for the procmail delivery agent
PROCMAIL_MAILER_FLAGS	§20.4.11[3ed]	Define the F= flags for the procmail delivery agent
PROCMAIL_MAILER_MAX	§20.4.11[3ed]	Define the M= limit for the procmail delivery agent
PROCMAIL_MAILER_PATH	§20.4.11[3ed]	Define the P= path for the procmail delivery agent
PROCMAIL_MAILER_QGRP	§20.4.11[3ed]	Define the Q= queue group for the procmail delivery agent
QPAGE_MAILER_ARGS	§20.4.12[3ed]	Define the A= arguments for the qpage delivery agent
QPAGE_MAILER_FLAGS	§20.4.12[3ed]	Define the F= flags for the qpage delivery agent
QPAGE_MAILER_MAX	§20.4.12[3ed]	Define the M= limit for the qpage delivery agent
QPAGE_MAILER_PATH	§20.4.12[3ed]	Define the P= path for the qpage delivery agent
QPAGE_MAILER_QGRP	§20.4.12[3ed]	Define the Q= queue group for the qpage delivery agent
QUEUE_DIR	§24.9.82[3ed]	Specify the directory or directories to use for queueing
QUEUE_GROUP( )	§11.4.3[3ed]	Define a queue group
RELAY_DOMAIN( )	§7.4.1.1[3ed]	Specify hosts for whom to relay
RELAY_DOMAIN_FILE( )	§7.4.1.2[3ed]	The file containing a list of hosts for whom to relay
RELAY_MAILER_ARGS	§20.4.13[3ed]	Define the A= arguments for the relay delivery agent
RELAY_MAILER_FLAGS	§20.4.13[3ed]	Define the F= flags for the relay delivery agent
RELAY_MAILER_MAXMSGS	§20.4.13[3ed]	Define the m= limit for the relay delivery agent
RELAY_MAILER_QGRP	§20.4.13[3ed]	Define the Q= queue group for the relay delivery agent
SITE( )	§4.6.5[3ed]	Declare sites for SITECONFIG *mc* macro (obsolete)
SITECONFIG( )	§4.6.6[3ed]	Set up local UUCP connections (obsolete)
SMART_HOST	§4.3.3.6[3ed]	Declare the machine that should be used as the ultimate relay
SMTP_MAILER_ARGS	§20.4.13[3ed]	Define the A= arguments for the smtp of delivery agents

Table 4-1. mc configuration macros and directives (continued)

Item	sendmail text reference	Description
SMTP_MAILER_CHARSET	§20.4.13[3ed]	Define the C= character set for the smtp suite of delivery agents
SMTP_MAILER_FLAGS	§20.4.13[3ed]	Define the F= flags for the smtp suite of delivery agents
SMTP_MAILER_MAX	§20.4.13[3ed]	Define the M= limit for the smtp suite of delivery agents
SMTP_MAILER_MAXMSGS	§20.4.13[3ed]	Define the m= limit for the smtp suite of delivery agents
SMTP_MAILER_MAXRCPTS	§20.4.13[3ed]	Define the r= recipient limit for the smtp suite of delivery agents
SMTP_MAILER_QGRP	§20.4.13[3ed]	Define the Q= queue group for the smtp of delivery agents
SMTP8_MAILER_ARGS	§20.4.13[3ed]	Define the A= arguments for the smtp8 delivery agent
SMTP8_MAILER_QGRP	§20.4.13[3ed]	Define the Q= queue group for the smtp8 delivery agent
STATUS_FILE	§24.9.106[3ed]	Specify the location of the statistics file
TLS_PERM_ERR	§10.10.8.2[3ed]	Redefine the STARTTLS errors to be permanent
TRUST_AUTH_MECH( )	§10.9.3[3ed]	List the mechanisms used to allow relaying
USENET_MAILER_ARGS	§20.4.14[3ed]	Define the A= arguments for the usenet delivery agent
USENET_MAILER_FLAGS	§20.4.14[3ed]	Define the F= flags for the usenet delivery agent
USENET_MAILER_MAX	§20.4.14[3ed]	Define the A= limit for the usenet delivery agent
USENET_MAILER_PATH	§20.4.14[3ed]	Define the P= path for the usenet delivery agent
USENET_MAILER_QGRP	§20.4.14[3ed]	Define the Q= queue group for the usenet delivery agent
UUCPSMTP	§4.6.7[3ed]	Define individual UUCP-to-network translations
UUCP_MAILER_ARGS	§20.4.15[3ed]	Define the A= arguments for the uucp suite of delivery agents
UUCP_MAILER_CHARSET	§20.4.15[3ed]	Define the C= character set for the uucp suite of delivery agents
UUCP_MAILER_FLAGS	§20.4.15[3ed]	Define the F= flags for the uucp suite of delivery agents
UUCP_MAILER_MAX	§20.4.15[3ed]	Define the M= limit for the uucp suite of delivery agents
UUCP_MAILER_PATH	§20.4.15[3ed]	Define the P= path for the uucp suite of delivery agents
UUCP_MAILER_QGRP	§20.4.15[3ed]	Define the Q= queue group for the uucp suite of delivery agents
UUCP_RELAY	§4.5.8[3ed]	Specify the UUCP relay host
VERSIONID( )	§4.2.3.1[3ed]	Version of the *mc* file
VIRTUSER_DOMAIN( )	§4.8.51.1[3ed]	Specify virtual domains to query in the virtusertable
VIRTUSER_DOMAIN_FILE( )	§4.8.51.2[3ed]	In a file, list the virtual domains to query in the virtusertable

CHAPTER 5
Companion Programs

The *sendmail* distribution comes complete with several companion programs that can help you use *sendmail*.

5.1 What's New with V8.13

Beginning with V8.13, *sendmail* offers expanded output for one program and new command-line switches for a couple of others:

- A new *mailstats* display (§5.1.1[V8.13]) includes a count of quarantined messages.
- A new *makemap* `-D` command-line switch (§5.1.2[V8.13]) allows you to define an alternative to # as a comment character.
- A new *vacation* `-j` command-line switch (§5.1.3[V8.13]) allows *vacation* to respond to messages, even if a user's name does not appear in a `To:` or `Cc:` header.
- A new *vacation* `-R` command-line switch (§5.1.4[V8.13]) allows you to redefine the envelope-sender address from <> to one of your own choice.

5.1.1 A New mailstats Display

As of V8.13, *sendmail* can quarantine messages based on the sender address so that they may be reviewed before being sent (§11.1.2[V8.13]). The *sendmail* program keeps track of the number of messages quarantined by updating the information in the *statistics* file (§24.9.106[3ed]), while the *mailstats* program (§5.4[3ed]) summarizes that information.

Prior to V8.13, the output produced by *mailstats* ended with the column that displayed the number of discarded messages (the `msgsdis` column). Beginning with V8.13, a new rightmost column has been added (called `msgsqur`) that shows the number of messages that have been quarantined:

```
# mailstats
Statistics from Sun Apr  6 09:47:44 2003
 M   msgsfr  bytes_from   msgsto    bytes_to  msgsrej msgsdis msgsqur  Mailer
 0   0       0K           15544     46975K    0       0       0        prog
 3   678     9590K        0         0K        62      0       0        local
 5   21430   264395K      1055      2082K     12969   0       0        esmtp
=====================================================================
 T    22108    273985K    16599     49057K    13031   0       0
 C    28551                          1980                     13031
```

The msgsqur column shows the number of messages (envelopes), if any, that have been quarantined since the *statistics* was cleared.

If you upgrade *mailstats* to V8.13 before you upgrade *sendmail*, *mailstats* will produce the following error when run:

```
mailstats version (4) incompatible with /etc/mail/statistics version (3)
```

5.1.2 New V8.13 makemap -D Switch

Normally, the *makemap* program (§5.5[3ed]) ignores lines of input that begin with the # character, but this can cause problems because some files use a different comment character. The *dig*(1) program, for example, produces output that uses a semicolon as the comment character:

```
;; ANSWERS:
host.domain.com   1845    CNAME   domain.com
```

To satisfy the need to build database-map files from such input, the -D command-line switch has been added to the *makemap* program. When you run *makemap* with the -D command-line switch, *makemap* will ignore lines of input that begin with a semicolon.

```
% makemap -D\; hash file.db < file.txt
```

Note that, we prefix the semicolon with a backslash to insulate it from interpretation by the shell.

5.1.3 New V8.13 vacation -j Switch

Ordinarily, the *vacation* program (§5.9[3ed]) will only auto-respond to messages that contain the recipient's address in the To: or Cc: headers. There will be instances, however, perhaps occurring as a result of aliasing or *~/.forward* file translation, when mail will be delivered with an address in one of those headers that is something other than the recipient's address. To illustrate, consider the following *aliases* file (§12.1.1[3ed]) entries:

```
root:          bob
bin:           root
sys:           root
webmaster:     root
hostmaster:    root
```

Here, the system administrator, bob, receives mail that is also sent to root, bin, sys, webmaster, and hostmaster. Normally, *vacation* will not respond to mail sent to any of these aliases. If *bob* wants *vacation* to respond even if the name bob is not found in the To: or Cc: headers, *bob* may cause it to do so by adding this -j command-line switch to his invocation of *vacation* in his *~/.forward* file:

```
|"/usr/ucb/vacation -j bob"
```

Henceforth, *vacation* will amend its recipient check* response (when otherwise able) to all messages, no matter to whom each is addressed.

But note, this switch can cause *vacation* to auto-reply to unexpected addresses so is better limited for use in restricted environments. Instead, when you know all possible addresses ahead of time (as you should, via the *aliases* file), use the *vacation* program's -a switch (§5.9.4.1[3ed]).

5.1.4 New V8.13 vacation -R Switch

There is always a chance that a *vacation* message will bounce. To prevent that, *vacation* (§5.9[3ed]) offers the -z command-line switch (§5.9.4.13[3ed]), which sets the return address for the message to be the null address:

```
<>
```

If you prefer a different return address, you may use the new V8.13 -R *vacation* command-line switch to define one. For example:

```
|"/usr/ucb/vacation -R bounce+vacation@bounce.yourhost.domain you"
```

Here, the -R command-line switch causes *vacation* to mail messages with a return address of *bounce+vacation@bounce.yourhost.domain*. Such a return address might be appropriate at a site that has a special address for all bounces.

You can also use this switch to have bounces sent to yourself at a plussed address. That way you can screen such bounces with *procmail*(1) or *slocal*(1), using a line like the following in your *~/.forward* file:

```
|"/usr/ucb/vacation -R you+bounce@yourhost.domain you"
```

5.2 Useful Tables

In this section, we have tables that contain the command-line switches for the following companion programs:

* The *vacation* program will still follow all of its other rules (except the recipient check). That is, it won't respond to a Precedence: header of junk or bulk; won't respond to list items; won't respond to mail from *postmaster*, *uucp*, *MAILER-DAEMON*, *mailer*, **-request*, **-owner*, or *owner-**; and finally, won't respond to a sender it has already responded to (within its response interval).

- The *Build* program (§5.2.1[V8.13])
- The *editmap* program (§5.2.2[V8.13])
- The *mail.local* program (§5.2.3[V8.13])
- The *mailstats* program (§5.2.4[V8.13])
- The *makemap* program (§5.2.5[V8.13])
- The *praliases* program (§5.2.6[V8.13])
- The *vacation* program (§5.2.7[V8.13])

5.2.1 The Build Program's Command-Line Switches

Even though the *Build* program is a shell script, it can use command-line switches just like a program. Table 5-1 lists the current *Build* command-line switches and describes what each does.

Table 5-1. Build command-line switches

Switch	sendmail text reference	Description
`-A`	§5.1.1[3ed]	Show the architecture for the build
`-c`	§5.1.2[3ed]	Clean out an existing object tree
`-E`	§5.1.3[3ed]	Pass environment variables to *Build*
`-f`	§5.1.4[3ed]	Use an *m4* build file in alternative directory
`-I`	§5.1.5[3ed]	Add additional include directories
`-L`	§5.1.6[3ed]	Add additional library directories
`-M`	§5.1.7[3ed]	Show the name of the object directory
`-m`	§5.1.8[3ed]	Show but don't create the directory
`-n`	§5.1.9[3ed]	Create the directory but don't compile[a]
`-O`	§5.1.10[3ed]	Specify the path of the object directory
`-Q`	§5.1.11[3ed]	Set prefix for the object directory
`-S`	§5.1.12[3ed]	Skip system-specific configuration
`-v`	§5.1.13[3ed]	Specify the build-variant

[a] The `-n` switch is not actually a part of *Build*. Instead, *Build* passes it to *make*(1).

5.2.2 The editmap Command-Line Switches

The command-line switches for *editmap* precede the *dbtype*:

```
% editmap -q switches dbtype dbfile key
% editmap -x switches dbtype dbfile key
% editmap -u switches dbtype dbfile key new_value
```

Switches are single characters, prefixed with a – character. They can also be combined:

```
-N -f          ← good
-Nf            ← also good
```

The complete list of switches is shown in Table 5-2. (See *getopt*(3) for additional information about the way they are handled.) We describe each switch in detail in the sections indicated in the table.

Table 5-2. editmap program's switches

Switch	sendmail text reference	Description
-C	§5.2.1.1[3ed]	Use an alternative *sendmail* configuration file
-f	§5.2.1.2[3ed]	Don't fold uppercase to lowercase
-N	§5.2.1.3[3ed]	Append a null byte to all keys
-q	§5.2.1.4[3ed]	Query for specified key
-u	§5.2.1.5[3ed]	Update the key with a new value
-v		Run in verbose mode (a no-op as of V8.13)
-x	§5.2.1.6[3ed]	Delete key from database

5.2.3 The mail.local Command-Line Switches

The *mail.local* program has a small set of command-line switches that modify its behavior. They are summarized in Table 5-3 and detailed in the sections indicated.

Table 5-3. The mail.local program's switches

Switch	sendmail text reference	Description
-7	§5.3.3.1[3ed]	Don't advertise 8BITMIME in LMTP
-b	§5.3.3.2[3ed]	Mailbox over quota error is permanent, not temporary
-d	§5.3.3.3[3ed]	Allow old-style -d execution
-D	§5.3.3.4[3ed]	Specify mailbox database type
-f	§5.3.3.5[3ed]	Specify the envelope sender
-h	§5.3.3.6[3ed]	Store mail in user's home directory
-l	§5.3.3.7[3ed]	Turn on LMTP mode
-r	§5.3.3.8[3ed]	Specify the envelope sender (deprecated)

5.2.4 The mailstats Program's Command-Line Switches

The *mailstats* program has a modest number of command-line switches. They are summarized in Table 5-4 and described more fully in the sections indicated.

Table 5-4. The mailstats program's switches

Switch	sendmail text reference	Description
`-c`	§5.4.4.1[3ed]	Use *submit.cf* instead
`-C`	§5.4.4.2[3ed]	Specify the configuration file's location
`-f`	§5.4.4.3[3ed]	Specify another name for the *statistics* file
`-o`	§5.4.4.4[3ed]	Omit the delivery agent names
`-p`	§5.4.4.5[3ed]	Produce program-friendly output and clear *statistics* file
`-P`	§5.4.4.6[3ed]	Produce program-friendly output and don't clear *statistics* file

5.2.5 The makemap Program's Command-Line Switches

The command-line switches for *makemap* must precede the `dbtype` and the `outfile`:

```
# makemap switches dbtype outfile
```

Switches are single characters, prefixed with a – character. They can also be combined:

```
-N -o        ← good
-No          ← also good
```

The complete list of switches is shown in Table 5-5. (See *getopt*(3) for additional information about the way they are handled.)

Table 5-5. makemap program's switches

Switch	sendmail text reference	Description
`-c`	§5.5.1.1[3ed]	Set the cache size for `hash` and `btree`
`-C`	§5.5.1.2[3ed]	Use an alternative *sendmail* configuration file
`-d`	§5.5.1.3[3ed]	Allow duplicate keys in database
`-D`	§5.1.2[V8.13]	Define a new comment character (V8.13 and later)
`-e`	§5.5.1.4[3ed]	Allow empty data for keys
`-f`	§5.5.1.5[3ed]	Don't fold uppercase to lowercase
`-l`	§5.5.1.6[3ed]	List database types supported
`-N`	§5.5.1.7[3ed]	Append a null byte to all keys
`-o`	§5.5.1.8[3ed]	Append to, don't overwrite the file
`-r`	§5.5.1.9[3ed]	Replace (silently) duplicate keys
`-s`	§5.5.1.10[3ed]	Skip security checks
`-t`	§5.5.1.11[3ed]	Specify an alternative to whitespace for a delimiter
`-u`	§5.5.1.12[3ed]	Unmake (dump) the contents of a database
`-v`	§5.5.1.13[3ed]	Watch keys and data being added

5.2.6 The praliases Program's Command-Line Switches

The *praliases* program reads the *sendmail.cf* file to find the locations and types of *aliases* files. But a command-line switch allows you to point to a different configuration file, and another allows you to specify a particular *aliases* database file. Those switches are outlined in Table 5-6 and explained in the sections indicated.

Table 5-6. praliases command-line switches

Switch	sendmail text reference	Description
-C	§5.6.2[3ed]	Use an alternative configuration file
-f	§5.6.3[3ed]	Specify another name for the *aliases* file

5.2.7 The vacation Program's Command-Line Switches

The behavior of the *vacation* program can be modified with the command-line switches shown in Table 5-7. In the sections indicated, we explain each in greater detail.

Table 5-7. vacation command-line switches

Switch	sendmail text reference	Description
-a	§5.9.4.1[3ed]	Also handle mail for another name
-C	§5.9.4.2[3ed]	Specify an alternate configuration file
-d	§5.9.4.3[3ed]	Don't *syslog*(3) errors
-f	§5.9.4.4[3ed]	Use a different database file
-i or -I	§5.9.4.5[3ed]	Initialize the database file
-j	§5.1.3[V8.13]	Respond, no matter to whom it is addressed
-l	§5.9.4.6[3ed]	List the database's contents
-m	§5.9.4.7[3ed]	Use a different message file
-R	§5.1.4[V8.13]	Specify an alternative return address
-r	§5.9.4.8[3ed]	Change the notification interval
-s	§5.9.4.9[3ed]	Specify the sender in the command line
-t	§5.9.4.10[3ed]	Ignored for compatibility with Sun's vacation
-U	§5.9.4.11[3ed]	Don't look up the user in the *passwd*(5) file
-x	§5.9.4.12[3ed]	Exclude a list of addresses
-z	§5.9.4.13[3ed]	Set the sender to <>

CHAPTER 6

Tune Performance

When *sendmail* is installed with near-default settings, it provides excellent email services for most machines. But when installed to service high loads, high volumes, or high rates, special tuning becomes a requirement.

6.1 What's New with V8.13

There are a few new items in V8.13 that affect performance tuning. They are described in other chapters but referenced here. In this chapter, we augment some of the knowledge imparted in the third edition of the *sendmail* book.

- The `RequiresDirfsync` option (§24.1.12[V8.13]) turns off the `REQUIRES_DIR_FSYNC` (§3.4.47[3ed]) compile-time macro's setting at runtime. Turning off directory *fsyncs* increases performance—but at (possibly) increased risk.
- The existing `SuperSafe` option (§24.9.107[3ed]) now accepts a new `PostMilter` setting that delays `fsync()`ing the *df* file until after all Milters have reviewed the message. This improves performance when a great deal of email is rejected by Milters that review the message body.
- The `Timeout.queuereturn.dsn` (§24.1.15[V8.13]) and `Timeout.queuewarn.dsn` (§24.1.16[V8.13]) options have been added. Use them to lower bounce timeouts, and thereby to create less congested queues and increase performance.
- Some sites have developed delivery agents that receive messages using SMTP over standard input/output. Such delivery agents use the `P=[LPC]` equate (§20.5.11[3ed]) to achieve this effect. Beginning with V8.13, *sendmail* enables connection caching (§24.7.5[3ed]) for such delivery agents, thereby increasing delivery performance.

6.1.1 Queue Disk Mounts

Although this is not a V8.13 improvement, you can safely increase the performance of your queue disks under Solaris 7 and above, and other operating systems by mounting them with the following *mount*(1) options:

```
logging,noatime
```

Here, the `logging` causes transactions (such as creating and deleting files) to be stored in a log before they are applied to the disk. Once a transaction is logged, it can be applied to the underlying disk layout later. This speeds up disk I/O and can help a machine to reboot faster.

The `noatime` prevents inodes from being updated each time a file is read. This eliminates a disk write that has no significant value. The speed increase will be most noticeable when many queued files are being retried in parallel.

One or the other of these *mount*(1) options may not be available with your operating system. See your online documentation to find out which you can use.

6.2 Useful Tables

There are no tables from the third edition available for inclusion in this chapter.

CHAPTER 7

Handle Spam and Filter with Milter

7.1 What's New with V8.13

V8.13 has been augmented in several ways that benefit your ability to detect and reject spam email.

- The confREJECT_MSG *mc* macro no longer auto-inserts quotation marks around its value (§7.1.1[V8.13]).
- Envelope quarantining has been added as a means to hold mail for review. (See §11.1.2[V8.13] for a complete discussion of quarantining.)
- The Milter library has been enhanced by the addition of a smfi_quarantine() routine (§7.1.2.1[V8.13]), a smfi_progress() routine (§7.1.2.2[V8.13]), a smfi_stop() routine (§7.1.2.3[V8.13]), a smfi_setdbg() routine (§7.1.2.4[V8.13]), a smfi_setmlreply() routine (§7.1.2.5[V8.13]), a smfi_setbacklog() routine (§7.1.2.6[V8.13]) and a smfi_opensocket() routine(§7.1.2.7[V8.13]). Support for a 421 SMTP return (§7.1.2.9[V8.13]) has been added, the removal of the socket by *root* (§7.1.2.10[V8.13]) has been prevented, and macros may now be passed to a Milter's end-of-message routine (§24.1.17[V8.13]).
- The check_relay ruleset (§7.1.1[3ed]) is now called with the value of ${client_name} macro (§21.9.20[3ed]) so that it can deal with bogus DNS entries (§9.1.2[V8.13]).
- The new greet_pause feature allows protection from SMTP slamming (§7.1.3[V8.13]).
- The new (experimental) mtamark feature implements MTA marking by looking up TXT records in the in-addr.arpa domain (§7.1.4[V8.13]).
- The new use_client_ptr feature (§7.1.5[V8.13]) causes the check_relay rule set to use the ${client_ptr} macro as its first argument.

7.1.1 confREJECT_MSG

Prior to V8.13, the confREJECT_MSG *mc* macro was declared in *cf/proto.m4*, in part, like this:

```
ifdef(`confREJECT_MSG´, `$: "confREJECT_MSG"´, `$@ 5.7.1 $: "550 Access denied"´)
```

Any confREJECT_MSG macro specified in your *mc* file had quotation marks placed around its value when that value was inserted into your *cf* file. But beginning with V8.13, quotation marks are no longer automatically inserted. Instead, the value in confREJECT_MSG is inserted into your *cf* file as is (with no added quotation marks).

Note that if you previously depended on this auto-quoting in your *mc* file, you will now have to add quotation marks of your own.

7.1.2 The Milter Library

The Milter library has been enhanced by the addition of several new library functions:

- The smfi_quarantine() function (§7.1.2.1[V8.13]) can be used to quarantine envelopes.
- The smfi_progress() function (§7.1.2.2[V8.13]) can be called from within your xxfi_eom() routine to reset its timeout.
- The smfi_stop() function (§7.1.2.3[V8.13]) provides for a clean exit.
- The smfi_setdbg() function (§7.1.2.4[V8.13]) turns on Milter debugging.
- The smfi_setmlreply() function (§7.1.2.5[V8.13]) defines a multiline SMTP error reply message.
- The smfi_setbacklog() function (§7.1.2.6[V8.13]) sets the size of the listen(2) queue.
- The smfi_opensocket() function (§7.1.2.7[V8.13]) actually opens the Milter socket.
- The smfi_insheader() function (§7.1.2.8[V8.13]) inserts a new header into a message.

7.1.2.1 The new smfi_quarantine( ) routine

V8.13 *sendmail* has added a routine called smfi_quarantine() to the Milter library. It is used to quarantine (rather than to simply accept or reject) a message. Quarantining in general is described in §11.1.2[V8.13].

This new routine may only be called from the end-of-message handling routine:

```
struct smfiDesc smfilter =
{
    "YourFilter",      /* filter name */
    SMFI_VERSION,      /* version code */
    SMFIF_ADDHDRS,     /* flags */
```

```
        mlfi_connect,       /* connect info */
        mlfi_helo,          /* SMTP HELO command */
        mlfi_envfrom,       /* envelope sender */
        mlfi_envrcpt,       /* envelope recipient */
        mlfi_header,        /* header */
        mlfi_eoh,           /* end of header */
        mlfi_body,          /* body block */
        mlfi_eom,           /* end of message */          ← call from this routine
        mlfi_abort,         /* message aborted */
        mlfi_close,         /* connection cleanup */
};
```

But before you can use this new smfi_quarantine() routine, you must first add the new SMFIF_QUARANTINE flag to the flags part of the above smfiDesc declaration:

```
struct smfiDesc smfilter =
{
        "YourFilter",       /* filter name */
        SMFI_VERSION,       /* version code */
        SMFIF_ADDHDRS|SMFIF_QUARANTINE,      /* flags */    ← add here
```

Note that the flags are bitwise-ORed together (using the "|" character). Once this is done, you can use this new smfi_quarantine() routine inside your mlfi_eom() routine, like this:

```
smfi_quarantine(ctx, "Possible virus found in message body");
```

Also note that the routine's arguments are composed of the usual ctx pointer, followed by a string that specifies the reason the message should be quarantined. The string must be non-NULL and not empty.

7.1.2.2 The new smfi_progress( ) routine

When the Milter is called at the end-of-message, the default behavior (if you have not declared an alternative routine to handle that phase) is to return SMFIS_CONTINUE. But if you have declared a routine to handle the end-of-message phase, you may call this new smfi_progress() routine from inside it. This call to smfi_progress() causes *sendmail* to reset its timeouts so that your end-of-message routine has plenty of time to finish.

If your end-of-message routine requires far too much time to complete, you may call smfi_progress() again to gain any extra time needed. The single argument to smfi_progress() is the *ctx* pointer:

```
smfi_progress(ctx);
```

In general, it is best to write your end-of-message routines to be super swift, rather than requesting extra time from *sendmail*. When you request extra time, you risk that the connecting host will time out, causing all your work to be deferred.

7.1.2.3 The new smfi_stop( ) routine

When an error occurs while running your Milter (such as the inability to allocate memory* or a failure to write to a database) you would normally *syslog*(3) an error and call *exit*(3) to quit. But, a more graceful way to quit your Milter is by using the new `smfi_stop( )` routine. It is called like this:

```
(void) smfi_stop( );
```

The `smfi_stop()` routine always returns `SMFIS_CONINUE` no matter what, so you may safely ignore its returned value. The `smfi_stop()` routine sets an internal, global flag that causes all threads to return (exit) when each has finished the current connection. The result is a return from your call to `smfi_main()`, so that you can perform clean-up tasks before exiting or warm-restart the Milter.

Note that `smfi_stop()` returns, whereas *exit*(3) does not. Be sure your code can handle that difference before replacing *exit*(3) with `smfi_stop()`.

7.1.2.4 The new smfi_setdbg( ) routine

Inside the Milter library, selected actions by those library routines may be traced. You turn tracing on and off with this new `smfi_setdbg()` routine. It takes a single argument (which is a tracing level) to use:

```
(void) smfi_setdbg(level);
```

The `smfi_setdbg()` routine always returns `SMFIS_CONINUE` no matter what, so you may safely ignore its returned value. The `smfi_setdbg()` routine sets an internal, global variable that causes selected events to be logged or printed. The default is zero, which turns off tracing. The maximum is six,† which prints the most tracing. To see what is traced and how to interpret that tracing output, search for `dbg` in the *libmilter/*.c* source files.

7.1.2.5 The new smfi_setmlreply( ) routine

The new `smfi_setmlreply()` library routine allows your Milter to return errors that have multiple lines. It is used like this:

```
ret = smfi_setmlreply(ctx, smtpcode, dsncode, msg1, msg2, ..., NULL);
```

Here, *ctx* is the common context pointer, *smtpcode* is a string containing a three-digit SMTP reply code, and *dsncode* is a string containing three integers separated by two dots that form a DSN reply code. *msg1*, *msg2*, etc. are strings (or pointers to strings). Each string will occupy a separate line of the error message. Concluding this list of one or more strings is the literal NULL.

* You should try to allocate several times with a *sleep*(3) between each, just in case the problem is transient.

† Levels higher than six are interpreted the same as six.

The following, for example, causes *sendmail* to issue the maximum amount of information with each bounce of an offending message:

```
ret = smfi_setmlreply(ctx, "421", "4.7.1",
        "We do not accept spam from your site,",
        "Contact whitelist@our.domain to be whitelisted",
        "or telephone (555) 555-1234 for help.", NULL);
```

This setting will cause the message to be rejected like this:

```
421-4.7.1 We do not accecpt spam from your site,
421-4.7.1 Contact whiteliste@our.domain to be whitelisted
421 4.7.1 or telephone +1-555-555-1234 for help.
```

Note here that if the Milter returns SMFI_TEMPFAIL, the SMTP reply code 421 causes *sendmail* to drop the connection immediately after issuing this reply (see also §7.1.2.9[V8.13]).

See *libmilter/docs/smfi_setmlreply.html* in the source distribution for further details.

7.1.2.6 The new smfi_setbacklog( ) routine

The Unix C-library *listen*(2) function takes two arguments: the *socket* on which to listen and the *backlog* (maximum length) of the queue of pending connections.

```
listen(socket, backlog);
```

The new `smfi_setbacklog()` routine is used to define a new value for *backlog*. The default is 20. This `smfi_setbacklog()` routine can be called at any point to dynamically change the setting for *backlog* each time the Milter listens for a new connection.

Note that some kernels may have built-in defaults of their own for *backlog*, so calling `smfi_setbacklog()` may have no effect at all.

7.1.2.7 The new smfi_opensocket( ) routine

After you call `smfi_setconn()` to declare the socket on which the Milter will listen, you may call the new `smfi_opensocket()` library routine, which actually causes the Milter to set up that connection for listening. The new `smfi_opensocket()` library routine is called like this:

```
ret = smfi_opensocket(flag);
```

Here, the *flag* tells the Milter to remove an existing Unix domain socket before creating a new one. If the *flag* is true (non-zero), the socket is removed; otherwise, it is not. If the socket is not a Unix domain socket, this *flag* has no effect.

Any error in opening the socket will return a value other than `MI_SUCCESS`. If that occurs, you should print or log the error and close down the Milter. Note that if you don't use this new routine, the socket will still be opened automatically by `smfi_main()`.

See *libmilter/docs/smfi_opensocket.html* for additional information.

7.1.2.8 The new smfi_insheader( ) routine

Prior to V8.13, the only way to add a header to the message was by using either the `smfi_addheader()` or the `smfi_chgheader()` routine. The `smfi_addheader()` routine has special logic in which existing header names were examined to determine whether the new name already existed and, if it was neither a trace header (such as `Received:`) nor a client or Milter added header, *sendmail* silently replaced the existing header's value with the new value, rather than adding the new header. Beginning with V8.13, the new `smfi_insheader()` routine allows you to unconditionally insert a new header, even if that header already exists in the message.

The `smfi_insheader()` routine is used like this.

```
ret = smfi_insheader(ctx, index, name, value);
```

The `smfi_insheader()` routine's first argument is the common context pointer `ctx`. The next argument is *index*—an index into the list of existing headers. If *index* is zero, the new header will be added at the beginning of the list, before the first existing header. If *index* is greater than the number of existing headers, the new header will be inserted after the last existing header in the list. Otherwise, the new header will be inserted after the header with that *index* count into the list of existing headers.

The *name* is the name of the new header (such as `X-MyMilter`) and excludes the colon. The *value* is the field value of the new header. If either of these two arguments is NULL, `smfi_insheader()` will fail. Note that before you can use this new `smfi_insheader()` routine, you must first add the `SMFIF_ADDHDRS` flag to the flags part of the your `smfiDesc` declaration:

```
struct smfiDesc smfilter =
{
    "YourFilter",           /* filter name */
    SMFI_VERSION,           /* version code */
    SMFIF_ADDHDRS,          /* flags */          ← add here
```

Omitting this flag will cause `smfi_insheader()` to fail. Other possible failures can result from memory allocation errors or network errors.

Neither *sendmail* nor the Milter library ensures that your new header is valid. It is up to you to make sure the header you insert does not violate any RFCs. You should also make sure that it does not cause headers to parse incorrectly.

7.1.2.9 SMTP 421 and SMFIS_TEMPFAIL

The connection routine in a Milter can cause a connection to be rejected. Prior to V8.13 *sendmail*, connections were rejected in a gentle manner. The connecting site was given a 220 reply, and all subsequent commands from that connecting site were each given a 550 reply—except for QUIT (a 221 reply) and NOOP (a 250 reply). This roundabout approach was needed to prevent harming broken MTAs that could not handle a 550 rejection to the connection gracefully.

The reply code that *sendmail* uses to reject or defer the current message is set by calling the smfi_setreply() Milter library routine. That routine accepts four arguments:

```
smfi_setreply(ctx, rcode, xcode, message);
```

Here, the *rcode* specifies the SMTP reply number that *sendmail* should return.

Beginning with V8.13, *sendmail* will reject the message with a 421 SMTP reply if you set *rcode* to 421 and if your Milter returns SMFIS_TEMPFAIL. When rejecting a connection, 421 allows *sendmail* to drop the connection immediately, instead of being forced to use the gentle approach described above.

7.1.2.10 Root won't remove socket file

When a Milter shuts down, it automatically removes any Unix domain socket that was used as the communication port. The communication port is set with the smfi_setconn() Milter library routine. If the argument to that routine begins with unix: or local:, the path listed following that prefix defines the Unix domain socket to use.

Beginning with V8.13, the Milter library will refuse to remove a Unix domain socket on shutdown if the Milter is being run by, or as, *root*.

7.1.3 The greet_pause Feature

Slamming is a technique used by some senders of spam email. It allows spamming machines and hijacked proxies to send a great deal of spam email very rapidly, without the need to monitor for rejections.* This is a boon to spam email companies, but a bane to those who resent that behavior.

To slam, a spammer first opens a connection to the SMTP server (in our case, a listening *sendmail* daemon). Normally, the sending client will not send anything to the server until the server issues its initial greeting:

```
220 mail.example.com ESMTP Sendmail 8.13.1/8.13.1;
    Fri, 13 Aug 2004 07:45:41 -0700 (MST)
```

With slamming, however, the client does not wait for the initial greeting. Instead, the offending client sends its entire SMTP message all at once, then disconnects, before the server (*sendmail*) has a chance to review the message's contents.

The greet_pause feature has been added to V8.13 *sendmail* to combat slamming. You use the greet_pause feature like this:

```
FEATURE(`greet_pause´, `ms_pause´)
```

The greet_pause feature takes a single argument, an integer representation of the number of milliseconds to wait before *sendmail* may send its initial greeting. The *ms_*

* Hijacking worms, loaded into unsuspecting PCs, are often used as proxies to perform just this sort of rapid spam email attack.

pause sets the default wait (we cover this shortly). If *ms_pause* is missing, no default is set. If *ms_pause* is greater than five minutes, the wait is silently truncated to five minutes.*

If *sendmail* detects input from the client during this wait, that input is interpreted as an indication of slamming. If slamming is detected, the following rejection (instead of the initial greeting just shown) will be issued to the client:

```
554 server_host_name not accepting messages
```

Whenever a slamming site is rejected like this, the following is logged with *syslog*(3):

```
rejecting commands from client_host_name [client_ip_address] due to pre-greeting
traffic
```

In addition, if the offending site continues to send SMTP commands, each command will be rejected with the following:

```
554 5.5.0 Command rejected
```

The greet_pause feature may also take advantage of the *access* database. To do so, the greet_pause feature must be declared after the access_db feature (§7.5[3ed]) is declared. If greet_pause is declared before access_db (or if access_db is not declared), the *access* database cannot be used with this feature.

When use of the *access* database is enabled, *sendmail* looks up the connecting host in the *access* database just before it begins to wait. First, the hostname (as taken from the ${client_name} macro: §21.9.20[3ed]) is looked up to see whether the canonical host name is in the database. Then, the host part (to the left of the dot) is recursively stripped to see whether the domain part is listed in the database (*host.sub.domain*, then *sub.domain*, then *domain*). If nothing matches, the same lookups are performed for the client's IP address (as taken from the ${client_addr} macro: §21.9.18[3ed]). First, the full address is looked up, then the network portions on dot boundaries are looked up (192.168.2.5, then 192.168.2, then 192.168, then 192).

To put entries into the *access* database's source file, prefix each line with a literal GreetPause and a colon. Then specify the host, domain, or IP address followed by a tab,† then an ASCII representation of the number of milliseconds to wait. For example:

```
GreetPause:host.domain        5000
GreetPause:domain             0
GreetPause:127.0.0.1          0
GreetPause:192.186.2          5000
```

Here, the first entry tells *sendmail* to wait 5,000 milliseconds (5 seconds) before issuing its initial greeting to *host.domain* (a hostname). The second entry tells *sendmail* to not wait at all (zero milliseconds) for the *domain* listed. The third entry tells *sendmail*

* RFC2821 defines five minutes as the maximum timeout for the 220 greeting.

† Unless you set a different column delimiter with the -t command-line switch for *makemap*.

to not wait when the connection is from the loopback interface (a memory interface on the local machine). And the last line tells *sendmail* to wait 5,000 milliseconds before sending its initial greeting to any host on the 192.168.2 network.

If a connecting client is not found in the *access* database, the wait used is taken from the second argument to the greet_pause feature:

```
FEATURE(`greet_pause´, `ms_pause´)
```

Here, *ms_pause* sets the default number of milliseconds to pause for any host, domain, or IP number that is not found in the *access* database.

Note that any detection of slamming will result in no Milter being called as well as prevent checkcompat() from being called.

7.1.4 The mtamark Feature (Experimental)

One way to reduce spam email is to set up a mechanism for marking each MTA as an MTA. To illustrate, consider a spam email received from a host with the IP number 192.168.123.45, which claims to be a legitimate MTA. Currently, *sendmail* can only look up that address using various open relay sites to see whether the IP number corresponds to an open relay, and to reject the message if it does. Under the new MTA mark proposal,* *sendmail* can look up a special TXT record associated with that address to see whether that IP address is marked as that of an MTA. You may emulate this lookup using *dig*(1) like this:

```
% dig txt _perm._smtp._srv.45.123.168.192.in-addr.arpa
```

Here, the _perm._smtp._srv is a literal defined by the MTA mark proposal. The 45.123.168.192 is the original IP address reversed, and the in-addr.arpa is the special domain used to treat IP numbers like domain names.

This lookup can return one of two possible TXT records. A "1" means that this IP number is that of an MTA. A "0" (or any other character) means that this IP number is not that of an MTA. Mail from an unmarked MTA may, under this proposal, be rejected.

Once this proposal is in place, spam sites are no longer able to send spam email via hijacked PCs, via hired PCs, or via worms implanted in PCs. When spam email does arrive, you will be certain that it is from a marked MTA only. Then by blocking email from that IP number, you will be able to turn off that site's spam at the source.

One problem with this approach is that many ISPs refuse to change PTR records for customers,† and this proposal must be implemented by those who control the IP numbers and not by those who control the domain names. Without control of your

* As of this writing, see *http://www.ietf.org/internet-drafts/draft-stumpf-dns-mtamark-01.txt*

† SBC, Qwest, and Hughs, just to name a few.

own PTR records, you cannot list an email server under this proposal. A glaring omission in this proposal is that it does not require an owner of IP numbers to create these records on the demand of legitimate businesses. Over time, this proposal and others like it will force everyone to use fewer and fewer large providers as their outbound relays, and eventually force email into a position where tolls and tariffs may be easily imposed by those large providers.

This experimental mtamark feature enables use of this proposal, but it should not be used unless you are willing to experiment. It is declared like this:

```
FEATURE(`mtamark', `reject', `tempfail')
```

Here, *reject* is either a rejection message of your own or, if it is omitted, a default that looks like this:

```
550 Rejected: $&{client_addr} not listed as MTA
```

Here, the ${client_addr} macro (§21.9.18[3ed]) contains the IP number of the connecting host that was looked up.

The second argument, *tempfail*, is either a literal "t" or a temporary failure message of your own. The "t" causes the following default to be used:

```
451 Temporary lookup failure of _perm._smtp._srv.$&{client_addr}
```

Thus, if the lookup returns a "0", the *reject* text is used and the message is rejected. If the lookup fails for a temporary (recoverable) reason, the *tempfail* text is used and the message's acceptance is deferred.

If the proposal is revised at a later date, the _perm._smtp._srv may need to be changed. If so, you may replace it by adding a third argument to the feature declaration:

```
FEATURE(`mtamark', `reject', `tempfail', `_perm._smtp._srv')
```

The default timeout for the lookup is five seconds. If that turns out to be too short for your needs, you may increase it by defining the MTAMARK_TO *mc* macro:

```
define(`MTAMARK_TO', `20')
FEATURE(`mtamark', `reject', `tempfail')
```

Note that the timeout must be defined before you declare the feature.

7.1.5 The use_client_ptr feature

The check_relay rule set (§7.1.1[3ed]) is used to screen incoming network connections and accept or reject them based on the hostname, domain, or IP number. The check_relay rule set is called with a workspace that looks like this:

```
host $| IPnumber
```

host and *IPnumber* are separated by the $| operator. As of V8.13, the new use_client_ptr feature causes a new rule to be inserted as the first rule under the check_relay rule set, which substitutes the value of the new ${client_ptr} macro (§21.1.3[V8.13]) for the prior host value passed.

Essentially, this causes V8.13 *sendmail* to behave like earlier versions of *sendmail* that did not use the delay_checks feature.

7.2 Useful Tables

Two tables are of interest for aiding the suppression of spam:

- Table 7-1 lists the *mc* configuration features useful for regulating relaying
- Table 7-2 lists the righthand-side values useful in the *access* database

7.2.1 Relay Features

Several *mc* configuration features affect relaying. Table 7-1 lists the features that determine how mail will, or will not, be relayed.

Table 7-1. Relay features

Feature	sendmail text reference	Description
access_db	§7.5[3ed]	Screen addresses and set policy
loose_relay_check	§7.4.2[3ed]	Allow percent-hack relaying
promiscuous_relay	§7.4.3[3ed]	Allow all relaying
relay_based_on_MX	§7.4.4[3ed]	Relay for any site for which you are an MX server
relay_entire_domain	§7.4.5[3ed]	Relay based on $=m
relay_hosts_only	§7.4.6[3ed]	Interpret domains in relay-domains and access database as hosts
relay_local_from	§7.4.7[3ed]	Relay if SMTP MAIL domain is in $=w
relay_mail_from	§7.4.8[3ed]	Relay if SMTP MAIL address is RELAY in access database, and provided the entry is properly tagged

7.2.2 Access Database Righthand-Side Values

The *access* database was introduced in V8.9 *sendmail* and improved upon in V8.10. It provides a single, central database with rules to accept, reject, and discard messages based on the sender name, address, or IP number. It is enabled with the access_db feature.*

In Table 7-2, we list the possible *access* database righthand-side values (which can be keywords or values) and describe the affect each has when it is invoked.

* Another feature, blacklist_recipients (§7.5.5[3ed]), allows recipients to also be rejected. Yet another feature, delay_checks, (§7.5.6[3ed]), allows even finer tuning based on the desires of individual recipients.

Table 7-2. Access database righthand-side values

Righthand-side value	sendmail text reference	Description
OK	§7.5.2.1[3ed]	Accept the lefthand-side entry
RELAY	§7.5.2.2[3ed]	Allow the lefthand-side entry to relay mail through this machine
REJECT	§7.5.2.3[3ed]	Reject the lefthand side entry (bounce the message)
DISCARD	§7.5.2.4[3ed]	Discard mail from the lefthand side
SKIP	§7.5.2.5[3ed]	Stop looking for the key, and don't look for any future parts of the key
XYZ text (deprecated)	§7.5.2.6[3ed]	Reject with custom SMTP code and message
ERROR:*XYZ text*	§7.5.2.7[3ed]	Reject with optional custom SMTP code and message
ERROR:*D.S.N*:*XYZ text*	§7.5.2.8[3ed]	Reject with a more precise DSN code
SUBJECT	§10.10.8.1[3ed]	Also look up the CERT subject
VERIFY	§10.10.8.2[3ed]	Verify the certificate
VERIFY:*bits*	§10.10.8.2[3ed]	Verify the certificate and require minimum number of encryption bits
ENCR:*bits*	§10.10.8.2[3ed]	The minimum number of encryption bits
QUARANTINE:*reason*	§11.1.4[V8.13]	Quarantine an envelope using this reason
milliseconds	§7.1.3[V8.13]	Milliseconds to pause before issuing the 220 SMTP greeting

CHAPTER 8

Test Rule Sets with -bt

The *sendmail* program offers a mode of operation (called *rule-testing mode*) that allows you to observe the flow of addresses through rule sets. The `-bt` command-line switch causes *sendmail* to run in rule-testing mode.

8.1 What's New with V8.13

V8.13 offers no new commands to aid in rule-testing.

8.2 A Useful Table

Beginning with V8.7 *sendmail*, rule-testing mode offers 13 simple commands that will help you understand your configuration file. They are listed in Table 8-1.

Table 8-1. Available -bt commands

Command	sendmail text reference	Description
`.D`	§8.2.1[3ed]	Give a macro a value
`.C`	§8.2.2[3ed]	Add a value to a class
`=S`	§8.4.1[3ed]	Show a rule set's rules
`=M`	§8.4.2[3ed]	List all delivery agents
`-d`	§16.1[3ed]	Turn debugging on or off
`$`	§8.3.1[3ed]	Show a macro's value
`$=`	§8.3.2[3ed]	List a class's contents
`/canon`	§8.5.1[3ed]	Canonify a host
`/mx`	§8.5.2[3ed]	Look up MX records
`/map`	§8.5.3[3ed]	Look up a database item

Table 8-1. Available -bt commands (continued)

Command	sendmail text reference	Description
`/tryflags`	§8.5.4[3ed]	Select whom to */parse* or */try*
`/parse`	§8.5.5[3ed]	Parse an address
`/try`	§8.5.6[3ed]	Try a delivery agent

CHAPTER 9

DNS and sendmail

DNS stands for Domain Name System. A *domain* is any logical or physical collection of related hosts or sites, such as *example.gov* or *www.example.gov*.

9.1 What's New with V8.13

- The `dnsbl` feature (§7.2.1[3ed]) no longer uses the `host` database-map type to look up addresses. Instead, it uses the `dns` database-map type (§9.1.1[V8.13]).
- The `DNSBL_MAP_OPT` *mc* macro (§9.1.1[V8.13]) has been added so that you may tune the database-map flags used with the `dnsbl` feature.
- The `check_relay` rule set (§7.1.1[3ed]) is now called with the value of `${client_name}` macro (§21.9.20[3ed]), allowing it to deal with bogus DNS entries (§9.1.2[V8.13]).

9.1.1 Feature dnsbl Uses dns Database-Map

The `dnsbl` feature (§7.2.1[3ed]) is used to enable the blocking of email from open relay sites, dial-up sites, or known spamming sites. It does so by invoking the RBL technique, which is discussed in §7.2[3ed].

Prior to V8.13, the `dnsbl` feature employed the `host` database-map type (§23.7.9[3ed]) to look up addresses. Beginning with V8.13, this feature now uses the `dns` database-map type (§23.7.6[3ed]).

The default declaration for the `dns` database-map for this feature looks like this:

```
Kdnsbl dns -R A -T<TMP>
```

If you wish to change the type of the lookup, you may redefine the `dns -R A` part of the expression:

```
define(`DNSBL_MAP´, `dns -R TXT´)
FEATURE(dnsbl, ...)
```

Here, the DNSBL_MAP redefines the lookup so that it performs TXT record lookups instead of A record lookups. Note that DNSBL_MAP must be defined before this feature is declared for the feature to have any effect.

You may also list additional arguments for the dns database-map used with this feature. Those additional arguments will follow the -T<TMP> part in the declaration and are specified like this:

```
define(`DNSBL_MAP_OPT´, `-d1s´)
FEATURE(dnsbl, ...)
```

Here, the -d1s tells *sendmail* to reduce the res_search() _res.retry interval to one second from the default of five seconds. Note that DNSBL_MAP_OPT must be defined before this feature is declared for the feature to have any effect.

9.1.2 Call check_relay with ${client_name}

Prior to V8.13, the check_relay rule set (§7.1.1[3ed]) was called with a workspace that looked like this:

```
host $| IPnumber
```

The *host* and *IPnumber* were separated by the $| operator. The *host* was the fully qualified canonical name of the connecting host. The *IPnumber* was the IP number of that host in dotted-quad form without surrounding square brackets, or the IPv6 number prefixed with a literal IPv6:. Because these values were looked up with DNS before the rule set was called, there was a possibility that those values could be falsely represented.

But, beginning with V8.13 *sendmail*, this problem is solved. The check_relay rule set is now called with a workspace that contains the value of the ${client_name} macro (§21.9.20[3ed]), which is assigned its value when a host connects to the listening daemon. This value is the canonical hostname of the connecting host, which is the same as the hostname stored in the $_ macro (§21.9.1[3ed]).

If you created your own Local_check_relay rule set, which relied on the old style workspace contents, you will need to redesign that rule set to use the new style workspace.

9.2 Useful Tables

There are no tables from the third edition available for inclusion in this chapter.

CHAPTER 10

Maintain Security with sendmail

When the administrator is not careful, the misuse or misconfiguration of *sendmail* can lead to an insecure and possibly compromised system.

10.1 What's New with V8.13

- A Milter no longer removes its socket when the Milter is run by *root*; see §7.1.2.10[V8.13].
- As of V8.13, AUTH information is no longer included in bounced email when *sendmail* is configure to use SMTP AUTH (§10.9[3ed]). This change was made to avoid the risk of leaking sensitive information.

10.2 A Useful Table

Table 10-1 shows recommended permissions and ownerships.

10.2.1 Recommended Permissions

Table 10-1 shows the recommended ownerships and permissions for all the files and directories in the *sendmail* system. The path components will vary depending on the vendor version of *sendmail* you are running. For example, while we might show the */usr/sbin/sendmail* path, your site might use */usr/lib/sendmail*, or even */usr/lib/mail/sendmail*.

In the "Owner" column of Table 10-1, the owner is indicated with a `root`, a `T`, an `R`, or some combination thereof. A `T` means the owner can be the user listed with the `TrustedUser` option (§24.9.112[3ed]). An `R` means the owner must be the one specified by the `RunAsUser` option (§24.9.94[3ed]) if that option was specified. We show `:group` when the group is important.

Table 10-1. Recommended permissions for V8.12 and above

Path	Type	Owner	Octal mode	ls(1) mode
/	Directory	root	0755	drwxr-xr-x
/usr	Directory	root	0755	drwxr-xr-x
/usr/sbin[a]	Directory	root	0755	drwxr-xr-x
/usr/sbin/sendmail	File	root:smmsp	2555	-r-xr-sr-x[b]
/etc	Directory	root	0755	drwxr-xr-x
/etc/mail	Directory	root,T	0755	drwxr-xr-x
/etc/mail/sendmail.cf	File	root,T	0644 or 0640	-rw-r--r--
/etc/mail/statistics	File	root,T,R	0600	-rw-------
/etc/mail/helpfile	File	root,T	0444	-r--r--r--
/etc/mail/aliases	File	root,T	0640	-rw-r-----
/etc/mail/aliases.pag	File	root,T,R	0640	-rw-r-----
/etc/mail/aliases.dir	File	root,T,R	0640	-rw-r-----
/etc/mail/aliases.db	File	root,T,R	0640	-rw-r-----
F/path[c]	Directory	root,T	0755	drwxr-xr-x
/var	Directory	root	0755	drwxr-xr-x
/var/spool	Directory	root	0755	drwxr-xr-x
/var/spool/mqueue	Directory	root,R	0700[d]	drwx------
/var/spool/clientmqueue	Directory	smmsp:smmsp	0770	drwxrwx---
:include:/path	Directories	root	0755	drwxr-xr-x
:include:/path/list	File	n/a	0644	-rw-r--r--

[a] The *sendmail* program sometimes lives in /usr/lib or in some other directory. If so, adjust this path accordingly.

[b] As of V8.12, *sendmail* is no longer `set-user-id root`, but is instead `set-group-id smmsp` or the like, and *sendmail* is only `root` when it is run by `root`. On some systems, older versions of *sendmail* might need to be `set-group-id kmem` for the load average to be checked.

[c] The *F* configuration command reads a class from a file.

[d] CERT (Computing Emergency Response Team) and the *sendmail* document *doc/op/op.me* recommend that the queue directories be mode `0700` to prevent potential security breaches.

CHAPTER 11

Manage the Queue

Mail messages can be either delivered immediately or held for later delivery. Held messages are referred to as *queued*. They are placed into either a single holding directory (usually called *mqueue*) or several directories from which they are later delivered.

11.1 What's New with V8.13

- The *qf* file's V line has been bumped to V8 in support of queue quarantining (§11.1.1[V8.13]).
- Queue quarantining is now officially supported (§11.1.2[V8.13]).
- The *qf* file's new q line lists the quarantine reason (§11.1.5[V8.13]).
- You may now manage lost (*Qf* file) envelopes (§11.1.6[V8.13]).
- Tunable queue-processing delays (§11.1.4[V8.13]).
- The new `confTO_QUEUERETURN_DSN` *mc* macro (see §4.1.3[V8.13]).
- The new `confTO_QUEUEWARN_DSN` *mc* macro (see §4.1.4[V8.13]).

11.1.1 The qf File's V Line

The `V` line (§11.11.19[3ed]) in the *qf* file (§11.2.5[3ed]) corresponds to the version of *sendmail* that created it. Table 11-1 compares `V` line *qf* file versions to corresponding *sendmail* versions.

Table 11-1. Queue qf file versions

V version	sendmail version
1	8.6 and earlier
2	8.7 and 8.8
3	8.9
4	8.10 and 8.11 built with `-D_FFR_QUEUEDELAY` not defined
5	8.10 and 8.11 built with `-D_FFR_QUEUEDELAY` defined

Table 11-1. Queue qf file versions (continued)

V version	sendmail version
6	8.12 built with -D_FFR_QUEUEDELAY not defined
7	8.12 built with -D_FFR_QUEUEDELAY defined
8	8.13

Note that the *qf* file's V8 line corresponds to V8.13 *sendmail*, which added official support for queue quarantining.

11.1.2 Queue Quarantining

Queue quarantining is the process by which envelopes in the queue are marked as being ineligible for delivery. Such envelopes may then be manually or automatically reviewed. If review permits, each such envelope may then be delivered, bounced, or discarded. Queue quarantining employs the queue's *qf* file, command-line switches, and the *access* database. Lost envelopes (covered in the next section) are also a part of this system.

11.1.2.1 Overview of quarantining

A *quarantined message* is an envelope containing one or more recipients that is held in the queue pending review. It can either be an inbound or outbound envelope that, for policy or security reasons, should not be sent or delivered immediately and should not be sent or delivered as is.

For example, consider a user who has a history of sending offensive email. You might want to intercept such a user's email on its way out, so it can be screened for certain words or phrases about which the user has been previously warned.

V8.13 *sendmail* implemented quarantining by creating a new kind of queued file. Instead of storing the envelope information in a *qf* file, a quarantined message has its envelope information stored in an *hf* file. The different file allows *sendmail* to process messages normally (quarantined messages are invisible) unless you specifically ask it to handle quarantined messages (make them visible).

Note that the *mailstats* program (§5.1.1[V8.13]) is an exception because it automatically includes the total count of quarantined messages in its output.

To insure that the reason for quarantining a message is not lost, a new *qf* file* line has been introduced. Called a q line (§11.1.5[V8.13]), it stores the reason the message was quarantined. In parallel, a new macro has also been added. Called ${quarantine} (§21.1.7[V8.13]), and intended for use in rule sets, it also contains the reason the envelope was quarantined.

* We say *qf* file, even though this new line appears only in the new *hf* file type.

Note that quarantining integrates well with all the other queuing facilities of *sendmail* and even works with envelope splitting.

In the following sections, we discuss how:

- Command-line switches manage quarantined envelopes (§11.1.2.2[V8.13])
- The *mailq* command displays quarantined envelopes (§11.1.2.3[V8.13])
- Milters can cause messages to be quarantined (§11.1.2.4)
- You may quarantine via the access database (§11.1.2.5)
- Quarantining can be determined via rules and rule sets(§11.1.2.6)

11.1.2.2 Quarantine command-line switches

The command-line can be used to quarantine and de-quarantine envelopes. V8.13 has added one new command-line switch and modified another. We will show the use of the modified switch first, then the new one.

The -qQ command-line switch. Normally, the queue is processed by invoking a `-q` command-line switch (§11.8.1[3ed]). This switch causes all the normally scheduled (nonquarantined) envelopes to be processed. By combining that switch with a `Q` argument, you tell *sendmail* to process quarantined messages instead.

Note that it is not possible to operate on both normal and quarantined envelopes at the same time. That is, listing `-q` then `-qQ` does not process both, but only quarantined messages.

Unless limited with other `-q` letters, the `-qQ` switch processes all the quarantined envelopes currently in the queue. To further limit the envelopes to be processed, specify any of these additional switches in the same command line:

```
-qIident      ← match any queue ID that contains ident  (§11.8.2.3[3ed])
-q!Iident     ← match any queue ID that does not contain ident  (§11.8.2.4[3ed])
-qRrecip      ← match any recipient address that contains recip  (§11.8.2.3[3ed])
-q!Rrecip     ← match any recipient address that does not contain recip  (§11.8.2.4[3ed])
-qSfrom       ← match any sender address that contains from  (§11.8.2.3[3ed])
-q!Sfrom      ← match any sender address that does not contain from  (§11.8.2.4[3ed])
-qGname       ← match any queue group with the name name  (§11.8.2.5[3ed])
-qQreason     ← match any queue group with the name name  (§11.1.2.2[V8.13]
```

For example, the following command line processes only quarantined envelopes in the queue group `okayclients` that were sent by the user `bob`:

```
/usr/sbin/sendmail -qQ -qGokayclients -qSbob
```

The same switches can also be used to determine what the *mailq* command will print. For example, the following prints the status of all the currently quarantined envelopes:

```
mailq -qQ
```

The -Q command-line switch. When the -Q command-line switch is used with an argument (such as -Q"reason"), it causes the specified envelopes to become quarantined. When used without an argument, it causes the specified envelopes to become de-quarantined.

For example, the following command line causes all currently queued envelopes sent by the user bob to become quarantined:

```
/usr/sbin/sendmail -qSbob@your.domain -Q"Bob resigned today"
```

Here, the -qSbob@your.domain causes the queue to be searched for all envelopes that are from the sender (the -qS) bob at your domain. -Q is followed by the argument "Bob resigned today" so all those messages are quarantined using "Bob resigned today" as the reason.

To de-quarantine those same messages, you might use a command line such as the following, where the -Q is not followed by an argument:

```
/usr/sbin/sendmail -qQ -qSbob@your.domain -Q
```

Here, the -qQ tells *sendmail* to operate only on quarantined envelopes. The -qS causes *sendmail* to search the quarantined envelopes for those from the sender bob at your domain. And finally, the -Q, without an argument, tells *sendmail* to de-quarantine all the envelopes found.

11.1.2.3 The mailq command's display

When the -qQ command-line switch is specified, the *mailq* command displays only quarantined messages and the reason each was quarantined. For example:

```
# mailq -qQ
                /var/spool/mailqueue (1 request)
-----Q-ID----- --Size-- -----Q-Time----- ------------Sender/Recipient---------
h2VJcN3M012024   875429 Thu Mar 24 16:44 bob@your.domain
     QUARANTINE: Bob resigned today
                                         fred@competitor.domain
                Total requests: 1
```

Here, the -qQ command-line switch causes *mailq* to print only the messages (there is only one in this example) that were quarantined in the queue. Information about the message is printed first. The reason the message was quarantined is printed next. Then the recipient or recipients of the message are printed last.

If you have set up a Milter to automatically quarantine messages (§7.1.2.1[V8.13]), set up the *access* database to automatically quarantine messages (§11.1.2.5[V8.13]), or have created rule sets to automatically quarantine messages (§11.1.2.6[V8.13]), you should run *mailq* with this -qQ command-line argument periodically to discover whether anything has been automatically quarantined.

11.1.2.4 Use Milter to quarantine

The end-of-message handler, inside a Milter, can call smfi_quarantine() to quarantine the envelope being screened. (This Milter routine is described in §7.1.2.1[V8.13].)

11.1.2.5 Use the access database to quarantine

The *access* database (§7.5[3ed]) provides a single, central database with rules to accept, reject, and discard messages based on the sender name, address, or IP number. It is enabled with the access_db *mc* configuration feature (§7.5.1[3ed]).

A source text file used to create an *access* database might look (in part) like the following. Note that each line is composed of a key on the left and a value on the right, separated by tabs:*

```
Connect:192.167.23.45    REJECT
To:friend.gov            RELAY
From:we-spam-you.com     REJECT
```

Here, the first line says to reject the connection from the sending host that has the address 192.168.23.45. The second line says that it is okay to relay anything that is intended for delivery to (the SMTP RCPT TO:) the domain *friend.gov*. The last line says to reject any message that is from (the SMTP MAIL FROM:) the domain *we-spam-you.com*.

Beginning with V8.13 *sendmail*, the *access* database may also be used to quarantine envelopes. The key on the left may be any normally legal key (§7.5.2[3ed]). To quarantine the envelope defined by that key, use the new term QUARANTINE as the value on the right.

```
key            QUARANTINE
key            QUARANTINE:reason
```

Note that the QUARANTINE term on the right may optionally be followed by a colon and the *reason* the envelope is being quarantined. The *reason* may contain whitespace but must not contain newlines and should not be quoted.

For example, consider the three following entries in a source file for an *access* database:

```
Connect:192.168.1.23        QUARANTINE:Bob's PC
To:your.competitor.gov      QUARANTINE:Review mail to our competitor
From:head.hunter.domain     QUARANTINE:Employee theft?
```

In the first line, Bob's PC sends email by connecting to the SMTP port on the central mail server. Because of past behavior, or perhaps because of a worm or virus on Bob's PC, we want to quarantine all outbound mail from that machine.

* Or other separation character specified by the -t command-line switch with *makemap*.

In the second line, management has requested that all mail (using an SMTP RCPT TO:) to the domain *your.competitor.gov* be quarantined for review before it is allowed to be sent.

The last line says that inbound mail addressed (using an SMTP MAIL FROM:) from the domain *head.hunter.domain* be quarantined so that it may be reviewed to see whether employee theft is being attempted.

One limitation of the *access* database is that it cannot conveniently be used to combine tests. If your tests are more complex than the *access* database can handle, you may employ rules in rule sets too.

11.1.2.6 Use rule sets to quarantine

Any of the `check_` rule sets (§7.1[3ed])* and any of the header screening rule sets (§25.5[3ed]) may be used to quarantine envelopes. Any rule set that returns a `$#error` (§20.4.4[3ed]) with a `$@` part (§19.5[3ed]) that is the literal `quarantine` will cause the message to be quarantined.

```
R $* < @ bad.site > $*          $#error $@ quarantine $: reason
```

Here, we show a rule in a rule set that returns a `$#error`. Because the `$@` part is the literal `quarantine`, the message will be quarantined. Note that the `$:` part contains the reason the message is being quarantined.

Note that rule set quarantining affects all recipients of that envelope.

To illustrate rule set quarantining, consider the following *mc* configuration lines that cause any message that contains a special `X-review:` header to be held for review:

```
LOCAL_CONFIG
HX-review: $>Xreview

LOCAL_RULESETS
SXreview
R YES            $#error $@ quarantine $: X-review held for review
```

The first part of our example, the `LOCAL_CONFIG` part, defines a header. This header definition tells *sendmail* to pass all `X-Review:` header values through the `Xreview` rule set as specified using the `$>` with the `H` command.

The second part (`LOCAL_RULESETS`) defines the `Xreview` rule set (the `S` line), which contains a single rule that looks for a value that is the literal word `YES`. If that header's value is `YES`, the message is quarantined with the reason shown. If that header is missing, or if it has any other value, this quarantine step is skipped.

Note that rules sets can detect whether a message has already been quarantined by checking the `${quarantine}` *sendmail* macro (§21.1.7[V8.13]). If that macro has a value, the message is already quarantined.

* Except the `check_compat` rule set.

11.1.3 Logging

Whenever a message is quarantined, the fact that it was quarantined and the reason for doing so is logged using *syslog*(3). One log line is produced to record the quarantine event. Another is produced for each recipient to show that each was also quarantined.

The information logged for the quarantine event varies depending on the method used to quarantine. If a rule set is used, for example, a log line such as the following might be produced:

```
Oct  9 11:26:00 your.domain sendmail[4788]: f99IPuIH004788: ruleset=check_mail,
arg1=bob@competitor.gov, quarantine=Hold mail from competitor.gov
```

This line (wrapped to fit the page) shows that the `check_mail` rule set found the address *bob@competitor.gov* in its workspace and quarantined the message for the reason shown.

A Milter can also cause messages to be quarantined. The log line, produced by such a Milter event, might look like the following:

```
Oct  23 09:25:59 monkeyboy sendmail[52314]: f99IPuIH004787: milter=DocMilter,
quarantine=Suspect application/ms-word attachment
```

Here, the Milter named `DocMilter` found a MIME type that indicated a possible Microsoft Word document was included as an attachment.

In addition to event logging, each recipient is also logged. For example, consider the following log line:

```
Nov 21 09:32:13 your.domain sendmail[33522]: fALHVwAQ033522: to=<bob@your.domain>,
delay=00:00:06, mailer=local, pri=30029, quarantine=Suspect application/ms-word
attachment, stat=quarantine
```

Here the `quarantine=` equate shows the reason the message was quarantined, and the `stat=` equate prints the literal word `quarantine`.

When Milters, the *access* database, and rule sets are used to automatically quarantine messages, a script may be devised to detect the `quarantine=` equate in logging output. When run nightly, such a script might email the *postmaster* with a summary of quarantined messages for that day.

11.1.4 Manage Quarantined Envelopes with qtool.pl

The *qtool.pl* program is located in the *contrib* subdirectory of the source distribution. It is a *perl*(1) script that allows you to move envelopes between queues, bounce envelopes, and remove envelopes.

In general, if you use queue groups (§11.4[3ed]), you should not use *qtool.pl* to move queued messages. However, it is always safe to move quarantined messages, because they are invisible to *sendmail* unless you manually cause *sendmail* to recognize them.

As of V8.13, the -Q command-line switch tells *qtool.pl* to operate on quarantined messages rather than on normal messages. For example, the following command causes all the quarantined messages in the main queue to be moved to a holding queue.

```
#./qtool.pl -Q /var/spool/hold /var/spool/mqueue
```

Also, as of V8.13, a new %msg hash variable has been introduced. Called quarantine_reason, it can be used to match strings in the quarantine reason. To illustrate, consider the need to bounce all messages that were quarantined with a reason that contained the word Virus.

```
#./qtool.pl -b -Q -e '$msg{quarantine_reason} =~ m/Virus/'
```

See the online manual for the *qtool.pl* program (*contrib/qtool.8*) for a complete guide to using that program.

11.1.5 The qf File's q Line

As of V8.13, the *qf* file's q line is used to store the reason that an envelope was quarantined. The q line should only appear in quarantined envelopes—that is, in *hf* files, not in *qf* files. If a q line appears in a *qf* file, that file will be silently converted into an *hf* file. Thus, it does no good to simply rename an *hf* file into a *qf* file.

The format of a q line looks like this:

```
qreason
```

There may only be one q line in an *hf* file. The *reason* is the reason the envelope was quarantined.

11.1.6 Handle Lost Envelopes

A problem with a *qf* file (such as a missing ending dot) can result in the loss of that file. When *sendmail* looses a *qf* file, it changes the first part of the filename into a *Qf* and logs that it did so. Other reasons an envelope can be lost are covered in §11.5[3ed].

You may now use command-line switches to handle lost envelopes. Note, however, that handling lost envelopes, without first repairing the problem that caused the loss, can be risky.

Beginning with V8.13, the new -qL command-line switch allows you to view and handle lost files.* One use for this new switch is to examine the mail queue to see whether any lost files exist:

```
% mailq -qL
                /var/spool/mqueue (1 request)
-----Q-ID----- --Size-- -----Q-Time----- ------------Sender/Recipient-----------
```

* But not using *qtool.pl*, which handles only quarantined files, not lost files.

```
h7AJG4kr009003?     235 Sun Aug 10 13:16 <you@your.domain>
                                          <bob@other.domain>
                Total requests: 1
```

Here, the -qL command-line switch was used with the *mailq* command to see whether any lost files were present. This output shows a lost file (called Qfh7AJG4kr009003) located in the */var/spool/mqueue* directory. The ? character following the file's name indicates that it is a lost envelope.

This -qL switch can be combined with other queue-handling switches (§11.8.2.3[3ed]) to further limit what can be shown.

11.2 Useful Tables

- Table 11-2 shows the parts of a queued message.
- Table 11-3 shows the meaning of each line in the *qf* file, by key letter.

11.2.1 Parts of a Queued Message

When a message is stored in the queue, it is split into pieces. Each piece is stored as a separate file in the queue directory. That is, the header and other information about the message are stored in one file, while the body (the data) is stored in another. All told, eight different types of files can appear in the queue directory. The type of each is indicated by the first two letters of the filename, which begins with a single letter followed by an f character. The complete list is shown in Table 11-2.

Table 11-2. Queue file types

File	sendmail text reference	Description
df	§11.2.2[3ed]	Data (message body)
lf	§11.2.3[3ed]	Lock file (obsolete and removed as of V5.62)
nf	§11.2.4[3ed]	ID creation file (obsolete and removed as of V5.62)
tf	§11.2.6[3ed]	Temporary *qf* rewrite image
xf	§11.2.7[3ed]	Transcript file
qf	§11.2.5[3ed]	Queue control file (and headers)
Qf	§11.5[3ed]	*qf* file that has been lost
hf	§11.1.2[V8.13]	*qf* file that has been quarantined

The complete form for each filename is:

```
Xfident
```

The *X* is one of the leading letters shown in Table 11-2. The f is the constant letter f. The *ident* is a unique queue identifier associated with each mail message.

11.2.2 The qf File Internals

The *qf* file holds all the information that is needed to perform delivery of a queued mail message. The information contained in that file, and its appearance, changes in various releases of *sendmail*. Here, we document the *qf* file that is used with V8.13 *sendmail*. Note that V8.7 introduced a `V` version line that enabled later versions to correctly process older versions' queue files.

This section should be taken with a proverbial grain of salt. The internals of the *qf* file are essentially an internal interface to *sendmail* and, as such, are subject to change without notice. The information offered here is intended only to help debug *sendmail* problems. It is *not* intended (and we strongly discourage its use) as a guide for writing files directly to the queue.

The *qf* file is line oriented, containing one item of information per line. Each line begins with a single character (the "code" character), which specifies the contents of the line. Each code character is followed, with no intervening space,* by the information appropriate to the character. The complete list of code characters is shown in Table 11-3.

Table 11-3. qf file code characters

Code	sendmail text reference	Meaning	How many lines
A	§11.11.1[3ed]	AUTH= parameter	At most, one
B	§11.11.2[3ed]	Message body type	At most, one
C	§11.11.3[3ed]	Set controlling user	At most, one per R line
d	§11.11.4[3ed]	Data file directory	Exactly one
D	§11.11.5[3ed]	Data filename	Exactly one
E	§11.11.6[3ed]	Send errors to	Many
F	§11.11.7[3ed]	Saved flag bits	Exactly one
H	§11.11.8[3ed]	Header line	Many
I	§11.11.9[3ed]	Inode and device information for the *df* file	Exactly one
K	§11.11.10[3ed]	Time last processed	Exactly one
M	§11.11.11[3ed]	Message (why queued)	Many[a]
N	§11.11.12[3ed]	Number of times tried	At most, one
P	§11.11.13[3ed]	Priority (current)	At most, one
q	§11.1.5[V8.13]	Why the envelope was quarantined	At most, one
Q	§11.11.14[3ed]	The DSN ORCPT address	At most, one per R line
r	§11.11.15[3ed]	Final recipient	At most, one per R line

* Except the `H` (header) lines, which can be multiline, while header continuation lines do not begin with a character code and may indeed have intervening spaces at the beginning of each continuation line.

Table 11-3. qf file code characters (continued)

Code	sendmail text reference	Meaning	How many lines
R	§11.11.16[3ed]	Recipient address	Many
S	§11.11.17[3ed]	Sender address	Exactly one
T	§11.11.18[3ed]	Time created	Exactly one
V	§11.11.19[3ed]	Version	Exactly one
Z	§11.11.20[3ed]	DSN envelope ID	At most, one
!	§11.11.21[3ed]	Deliver-by specification	At most, one
$	§11.11.22[3ed]	Restore macro value	At most, one per macro
.	§11.11.23[3ed]	End of *qf* file	Exactly one

[a] Prior to V8.12, there could be only a single M line.

CHAPTER 12

Maintain Aliases

Aliasing is the process of replacing one recipient address with one or more different recipient addresses. The replacement address can be that of a single user, a list of recipients, a program, a file, or any mixture of these.

12.1 What's New with V8.13

There is one new aliasing item, but it is not covered until Chapter 23:

- Extend the default LDAP specifications for the `AliasFile` option and for file classes to include support for LDAP recursion by way of new attributes (see §23.1.2[V8.13]).

Here, we cover a topic that was only mentioned in a footnote in the third edition.

12.1.1 RFC2142 Common Mailbox Names

The name *postmaster* is required by RFC2822, and all sites must accept mail to that address.* RFC2142 takes the concept of postmaster one step further by recognizing that other roles now correspond to well-known email addresses. For example, most web sites that sell products also accept email to the address *sales*, which is now a well-known email address.

Table 12-1 shows all the newly required addresses defined by RFC2142. Of these, only *postmaster* is treated in a case-insensitive manner by *sendmail*.† That is, mail to *postmaster*, *Postmaster*, *POSTMASTER*, and *PoStMaStEr* will all be delivered to the same person.

* Some Internet sites (such as spews.org) fear mail to that address because of improper Internet behavior, and improperly reject mail to *postmaster*. Also, some sites (such as aol.com) reject all mail from residential sites, including mail to *postmaster* and *abuse*.

† Although RFC2142 requires that they all be treated in a case-insensitive manner.

Table 12-1. RFC2142-defined email addresses and aliases

Address	RFC	Description
abuse	RFC2142	Accepts reports of unacceptable behavior
ftp	RFC959	Accepts mail reporting ftp needs or problems
hostmaster	RFC1033 through RFC1035	Accepts mail reporting needs or problems with DNS
info	RFC2142	Who replies to requests for information about the business and its products and services
marketing	RFC2142	Handles marketing communications
news	RFC977	A synonym for Usenet
noc	RFC2142	Accepts mail for the network operations center that deals with network infrastructure problems and requests
postmaster	RFC2821 and RFC2822	Accepts mail describing email problems
sales	RFC2142	Replies with product or services information
security	RFC2142	Sends or receives security notices and answers security concerns
support	RFC2142	Accepts mail describing problems with products or services
usenet	RFC977	Accepts email notification of problems with the Usenet News system; (note that abuse should be reported to the *abuse* address)
uucp	RFC976	For sites that support UUCP, accepts mail describing problems with that service
webmaster	RFC2068	Accepts mail describing problems with or requests for changes in web services
www	RFC2068	A synonym for *webmaster*

Each of these required addresses is actually required only if you offer the service indicated in the description (shown in Table 12-1). For example, if you do not run UUCP (as few do), you may safely ignore mail to *uucp*. If you later add UUCP services, you should add an alias for *uucp*.

RFC2142, then, suggests that a well-formed *aliases* file might contain the following entries:

```
info:        recipient
marketing:   recipient
sales:       recipient
support:     recipient
abuse:       recipient
noc:         recipient
security:    recipient
postmaster:  recipient
hostmaster:  recipient
usenet:      recipient
news:        recipient
webmaster:   recipient
www:         recipient
uucp:        recipient
ftp:         recipient
```

Note that *recipient* will be a person in some instances, and in others it will be a program or a file.

In addition to requiring specific recipient addresses, RFC2142 also requires that mailing lists always have a mailbox that can be reached using the literal suffix `-request`. That is, if a mailing list is named *bobs*, the administrative address must be *bobs-request*.

This behavior is easy to maintain using *sendmail* (with the process is covered in §12.1[3ed]) and could be implemented in an *aliases* file entry that looks like this:

```
testlist:          :include:/mail/lists/testlist
owner-testlist:    postmaster
testlist-request:  bob
```

Here, the first line defines the actual mailing list as a list of addresses read from the file */mail/lists/testlist*. The second line defines the address that should process bounced email generated by this list. The third line defines the `-request` address that will receive administrative email concerning the list.

12.2 Useful Tables

There are no tables from the third edition available for inclusion in this chapter.

CHAPTER 13

Mailing Lists and ~/.forward

A *mailing list* is the name of a single recipient* that, when expanded by *sendmail* aliasing, becomes a list of many recipients. Mailing lists can be internal (in which all recipients are listed in the *aliases* file), external (in which all recipients are listed in external files), or a combination of the two. The list of recipients that forms a mailing list can include users, programs, and files.

13.1 What's New with V8.13

There is one new addition to mailing lists, but it is not covered until Chapter 23:

- Extend the use of LDAP to include aliases files so that LDAP recursion can be used to automate mailing list creation via LDAP queries (§23.1.2[V8.13]).

Here, we cover a few of the do's and don'ts of mailing list management that were omitted from the third edition.

13.1.1 Mail List Etiquette

Managing your own mailing lists can become tricky, especially in light of the recent explosion of spam email and the effort and cost of fighting it. In this section, we cover positive behaviors associated with mailing lists that will help you avoid being labeled a spam emailer.

- Clearly indicate subscription and management information
- Keep messages small
- Don't use the `To:` or `Cc:` headers to create lists
- Let software do the job for you
- Boot members who send spam email

* RFC defines a mailing list as a pseudouser's address that expands to multiple real email addresses. As you should recall, with the *~/.forward* file, real email addresses also can expand to mailing lists.

Before we begin, however, we need to mention the difference between an "open list" and a "closed list." An *open list* allows anyone interested in it to subscribe through some (usually) automatic process. A *closed list* is intended for subscribers only and is usually tied to some controlled membership mechanism.

In this section, we chiefly discuss open lists, although the lessons taught can often apply equally to closed lists.

13.1.1.1 Offer subscription and management information

Each mailing to a list should contain clear information describing how a subscriber may be removed from the list and to whom to send questions or complaints.

Subscribers must find it easy to unsubscribe for a wide variety of legitimate reasons:

- The subscriber's interest has flagged or the original reason for joining no longer applies.
- The subscriber left a workstation unguarded and a jokester subscribed that subscriber.
- The subscriber abandoned the email address and someone else inherited it.
- The subscriber moved, and the old address could not be forwarded.

Similarly, it is important that the manager of the list is easy to contact, because that person can uniquely fix a number of common problems:

- Someone on the list sent a spam email and must be removed from the list.
- The mechanism used to unsubscribe is broken.
- A member is receiving duplicate messages or omissions.

In general, there are only two places in a message that can contain such information: the message headers and the message body.

Some mailing list software inserts the information into custom `X-` headers on your behalf. For example:

```
X-Unsubscribe: remove@mailing.list.domain
X-Owner: list-request@mailing.list.domain
```

Others arrange for standard headers to work. For example:

```
From: list-request@mailing.list.domain
```

Here, merely replying to this message will get the subscriber's comments delivered directly to the list administrator (see §12.1.1[V8.13] for a discussion of the `-request` suffix).

Other mailing list software appends a standard footer to the body of every message. For example:

```
This list is brought to you by the power of mailing.list.domain.
To unsubscribe visit http://www.mailing.list.domain/unsubscribe
```

```
or send email to unsubscribe@mailing.list.domain. To report
abuse or problems, send email to abuse@mailing.list.domain. In
the event email fails you may also telephone +1-800-555-1234 or send
surface mail to MailingList, Inc.,
P.O. Box 555, City, CA 12345
```

This footer solves most of a mailing list's needs. It allows the recipient to unsubscribe either via a web site or by sending email to a clearly indicated email address. It also indicates to whom to send complaints and notices of problems. It is vital (and required) that if you send email from your site, you maintain for the user an alias named *abuse*, which causes mail for that name to be delivered to an actual person. If email fails, there is a telephone number and surface mail address to fall back on.

We recommend that you adopt as many of these techniques as you can. A recipient should be able to communicate with the administrator of the list by simply sending a message to the name of the list suffixed with a `-request`. Also, information about unsubscibing should be placed in clear text in the body of every message.

We don't show you how to fulfill those needs in this book. There are simply too many public and custom pieces of mailing-list software available. Rather, we leave the details of implementation to the reader.*

13.1.1.2 Keep messages small

Many businesses routinely reject messages that contain attachments or accept them and silently strip attachments. Mailing list management should adopt a similar strategy when accepting messages that will be broadcast to subscribers. To protect the recipients of the mailing list, either reject submissions that contain attachments or silently remove attachments (perhaps with an indication of that removal placed in the body of the message).

The method for rejecting or removing attachments varies depending on the type of mailing list software you use; therefore, we leave the discovery of that method up to you.

Some lists discuss matters that, by their very nature, require readers to view or hear examples. For lists that discuss images or sounds, for example, try to encourage list members to send web references instead of imbedding the images or sounds directly into each message. The following lines illustrate one appropriate technique:

```
I put my latest 3D images up for you to see at
http://www.my.domain/3d/bob/newimages. Let me know
if you like them.
```

Here, a half kilobyte message distributes images vastly more efficiently than would 2- or 3-megabyte message that imbedded the images directly inside itself. Because of that efficiency, use of references is kinder on ISP machines, and reduces the risk that the images will be removed or rejected because they are attachments.

* See §13.1[3ed] for a discussion of how to properly set up a mailing list with *sendmail*.

13.1.1.3 Don't pack addresses in headers

Hands down, the most offensive way to email a message to a mailing list is by placing all the recipients into a `To:` or `CC:` header, or into both. Not only will this likely mark you as a spammer, it also risks that your site will become listed at one or more blacklisting sites.

Never send mail to a mailing list like this:

```
To: list-owner@mailing.list.domain
Cc: bob@a.domain, ben@another.domain, bill@yet.another.domain,
      carrie@somewhere.gov, jose@there.domain, ...
      ... etc. to form hundreds of addresses
```

There are two serious problems with this approach. First, it reveals all the members of the list to every recipient on the list. This violates the privacy of each recipient. Most who join an organization or mailing list expect that their membership will be private and not advertised to others.

Second, messages with too many header recipients (typically more than 25 or so) are consider spam email by many sites. Mailing list messages are not spam email and therefore should never appear to be.

See §13.1[3ed] to learn the correct way to set up mailing lists using *sendmail*.

13.1.1.4 Let software do the job for you

As mailing lists become large, or emailings to them become frequent, lists eventually need to be moved from self-serviced lists to fully automated lists. There are three classes of software available for this transition. Open source software for Unix is mature and well written. Commercial software for Unix and Windows is widely available. Commercial services (some free with advertising included in each message) are also available.

A solution suitable to your needs can quickly be found by simply googling for one.

13.1.1.5 Maintain a clear policy

Each subscriber that joins your mailing list should be made aware of your list's policies from the beginning. One common way to distribute policy to subscribers is to include it in the initial greeting sent to a new subscriber. Another common method is to post it on a web site. Naturally, we encourage you to do both.

Your published policy should include many of the following points:

- The mailing list shall not be used to send unsolicited commercial email (spam email) to its members.
- Mailings to the list shall remain on topic and of general interest to the list as a whole.

- Members shall not engage in name calling, anger, or offensive language. Members shall not post messages to the list that could be construed as defamatory, libellous, or offensive to individuals, organizations, or institutions.
- Mailings to members of the list shall be sent directly to each, rather than broadcasted to the list as a whole.
- Members who violate these policies shall be removed from the list.
- Subscribers whose addresses continue to bounce for over a week shall be removed from the list.

13.1.1.6 Boot off offending members

As the administrator of a mailing list, it is your job to police that list. Any time a subscriber sends an offensive or spam email message to the list, you should immediately contact that subscriber and take corrective action. Many administrators will immediately unsubscribe the offender. Some administrators must find other solutions, because members may have to pay to subscribe.

Find out what your rights are as an administrator before you accept the job or before you set up the mailing list. Make certain you can remove offending subscribers in a timely manner to protect the remainder of your subscriber base.

As a courtesy to your remaining subscribers, you should let them know that you handled a certain problem and that the offending subscriber won't post to the list again.

13.2 Useful Tables

There are no tables from the third edition available for inclusion in this chapter.

CHAPTER 14
Signals, Transactions, and Syslog

The *sendmail* program can keep the system administrator up to date about many aspects of mail delivery and forwarding. It does this by logging its activities using the *syslog*(3) facility.

14.1 What's New with V8.13

There is one new option that effects logging, but it is covered in Chapter 24:

- The RejectLogInterval option (§24.1.11[V8.13]) tells *sendmail* how often (at what intervals) it should log a message saying that connections are still being refused.

Two equates that were not covered in the third edition and are covered here, along with a new one that is available with V8.13:

- The milter= equate, new since V8.12, shows the name of the Milter (§14.1.1[V8.13]).
- The action= equate, new since V8.12, shows the Milter's phase (§14.1.2[V8.13]).
- The quarantine= equate, new since V8.13, shows why a message was quarantined (§14.1.3[V8.13]).

14.1.1 The milter= Equate

The milter= equate (new since V8.12) shows the name of the Milter that was used to prevent the message from being sent. That name was set by the X configuration command when your configuration file was created. For example, the following sets the name of the Milter to Milter1:

```
INPUT_MAIL_FILTER(`Milter1´, `S=local:/var/run/f1.sock, F=R´)
```

If a message is prevented from being delivered by this Milter, the following equate will be logged:

```
milter=Milter1
```

This equate is most useful when you run multiple Milters.

14.1.2 The action= Equate

The action= equate (new since V8.12) specifies the Milter phase that was in effect when the message was prevented from being delivered. The phases correspond to the xxfi routines in the Milter documentation. For example, if the xxfi_header() routine was used to reject the message based on a header, the following action= will be logged:

```
action=header
```

14.1.3 The quarantine= Equate

The new quarantine= equate is used to log the reason that an envelope was quarantined (§11.1.2[V8.13]). For example, the following log line shows that this particular envelope was quarantined because it was destined for a competitor's site:

```
Oct  9 11:26:00 your.domain sendmail[4788]: f99IPuIH004788: ruleset=check_mail,
arg1=bob@competitor.gov, quarantine=Held, mail from competitor.gov
```

The use of this new equate is fully demonstrated in §11.1.3[V8.13]. Note that the reason for quarantining, that is printed following this equate, may contain spaces, equal signs, and commas, possibly making this output more difficult to parse.

14.2 A Useful Table

There is only one table in this chapter.

14.2.1 Logging Equates

When the LogLevel option level is 9 or above (§24.9.56[3ed]), *sendmail* logs one line of information for each envelope sender and one line of information for each recipient delivery or deferral. See Table 14-1.

Table 14-1. what= in syslog output lines

what=	sendmail text reference	Description
action=	§14.1.2[V8.13]	The Milter phase in effect
arg1=	§14.5.1[3ed]	The argument to a check_ rule set
bodytype=	§14.5.2[3ed]	The body type of the message
class=	§14.5.3[3ed]	The Precedence: header's value
ctladdr=	§14.5.4[3ed]	The controlling user
daemon=	§14.5.5[3ed]	The name of the sender's daemon
delay=	§14.5.6[3ed]	Total time to deliver
dsn=	§14.5.7[3ed]	Show DSN status code

Table 14-1. what= in syslog output lines (continued)

what=	sendmail text reference	Description
`from=`	§14.5.8[3ed]	The envelope sender
`len=`	§14.5.10[3ed]	The length of a too-long header value
`mailer=`	§14.5.11[3ed]	The delivery agent used
`milter=`	§14.1.1[V8.13]	The name of the Milter used to inhibit delivery
`msgid=`	§14.5.12[3ed]	The `Message-Id:` header identifier
`nrcpts=`	§14.5.13[3ed]	The number of recipients
`ntries=`	§14.5.14[3ed]	The number of delivery attempts
`pri=`	§14.5.15[3ed]	The initial priority
`proto=`	§14.5.16[3ed]	The protocol used in transmission
`quarantine=`	§14.1.3[V8.13]	The reason a message was quarantined
`reject=`	§14.5.17[3ed]	The reason a message was rejected
`relay=`	§14.5.18[3ed]	The host that sent or accepted the message
`ruleset=`	§14.5.19[3ed]	The `check_` rule set
`size=`	§14.5.20[3ed]	The size of the message
`stat=`	§14.5.21[3ed]	The status of delivery
`to=`	§14.5.22[3ed]	The final recipient
`xdelay=`	§14.5.23[3ed]	The transaction delay for this address only

CHAPTER 15

The sendmail Command Line

The initial behavior of *sendmail* is determined largely by the command line used to invoke it. The command line can, for example, cause *sendmail* to use a different configuration file or to rebuild the *aliases* file rather than deliver mail. The command line can be typed at your keyboard, executed from a boot-time script, or even executed by an MUA when sending mail.

15.1 What's New with V8.13

V8.13 *sendmail* introduced five new command-line switches and modified the way one existing command-line switch worked. Of these, the first is covered in this chapter and the last four are covered in Chapters 11 and 16.

- The modified `-v` verbose switch with the MSP (see §15.1.1[V8.13])
- The new `-D` debug file switch (see §16.1.1[V8.13])
- The new `-Q` quarantining switch (see §11.1.2.2[V8.13])
- The new `-qQ` switch to handle quarantined messages (see §11.1.2.2[V8.13])
- The new `-qL` switch to handle lost files (see §11.1.6[V8.13])

15.1.1 The Modified -v Verbose Switch with the MSP

Since V8.12, *sendmail* has run as `non-set-user-id` *root* (§10.1[3ed]). One problem with this scheme is that only the connection between the MSP *sendmail* and the local listening daemon is viewable when using the `-v` command-line switch. This restriction made it difficult to diagnose certain sending problems in the traditional manner.

Beginning with V8.13, the `-v` command-line switch causes the MSP *sendmail* to send the SMTP VERB (verbose) command to the local listening daemon. This causes the local listening daemon to print (as part of its SMTP replies) each step of what it is doing to send the message out over the Internet.

In the following examples, we show a verbose run with V8.12 *sendmail*:

```
% /usr/sbin/sendmail -v you@someother.site < /dev/null
you@someother.site... Connecting to localhost via relay...
220 your.site ESMTP Sendmail 8.12.9/8.12.9; Sun, 7 Sep 2003 15:48:23 -0600 (MDT)
>>> EHLO your.site
250-your.site Hello localhost [127.0.0.1], pleased to meet you
250-ENHANCEDSTATUSCODES
250-PIPELINING
250-8BITMIME
250-SIZE
250-DSN
250-ETRN
250-DELIVERBY
250 HELP
>>> MAIL From:<you@your.site>
250 2.1.0 <you@your.site>... Sender ok
>>> RCPT To:<you@someother.site>
250 2.1.5 <you@someother.site>... Recipient ok
>>> DATA
354 Enter mail, end with "." on a line by itself
>>> .
250 2.0.0 h87LmN09001068 Message accepted for delivery
you@someother.site... Sent (h87LmN09001068 Message accepted for delivery)
Closing connection to localhost
>>> QUIT
221 2.0.0 your.site closing connection
```

Note that under V8.12 all you could see was the conversation between the MSP *sendmail* and the local listening daemon. But beginning with V8.13, the -v command-line switch causes additional information to be printed by the listening daemon. That additional information is shown below, where each additional line is prefixed with a 050 SMTP reply code.

```
050 <you@someother.site>... Connecting to someother.site. via esmtp...
050 220 someother.site ESMTP Sendmail 8.13.0/8.13.0;
    Sun, 7 Sep 2003 15:55:35 -0600 (MDT)
050 >>> EHLO your.site
050 250-someother.site Hello your.site [192.168.5.12], pleased to meet you
050 250-ENHANCEDSTATUSCODES
050 250-PIPELINING
050 250-8BITMIME
050 250-SIZE
050 250-DSN
050 250-ETRN
050 250-DELIVERBY
050 250 HELP
050 >>> MAIL From:<you@your.site> SIZE=294
050 250 2.1.0 <you@your.site>... Sender ok
050 >>> RCPT To:<you@someother.site>
050 >>> DATA
050 250 2.1.5 <you@someother.site>... Recipient ok
050 354 Enter mail, end with "." on a line by itself
050 >>> .
```

```
050 250 2.0.0 h87LtZ9j053249 Message accepted for delivery
050 <you@someother.site>... Sent (h87LtZ9j053249 Message accepted for delivery)
```

The -v command-line switch will only put the local listening daemon into verbose mode if the configuration file for that daemon omits both the noverb (§24.9.80.10[3ed]) and goaway (§24.9.80.2[3ed]) PrivacyOptions option's settings.

```
define('confPRIVACY_FLAGS','noverb')      ← omit this
define('confPRIVACY_FLAGS','goaway')      ← omit this
```

If either option is declared, the local listening daemon will not go into verbose mode, and no additional information will print.

15.2 Useful Tables

There are two tables of interest for handling the *sendmail* command line:

- Table 15-1 shows the alternate names that *sendmail* will run under and the effect of each.
- Table 15-2 shows the command-line switches used by *sendmail* and describes the effect of each.

15.2.1 Alternative argv[0] Names

The *sendmail* program can exist in any of several places, depending on the version of the operating system you are running. Usually, it is located in the */usr/sbin* directory and is called *sendmail*,* but it can also be located in the */etc*, */usr/lib*, */usr/libexec*, or */usr/etc* directories. The location of the *sendmail* program can be found by examining the */etc/rc* files for BSD Unix or the */etc/init.d* files for Sys V Unix (§1.6.11[3ed]). Also, on some BSD-derived systems, the *mailwrapper* program and its */etc/mail/mailer.conf* file define where *sendmail* is located.

In addition to the name *sendmail*, other names (in other directories) can exist that alter the behavior of *sendmail*. Those alternative names are usually symbolic links to */usr/sbin/sendmail*. On some systems, they can be hard links, and in rare cases, you might actually find them to be copies. The complete list of other names is shown in Table 15-1.

Table 15-1. Alternative names for sendmail

Name	sendmail text reference	Mode of operation
hoststat	§15.1.1[3ed]	Print persistent host status (V8.8 and later)
mailq	§15.1.2[3ed]	Print the queue contents

* On SunOS 4.*x* systems, you can find */usr/lib/sendmail.mx* for use with the Domain Name System.

Table 15-1. Alternative names for sendmail (continued)

Name	sendmail text reference	Mode of operation
newaliases	§15.1.3[3ed]	Rebuild the *aliases* file
purgestat	§15.1.4[3ed]	Purge persistent host status (V8.8 and later)
smtpd	§15.1.5[3ed]	Run in daemon mode

15.2.2 Command-Line Switches

Command-line switches are command-line arguments that begin with a – character, and precede the list of recipients (if any). The forms for command-line switches, where X is a single letter, are:

```
-X                  ← Boolean switch
-Xarg               ← switch with argument
```

All switches are single letters. The complete list is shown in Table 15-2.

Table 15-2. Command-line switches

Switch	sendmail text reference	Version	Description
-A	§15.7.1[3ed]	V8.12 and later	Specify *sendmail.cf* versus *submit.cf*
-B	§15.7.2[3ed]	V8.1 and later	Specify message body type
-b	§15.7.3[3ed]	All versions	Set operating mode
-ba	§15.7.4[3ed]	Not V8.1 through V8.6	Use ARPAnet/Grey Book protocols
-bD	§15.7.5[3ed]	V8.8 and later	Run as a daemon, but don't fork
-bd	§15.7.6[3ed]	All versions	Run as a daemon
-bH	§15.7.7[3ed]	V8.8 and later	Purge persistent host status
-bh	§15.7.8[3ed]	V8.8 and later	Print persistent host status
-bi	§12.5.1[3ed]	All versions	Initialize alias database
-bm	§15.7.10[3ed]	All versions	Be a mail sender (the default)
-bP	§15.7.11[3ed]	V8.12 and later	Print number of messages in the queue
-bp	§11.6[3ed]	All versions	Print the queue
-bs	§15.7.13[3ed]	All versions	Run SMTP on standard input
-bt	§8.1[3ed]	All versions	Enter rule-testing mode
-bv	§15.7.15[3ed]	All versions	Verify: don't collect or deliver
-bz	§15.7.16[3ed]	Not V8	Freeze the configuration file
-C	§15.7.17[3ed]	All versions	Location of the configuration file
-c	§24.9.50[3ed]	(deprecated)	Set HoldExpensive option to true
-D	§16.1.1[V8.13]	V8.13 and later	Redirect debugging to a file
-d	§16.1[3ed]	All versions	Enter debugging mode

Table 15-2. Command-line switches (continued)

Switch	sendmail text reference	Version	Description
`-E`	§15.7.20[3ed]	Sony NEWS only	Allow Japanese font conversion
`-e`	§24.9.44[3ed]	(deprecated)	Set the `ErrorMode` option's mode
`-F`	§15.7.22[3ed]	All versions	Set the sender's full name
`-f`	§15.7.23[3ed]	All versions	Set sender's address
`-G`	§15.7.24[3ed]	V8.10 and later	Set gateway submission mode
`-h`	§15.7.25[3ed]	(deprecated)	Set the initial hop count
`-I`	§15.7.26[3ed]	(deprecated)	This switch is a synonym for `-bi`
`-i`	§15.7.27[3ed]	(deprecated)	Set the `IgnoreDots` option to true
`-J`	§15.7.28[3ed]	Sony NEWS only	Allow Japanese font conversion
`-L`	§15.7.29[3ed]	V8.10 and later	Define a *syslog*(3) label
`-M`	§21.2[3ed]	V8.7 and later	Define a *sendmail* macro on the command line
`-m`	§24.9.69[3ed]	Deprecated	Set the `MeToo` option to true
`-N`	§15.7.32[3ed]	V8.8 and later	Specify DSN NOTIFY information
`-n`	§12.6[3ed]	All versions	Don't do aliasing
`-O`	§24.2[3ed]	V8.7 and later	Set a multi-character option
`-o`	§24.2[3ed]	All versions	Set a single character option
`-p`	§15.7.36[3ed]	V8.1 and later	Set protocol and host
`-q`	§11.8.1[3ed]	All versions	Process the queue
`-Q`	§11.1.2.2[V8.13]	V8.13 and later	Quarantine or unquarantine messages
`-R`	§15.7.38[3ed]	V8.8 and later	Set what DSN info to return on a bounce
`-r`	§15.7.23[3ed]	(deprecated)	This switch is a synonym for `-f`
`-s`	§24.9.96[3ed]	(deprecated)	Set the `SaveFromLine` option to true
`-T`	§24.9.87[3ed]	(deprecated)	Set the `QueueTimeout` option
`-t`	§15.7.42[3ed]	All versions	Get recipients from message header
`-U`	§15.7.43[3ed]	V8.8 through V8.11	This is the initial MUA-to-MTA submission
`-V`	§15.7.44[3ed]	V8.8 and later	Specify the ENVID string
`-v`	§15.7.45[3ed]	All versions	Run in verbose mode
`-X`	§14.2[3ed]	V8.1 and later	Log transactions
`-x`	§15.7.47[3ed]	OSF and AIX 3.x only	This switch is ignored

CHAPTER 16

Debug sendmail with -d

The `-d` command-line switch allows you to observe *sendmail*'s inner workings in detail. But note that *sendmail's* various debugging switches differ from vendor to vendor and from version to version. This chapter is specific to V8.13 *sendmail*. These switches are perhaps best used with a copy of the *sendmail* source by your side.

Also note that many of the internal details shown here will change as *sendmail* continues to evolve and improve.

16.1 What's New with V8.13

Although there are no additional, useful debugging switch settings in V8.13, there is one new debugging command-line switch described next.

16.1.1 The New -D Debug File Switch

The `-D` command-line switch is used to redirect *sendmail*'s debugging output (§16.1[3ed]) into a file for later examination. It is used as in the following example, where *file* is the name of an existing or new file:

```
-D file
```

The `-D` command-line switch (if used) must precede the `-d` switch on the same command-line, otherwise the following error will print, and all debugging output will be printed to the standard output (possibly causing you to miss seeing the error):

```
-D file must be before -d
```

The *file* specified with `-D` must live in a directory that is writable by the user running *sendmail*. If the file does not exist, it will be created. If the file already exists, it will be silently appended to.

Extra care must be exercised when using the `-D` command-line switch as *root* because the target file will be appended to, even if it is a symbolic link to an important file.

For example, when */tmp/foo* is a nonroot owned symbolic link that points to */etc/passwd*, the following command-line, when run by *root*, will silently append debugging information to the */etc/passwd* file:

```
# /usr/sbin/sendmail -D /tmp/foo -d0.1 -bt < /dev/null
```

Using -D causes sendmail to drop privileges.

16.2 Useful Tables

There are two tables of useful information in this chapter:

- Table 16-1 lists all the -d categories in numerical order.
- Table 16-2 lists only those -d catagories that are considered useful to the day-to-day management of *sendmail*.

16.2.1 Table of All -d Categories

In Table 16-1, we list all the debugging switches by category, regardless of their usefulness to the administrator, and give a brief description of each. If you need more detail about those we do not document, we suggest you use *sendmail/TRACEFLAGS* as a guide to the appropriate source code files.

Table 16-1. Debugging switches by category

Category	Description
-d0	Display system configuration information
-d1	Show sender information
-d2	Trace *sendmail's* exit information
-d3	Print the load average
-d4	Trace disk-space calculations
-d5	Trace timed events
-d6	Show failed mail
-d7	Trace the queue filename
-d8	Trace hostname canonicalization
-d9	Trace *identd* exchanges
-d10	Trace recipient delivery
-d11	Trace delivery generally
-d12	Trace mapping of relative host
-d13	Trace the envelope and envelope splitting
-d14	Show header field commas
-d15	Trace incoming connections
-d16	Trace outgoing connections

Table 16-1. Debugging switches by category (continued)

Category	Description
-d17	Trace MX record lookups
-d18	Trace SMTP replies
-d19	Show ESMTP MAIL and RCPT parameters
-d20	Show delivery agent selection
-d21	Trace rules and rule sets
-d22	Show address tokenization
-d23	Unused
-d24	Trace assembly of address tokens
-d25	Trace the send-to list
-d26	Trace recipient queueing
-d27	Trace aliasing, *~/.forward* file handling, and controlling user
-d28	Trace the User Database
-d29	Trace `localaddr` rule set rewrite of local recipient
-d30	Trace header processing
-d31	Trace header validation
-d32	Show collected headers
-d33	Watch *crackaddr*( )
-d34	Trace header generation and skipping
-d35	Trace macro definition and expansion
-d36	Trace the internal symbol table
-d37	Trace setting of options and classes
-d38	Trace database processing
-d39	Display *digit* database-mapping
-d40	Trace processing of the queue
-d41	Trace queue ordering
-d42	Trace connection caching
-d43	Trace MIME conversions
-d44	Trace *safefile*( )
-d45	Trace envelope sender
-d46	Show *xf* file's descriptors
-d47	Trace effective/real user/group IDs
-d48	Trace calls to the `check_` rule sets
-d49	Trace *checkcompat*( )
-d50	Trace envelope dropping
-d51	Trace unlocking and prevent unlink of *xf* file
-d52	Trace controlling TTY

Table 16-1. Debugging switches by category (continued)

Category	Description
-d53	Trace *xclose*( )
-d54	Show error return and output message
-d55	Trace file locking
-d56	Trace persistent host status
-d57	Monitor *vsnprintf*( ) overflows
-d58	Trace buffered filesystem I/O
-d59	Trace XLA from contrib
-d60	Trace database-map lookups inside *rewrite*( )
-d61	Trace *gethostbyname*( )
-d62	Log file descriptors before and after all deliveries
-d63	Trace queue-processing forks
-d64	Trace MILTER interactions
-d65	Trace nonallowed user actions
-d66	Unused
-d67	Unused
-d68	Unused
-d69	Unused
-d70	Trace queue quarantining (V8.13 and above)
-d71	Unused
-d72	Unused
-d73	Unused
-d74	Unused
-d75	Unused
-d76	Unused
-d77	Unused
-d78	Unused
-d79	Unused
-d80	Trace `Content-Length:` header (Sun version)
-d81	Trace > option for remote mode (Sun version)
-d82	Unused
-d83	Unused
-d84	Unused
-d85	Unused
-d86	Unused
-d87	Unused
-d88	Unused

Table 16-1. Debugging switches by category (continued)

Category	Description
-d89	Unused
-d90	Unused
-d91	Log caching and uncaching connections
-d92	Unused
-d93	Unused
-d94	Force RSET failure
-d95	Trace AUTH= authentication
-d96	Allow `SSL_CTX_set_info_callback( )` call
-d97	Trace setting of auto mode for I/O
-d98	Trace timers (commented out in the code)
-d99	Prevent backgrounding the daemon

16.2.2 Table of Useful Categories

In Table 16-2, we provide a detailed description of debugging switches (by category) that we consider useful for the system administrator who is trying to solve an email problem. Categories that are only of interest to *sendmail* developers are omitted. If you have an unusual problem and need to use a category not listed here, you have to examine the source to find that category.

Table 16-2. Useful debugging switches by category

Category	sendmail text reference	Description
-d0.1	§16.6.1[3ed]	Print version, compilation, and interface information
-d0.4	§16.6.2[3ed]	Our name and aliases
-d0.10	§16.6.3[3ed]	Operating system defines
-d0.12	§16.6.4[3ed]	Print library (libsm) defines
-d0.13	§16.6.5[3ed]	Print `_FFR` defines
-d0.15	§16.6.6[3ed]	Dump delivery agents
-d0.20	§16.6.7[3ed]	Print network address of each interface
-d2.1	§16.6.8[3ed]	End with `finis( )`
-d2.9	§16.6.9[3ed]	Show file descriptors with `dumpfd( )`
-d4.80	§16.6.10[3ed]	Trace `enoughspace( )`
-d6.1	§16.6.11[3ed]	Show failed mail
-d8.1	§16.6.12[3ed]	DNS name resolution
-d8.2	§16.6.13[3ed]	Call to *getcanonname*(3)
-d8.3	§16.6.14[3ed]	Trace dropped local hostnames

Table 16-2. Useful debugging switches by category (continued)

Category	sendmail text reference	Description
-d8.5	§16.6.15[3ed]	Hostname being tried in getcanonname(3)
-d8.7	§16.6.16[3ed]	Yes/no response to -d8.5
-d8.8	§16.6.17[3ed]	Resolver debugging
-d11.1	§16.6.18[3ed]	Trace delivery
-d11.2	§16.6.19[3ed]	Show the user-id running during delivery
-d12.1	§16.6.20[3ed]	Show mapping of relative host
-d13.1	§16.6.21[3ed]	Show delivery
-d20.1	§16.6.22[3ed]	Show resolving delivery agent: `parseaddr()`
-d21.1	§16.6.23[3ed]	Trace rewriting rules
-d21.2	§16.6.24[3ed]	Trace $& macros
-d22.1	§16.6.25[3ed]	Trace tokenizing an address: `prescan()`
-d22.11	§16.6.26[3ed]	Show address before prescan
-d22.12	§16.6.27[3ed]	Show address after prescan
-d25.1	§16.6.28[3ed]	Trace "sendtolist"
-d26.1	§16.6.29[3ed]	Trace recipient queueing
-d27.1	§16.6.30[3ed]	Trace aliasing
-d27.2	§16.6.31[3ed]	Include file, self-reference, error on home
-d27.3	§16.6.32[3ed]	Forwarding path and alias wait
-d27.4	§16.6.33[3ed]	Print not safe
-d27.5	§16.6.34[3ed]	Trace aliasing with `printaddr()`
-d27.8	§16.6.35[3ed]	Show setting up an alias map
-d27.9	§16.6.36[3ed]	Show user-id/group-id changes with `:include:` reads
-d28.1	§16.6.37[3ed]	Trace user database transactions
-d29.1	§16.6.38[3ed]	Special rewrite of local recipient
-d29.4	§16.6.39[3ed]	Trace fuzzy matching
-d31.2	§16.6.40[3ed]	Trace processing of headers
-d34.1	§16.6.41[3ed]	Watch header assembly for output
-d34.11	§16.6.42[3ed]	Trace header generation and skipping
-d35.9	§16.6.43[3ed]	Macro values defined
-d37.1	§16.6.44[3ed]	Trace setting of options
-d37.8	§16.6.45[3ed]	Trace adding of words to a class
-d38.2	§16.6.46[3ed]	Show database-map opens and failures
-d38.3	§16.6.47[3ed]	Show passes
-d38.4	§16.6.48[3ed]	Show result of database-map open
-d38.9	§16.6.49[3ed]	Trace database-map closings and appends

Table 16-2. Useful debugging switches by category (continued)

Category	sendmail text reference	Description
-d38.10	§16.6.50[3ed]	Trace NIS search for `@:@`
-d38.12	§16.6.51[3ed]	Trace database-map stores
-d38.19	§16.6.52[3ed]	Trace switched map finds
-d38.20	§16.6.53[3ed]	Trace database-map lookups
-d41.1	§16.6.54[3ed]	Trace queue ordering
-d44.4	§16.6.55[3ed]	Trace `safefile( )`
-d44.5	§16.6.56[3ed]	Trace `writable( )`
-d48.2	§16.6.57[3ed]	Trace calls to the `check_` rule sets
-d49.1	§16.6.58[3ed]	Trace `checkcompat( )`
-d52.1	§16.6.59[3ed]	Show disconnect from controlling TTY
-d52.100	§16.6.60[3ed]	Prevent disconnect from controlling tty
-d60.1	§16.6.61[3ed]	Trace database-map lookups inside `rewrite( )`
-d99.100	§16.6.62[3ed]	Prevent backgrounding the daemon

CHAPTER 17

Configuration File Overview

The *sendmail* configuration file (usually called *sendmail.cf*, but for MSP submission, called *submit.cf*) provides all the central information that controls the *sendmail* program's behavior.

17.1 What's New with V8.13

There are no new configuration file commands as of V8.13.

17.2 Useful Tables

There is only one useful table in this chapter.

17.2.1 Table of Configuration File Commands

The *sendmail.cf* file is line-oriented, with one configuration command per line. Each configuration command consists of a single letter* that must begin a line. Each letter is followed by other information as required by that particular command.

The configuration file can also have lines that begin with a # to form a comment line, or with a tab or space character to form a continuation line. A list of all legal characters that can begin a line in the configuration file is shown in Table 17-1.

Table 17-1. sendmail.cf configuration commands

Command	sendmail text reference	Version	Description
#	§17.2[3ed]	All	A comment line, ignored
space	§17.4[3ed]	All	Continue the previous line

* A quick bit of trivia: initially, there was almost nothing in the configuration file except R rules (and there was only one rule set). Eric Allman recalls adding M and O fairly quickly. Commands such as K and V came quite late.

Table 17-1. sendmail.cf configuration commands (continued)

Command	sendmail text reference	Version	Description
tab	§17.4[3ed]	All	Continue the previous line
C	§22.1[3ed]	All	Define a class macro
D	§21.3[3ed]	All	Define a *sendmail* macro
E	§10.2.1[3ed]	V8.7 and above	Environment for agents
F	§22.1[3ed]	All	Define a class macro from a file or a pipe
H	§25.1[3ed]	All	Define a header
K	§23.2[3ed]	V8.1 and above	Create a keyed map entry
L		Obsolete	Extended load average
M	§20.1[3ed]	All	Define a mail delivery agent
O	§24.3[3ed]	All	Define an option
P	§25.10[3ed]	All	Define delivery priorities
Q	§11.4.2[3ed]	V8.12 and above	Declare queue groups
R	§18.2[3ed]	All	Define a transformation rule
S	§19.1[3ed]	All	Declare a rule-set start
T	§10.8.1.1[3ed]	All	Declare trusted users (ignored V8.1 through V8.6)
V	§17.5[3ed]	V8.1 and above	Version of configuration file
X	§7.6.2[3ed]	V8.12 and above	Define a mail filter for use

CHAPTER 18

The R (Rules) Configuration Command

Rules are like little if-then clauses* that exist inside rule sets, which test a given pattern against an address and change the address if the two match. The process of converting one form of an address into another is called *rewriting*. Most rewriting requires a sequence of many rules because an individual rule is relatively limited in what it can do.

18.1 What's New with V8.13

There is only one change in rules in V8.13:

- Balancing of special characters in rules is no longer checked when the configuration file is read (§18.1.1[V8.13]).

18.1.1 Rules No Longer Need to Balance

Prior to V8.13, special characters in rules were required to balance. If they didn't, *sendmail* would issue a warning and try to make them balance.

```
SCheck_Subject
R ----> test <----          $#discard $: discard
```

When a rule such as the above was read by *sendmail* (while parsing its configuration file), *sendmail* would issue the following warning:

```
/path/cffile: line num:  ----> test <----... Unbalanced '>'
/path/cffile: line num:  ----> test <----... Unbalanced '<'
```

Thereafter, *sendmail* would rewrite this rule internally to become:

```
R <----> test ----          $#discard $: discard
```

* Actually, they can either be if-then or while-do clauses, but we gloss over that complexity for the moment.

Clearly, such behavior made it difficult to write rules for parsing header values and for matching unusual sorts of addresses. Beginning with V8.13 *sendmail*, rules are no longer automatically balanced. Instead, unbalanced expressions in rules are accepted as is, no matter what.

The characters that were special prior to V8.13 but no longer need to balance are shown in Table 18-1.

Table 18-1. Former balancing characters

Begin	End
"	"
(	)
[	]
<	>

Note that if you have composed rules that anticipated and corrected this automatic balancing, you will need to rewrite those rules beginning with V8.13.

See the description of balancing (§25.1.1[V8.13]), which discusses this same change as it applies to the $>+ header operator.

18.2 Useful Tables

There are three useful tables in this chapter:

- Table 18-2 lists all the rule operators that you may use on the LHS of rule sets (§18.2.1[V8.13])
- Table 18-3 lists all the rule operators that you may use on the RHS of rule sets (§18.2.2[V8.13])
- Table 18-4 lists all the rule operators (§18.2.3[V8.13])

18.2.1 Table of LHS Operators

The LHS (lefthand side) of any rule is compared to the current contents of the workspace to determine whether the two match. Table 18-2 displays a variety of special operators offered by *sendmail* that make comparisons easier and more versatile.

Table 18-2. LHS operators

Operator	sendmail text reference	Description or use
$*	§18.9.21[3ed]	Match zero or more tokens
$+	§18.9.17[3ed]	Match one or more tokens
$-	§18.9.16[3ed]	Match exactly one token

Table 18-2. LHS operators (continued)

Operator	sendmail text reference	Description or use
$@	§18.9.2[3ed]	Match exactly zero tokens (V8 only)
$=	§22.2.1[3ed]	Match any tokens in a class[a]
$~	§22.2.2[3ed]	Match any single token not in a class
$#	§18.9.18[3ed]	Match a literal $#
$|	§18.9.23[3ed]	Match a literal $|
$&	§21.5.3[3ed]	Delay macro expansion until runtime

[a] Class matches either a single token or multiple tokens, depending on the version of *sendmail* (§22.2[3ed]).

18.2.2 Table of RHS Operators

The RHS (right-hand side) of a rule rewrites the workspace. To make this rewriting more versatile, *sendmail* offers several special RHS operators. The complete list is shown in Table 18-3.

Table 18-3. RHS operators

RHS	sendmail text reference	Description or use
`$digit`	§18.7.1[3ed]	Copy by position.
`$:`	§18.7.2[3ed]	Rewrite once (when used as a prefix), or specify the address in a delivery-agent "triple," or specify the default value to return on a failed database-map lookup.
`$@`	§18.7.3[3ed]	Rewrite and return (when used as a prefix), or specify the host in a delivery-agent "triple," or specify an argument to pass in a database-map lookup or action.
`$>set`	§18.7.4[3ed]	Rewrite through another rule set (such as a subroutine call that returns to the current position).
`$#`	§18.7.5[3ed]	Specify a delivery agent or choose an action, such as reject or discard a recipient, sender, connection, or message.
`$[ $]`	§18.7.6[3ed]	Canonicalize hostname.
`$( $)`	§23.4[3ed]	Perform a lookup in an external database, file, or network service, or perform a change (such as dequoting), or store a value into a macro.
`$&`	§21.5.3[3ed]	Delay conversion of a macro until runtime.

18.2.3 Table of Rule Operators

In this section, we list each rule operator. Note that we exclude operators that are not germane to rules (such as $?, §21.6[3ed]) and list (in Table 18-4) only those that can be used in rules. Because all rule operators are symbolic, we cannot list them in alphabetical order, so instead, we list them in the alphabetical order of pronunciation. That is, for example, $@ (pronounced dollar-at) comes before $: (pronounced dollar-colon).

Table 18-4. Operators in rules

Operator	sendmail text reference	RHS or LHS	Description or use
$&	§18.9.1[3ed]	LHS and RHS	Delay macro expansion until runtime
$@	§18.9.2[3ed]	LHS	Match exactly zero tokens (V8 only)
$@	§18.9.3[3ed]	RHS	Rewrite once and return
$@	§18.9.4[3ed]	RHS	Specify host in delivery-agent "triple"
$@	§18.9.5[3ed]	RHS	Specify DSN status in error-agent "triple"
$@	§18.9.6[3ed]	RHS	Specify a database-map argument
$:	§18.9.7[3ed]	RHS	Rewrite once and continue
$:	§18.9.8[3ed]	RHS	Specify address in delivery-agent "triple"
$:	§18.9.9[3ed]	RHS	Specify message in error- or discard-agent "triple"
$:	§18.9.10[3ed]	RHS	Specify a default database-map value
$*digit*	§18.9.11[3ed]	RHS	Copy by position
$=	§18.9.12[3ed]	LHS	Match any token in a class
$>	§18.9.13[3ed]	RHS	Rewrite through another rule set (subroutine call)
$[$]	§18.9.14[3ed]	RHS	Canonicalize hostname
$($)	§18.9.15[3ed]	RHS	Perform a database-map lookup or action
$-	§18.9.16[3ed]	LHS	Match exactly one token
$+	§18.9.17[3ed]	LHS	Match one or more tokens
$#	§18.9.18[3ed]	LHS	Match a literal $#
$#	§18.9.19[3ed]	RHS	Specify a delivery agent
$#	§18.9.20[3ed]	RHS	Specify return for a policy-checking rule set
$*	§18.9.21[3ed]	LHS	Match zero or more tokens
$~	§18.9.22[3ed]	LHS	Match any single token not in a specified class
$|	§18.9.23[3ed]	LHS and RHS	Match or return a literal $|

CHAPTER 19

The S (Rule Sets) Configuration Command

Rule sets in the configuration file, like subroutines in a program, control the sequence of steps *sendmail* uses to rewrite addresses. Inside each rule set is a series of zero or more individual rules. Rules are used to select the appropriate delivery agent for any particular address, to detect and reject addressing errors, to transform addresses to meet particular needs, to validate addresses and headers for the purpose of rejecting spam, and to make policy decisions.

19.1 What's New with V8.13

V8.13 has introduced one change in rule sets:

- New character commands were added to the svr_features rule set (§19.1.1[V8.13]).

19.1.1 More srv_features Return Values

The svr_features rule set (§19.1.3[3ed]) returns a $# followed by one or more of the characters defined in Table 19-1. Each character turns a feature on or off. If the character is lowercase, it turns the feature on. Uppercase turns the feature off. One character, the t, is special because it causes *sendmail* to temporarily fail the connection. Prior to V8.13, the characters listed in the table below (as documented in V8.13) were undocumented (and thus unsupported). They are now both documented and supported.

Table 19-1. Characters that set/clear server features

On	Off	Documented	Description
a	A	V8.12	Offer the AUTH SMTP extension
b	B	V8.13	Offer use of the SMTP VERB command
c	C	V8.12	"C" is the equivalent to AuthOptions=p; i.e., it doesn't permit mechanisms susceptible to simple passive attack (e.g., PLAIN, LOGIN), unless a security layer is active

Table 19-1. Characters that set/clear server features (continued)

On	Off	Documented	Description
d	D	V8.13	Offer the DSN SMTP extension
e	E	V8.13	Offer the ETRN SMTP extension
l	L	V8.13	Require the client to authenticate with AUTH
p	P	V8.12	Offer the PIPELINING SMTP extension
r	R	V8.13	Request a certificate
s	S	V8.12	Offer the STARTTLS SMTP extension
v	V	V8.12	Verify a client certificate
x	X	V8.13	Offer use of the SMTP EXPN command

19.2 A Useful Table

There is only one useful table in this chapter, which covers policy rule sets.

19.2.1 Policy Rule Sets

Beginning with V8.8, *sendmail* calls special rule sets internally to determine its behavior. These are called the *policy rule sets* and are used for such varied tasks as setting spam-handling, setting policy, or validating the conditions when ETRN should be allowed (to mention just a few). Table 19-2 shows the complete list of these policy rule sets.

Table 19-2. The policy rule sets

Rule set	sendmail text reference	Hook	Description
`authinfo`	§10.9.3.2[3ed]	None	Handle `AuthInfo:` lookups in the `access` database
`check_compat`	§7.1.4[3ed]	See discussion following the table	Validate just before delivery
`check_data`	§19.9.1[3ed]	None needed	Check just after DATA
`check_eoh`	§25.5.3[3ed]	None needed	Validate after headers are read
`check_etrn`	§19.9.2[3ed]	None needed	Allow or disallow ETRN
`check_expn`	§19.9.3[3ed]	None needed	Validate EXPN
`check_mail`	§7.1.2[3ed]	`Local_check_mail`	Validate the envelope-sender address
`check_rcpt`	§7.1.3[3ed]	`Local_check_rcpt`	Validate the envelope-recipient address
`check_relay`	§7.1.1[3ed]	`Local_check_relay`	Validate incoming network connections
`check_vrfy`	§19.9.3[3ed]	None needed	Validate VRFY
`queuegroup`	§11.4.5[3ed]	See discussion following the table	Select a queue group

Table 19-2. The policy rule sets (continued)

Rule set	sendmail text reference	Hook	Description
srv_features	§19.1.3[3ed]	None needed	Tune server setting based on connection information
tls_client	§10.10.8.2[3ed]	LOCAL_TLS_CLIENT	With the *access* database, validate inbound STARTTLS or MAIL FROM SMTP command
tls_rcpt	§10.10.8.3[3ed]	LOCAL_TLS_RCPT	Validate a server's credentials based on the recipient address
tls_server	§10.10.8.2[3ed]	LOCAL_TLS_SERVER	Possibly with the *access* database, validate the inbound and outbound connections
trust_auth	§10.9.4[3ed]	Local_trust_auth	Validate that a client's authentication identifier (authid) is trusted to act as (proxy for) the requested authorization identity (userid).
try_tls	§10.10.8.4[3ed]	LOCAL_TRY_TLS	Disable STARTTLS for selected outbound connected-to hosts
Hname:$>	§25.5[3ed]	N/A	Reject, discard, or accept a message based on a header's value

Note that some of these rule sets are omitted from your configuration file by default. For those, no hook is needed. Instead, you merely declare the rule set in your *mc* file and give it the appropriate rules:

```
LOCAL_RULESETS
Scheck_vrfy
... your rules here
```

Those with a Local_ hook, as shown in the table, are declared by default in your configuration file. To use them yourself, you need only declare them with the Local_ hook indicated:

```
LOCAL_RULESETS
SLocal_check_rcpt
... your rules here
```

Those with a LOCAL_ hook, as shown in the table, are declared directly with that hook, so there is no need to precede the hook with LOCAL_RULESETS. For example:

```
LOCAL_TRY_TLS
... your rules here
```

The two exceptions are the check_compat and queuegroup rule sets. Each of these is automatically declared when you use the corresponding check_compat or queuegroup feature, but not declared if you don't use that feature.

All of these rule sets are handled in the same manner. If the rule set does not exist, the action is permitted. If the rule set returns anything other than a #error or a #discard delivery agent, the message, identity, or action is accepted for that rule set (although it can still be rejected or discarded by another rule set).* Otherwise, the #error delivery agent causes the message, identity, or action to be rejected (§20.4.4[3ed]) or quarantined (§11.1.2.6[V8.13]), and the #discard delivery agent causes the message to be accepted, then discarded (§20.4.3[3ed]).

* Note that #error and #discard do not apply to all of the rule sets listed in Table 19-2.

CHAPTER 20

The M (Mail Delivery Agent) Configuration Command

Other than relaying mail via SMTP or LMTP, the *sendmail* program does not perform the actual delivery of mail.* Instead, it calls other programs (called *mail delivery agents*†) to perform that service. Because the mechanics of delivery can vary widely from delivery agent to delivery agent, *sendmail* needs a great deal of information about each one. The *sendmail* `M` configuration command defines a mail delivery agent and provides the information that *sendmail* needs.

20.1 What's New with V8.13

V8.13 *sendmail* has made four changes regarding delivery agents, three of which are described here and two of which are described in the specified sections:

- The `#error` agent can now return a `$@ quarantine` with a reason (§11.1.2.6[V8.13]).
- Connections caching for the LPC delivery agent (§6.1[V8.13]) is now provided.
- The new `F=B` delivery agent flag strips all leading backslashes (§20.1.1[V8.13])
- The `F=f` flag has been removed from the defaults for `local_lmtp` (§20.1.2[V8.13])
- The new `F=W` delivery agent flag causes persistent host status to be ignored for an individual delivery agent (§20.1.3[V8.13])

20.1.1 New F=B Delivery Agent Flag

The `F=s` (§20.8.43[3ed]) delivery agent flag causes *sendmail* to dequote the recipient's address before passing it to the selected delivery agent. Dequoting causes all quotation marks (") and all leading backslashes (\) to be removed. But when a lighter

* For the purpose of this discussion, we gloss over the fact that *sendmail* actually can deliver directly to files (§12.2.2[3ed]).

† These are misleadingly called "mailers" by the internal documentation supplied with *sendmail*.

touch is needed, you may use this new F=B flag instead, which just removes all leading backslashes. For example:

```
"\\\user"@relayhost     with F=s becomes     user@relayhost
"\\\user"@relayhost     with F=B becomes     "user"@relayhost
```

Note that because F=B is a subset of F=s, you are discouraged from using both flags at the same time.

20.1.2 No F=f for local_lmtp mc config

Prior to V8.13, the `local_lmtp` feature (§4.8.19[3ed]) set the default `LOCAL_MAILER_FLAGS` (§20.5.6.2[3ed]) to `F=PSXfmnz9`. Beginning with V8.13, the `F=f` flag (§20.8.24[3ed]) is no longer set as part of that default. Recall that if *sendmail* is run with a `-f` command-line argument (§15.7.23[3ed]), and if the `F=f` delivery agent flag is specified, the `A=` for this local delivery agent will have the two additional arguments `-f` and `$g` inserted between its `argv[0]` and `argv[1]`.

20.1.3 The New F=W Flag

The `HostStatusDirectory` option (§24.9.52[3ed]) defines where long-term host status should be maintained. If you prefer a particular delivery agent to ignore that status, you may do so by defining this `F=W` flag. When defined, it acts as though the `HostStatusDirectory` option were undefined for that particular delivery agent.

20.2 Useful Tables

There are three useful tables in this chapter.

- Table 20-1 lists all the delivery agents by name (§20.2.1[V8.13]).
- Table 20-2 lists all the delivery agent equates (§20.2.2[V8.13]).
- Table 20-3 lists all the delivery agent F= flags (§20.2.3[V8.13]).

20.2.1 Delivery Agents by Name

In Table 20-1, we list the standard and special delivery agents in alphabetical order, along with a convenient description of each.

Table 20-1. Delivery agents described by name

MAILER( )	Agents declared	Description
cyrus	*cyrus* and *cyrusbb* (§20.4.1[3ed])	Deliver to a local cyrus user. Handles *user+where@local.host* syntax to the user's IMAP V1 mailbox.
cyrusv2	*cyrusv2* (§20.4.2[3ed])	Somewhat like cyrus, but delivers using LMTP via a Unix-domain socket, and requires Cyrus V2.

Table 20-1. Delivery agents described by name (continued)

MAILER( )	Agents declared	Description
none	*discard* (§20.4.3[3ed])	Causes the message to be accepted and discarded.
none	*error* (§20.4.4[3ed])	Causes the message to be rejected or quarantined (§11.1.2.6[V8.13]).
`fax`	*fax* (§20.4.5[3ed])	Delivers to a program that handles fax delivery.
none	**file** and **include** (§20.4.6)[3ed]	Performs delivery by appending to a file and handles delivery through `:include:` lists.
`local`	*local* (§20.4.7.1[3ed]), *prog* (§20.4.7.2[3ed])	Performs final, local delivery, either to a user's mailbox or through a program.
`mail11`	*mail11* (§20.4.8[3ed])	Allows use of the *mail11* program for delivery to DECnet addresses.
`phquery`	*ph* (§20.4.9[3ed])	Delivery is through the *phquery* program, which looks up user information in the CCSO nameserver database, and then provides appropriate information for delivery (deprecated).
`pop`	*pop* (§20.4.10[3ed])	Delivery for POP users who lack local accounts using MH's *spop*.
`procmail`	*procmail* (§20.4.11[3ed])	Delivers via *procmail*, which allows additional processing for local or special delivery needs.
`qpage`	*qpage* (§20.4.12[3ed])	Part of a client/server software package that allows messages to be sent via an alphanumeric pager.
`smtp`	*smtp* (§20.4.13[3ed]), *esmtp* (§20.4.13.2[3ed]), *smtp8* (§20.4.13.3[3ed]), *dsmtp* (§20.4.13.4[3ed]), and *relay* (§20.4.13.5[3ed])	The internal SMTP delivery agents.
`usenet`	*usenet* (§20.4.14[3ed])	The usenet delivery agent is used to post messages to the USENET by means of the *inews* program.
`uucp`	*uucp* (§4.6.1[3ed]), *uucp-old* (§4.6.1[3ed]), *uucp-new* (§4.6.2[3ed]), *suucp* (§4.6.2[3ed]), *uucp-dom* (§4.6.3[3ed]), *uucp-uudom* (§4.6.4[3ed])	The delivery agents used to send UUCP mail.

20.2.2 Delivery Agent Equates

Recall that the form for the `M` *cf* configuration command is:

```
Msymname, equate, equate, equate, ...
```

And that each *equate* expression is of the form:

```
field=arg
```

Here, the *`field`* is one of those in Table 20-2. Only the first character of the *`field`* is recognized. For example, all of the following are equivalent:

```
S=21
Sender=21
SenderRuleSet=21
```

The *field* is followed by optional whitespace, the mandatory = character, optional whitespace, and finally the *arg*. The form of the *arg* varies depending on the *field*. The *arg* might or might not be required.

Special characters can be embedded into the *field*, as shown in Table 21-1 of §21.3.1[3ed]. For example, backslash notation can be used to embed commas into the A= delivery agent equate like this:

```
...              A=eatmail -FO\,12\,99
```

The complete list of delivery agent equates is shown in Table 20-2. A full description of each begins in the next section. Note that they are presented in alphabetical order, rather than the order in which they would appear in typical delivery agent definitions.

Table 20-2. Delivery agent equates

Equate	Field name	sendmail text reference	Meaning
/=	/path	§20.5.1[3ed]	Set a *chroot* directory (V8.10 and above)
A=	Argv	§20.5.2[3ed]	Delivery agent's command-line arguments
C=	CharSet	§20.5.3[3ed]	Default MIME character set (V8.7 and above)
D=	Directory	§20.5.4[3ed]	Delivery agent working directory (V8.6 and above)
E=	EOL	§20.5.5[3ed]	End-of-line string
F=	Flags	§20.5.6[3ed]	Delivery agent flags
L=	LineLimit	§20.5.7[3ed]	Maximum line length (V8.1 and above)
M=	MaxMsgSize	§20.5.8[3ed]	Maximum message size
m=	maxMsgsPerConn	§20.5.9[3ed]	Max messages per connection (V8.10 and above)
N=	Niceness	§20.5.10[3ed]	How to *nice*(2) the agent (V8.7 and above)
P=	Path	§20.5.11[3ed]	Path to the delivery agent
Q=	QueueGroup	§20.5.12[3ed]	The name of the queue group to use (V8.12 and above)
R=	Recipient	§20.5.13[3ed]	Recipient rewriting rule set
r=	recipients	§20.5.14[3ed]	Maximum recipients per envelope (V8.12 and above)
S=	Sender	§20.5.15[3ed]	Sender rewriting rule set
T=	Type	§20.5.16[3ed]	Types for DSN diagnostics (V8.7 and above)
U=	UID	§20.5.17[3ed]	Run agent as `user-id:group-id` (V8.7 and above)
W=	Wait	§20.5.18[3ed]	Timeout for a process wait (V8.10 and above)

20.2.3 Delivery Agent F= Flags

In Table 20-3, we detail each delivery agent flag, presented in alphabetical order, where lowercase letters precede uppercase letters for each delivery agent flag.

Note that, when configuring with the *mc* technique, you should examine *cf/README* to determine which delivery agent flags are set by default for which delivery agents.

Table 20-3. Delivery agent F= flags

Flag	sendmail text reference	Meaning
%	§20.8.1[3ed]	Hold delivery until ETRN or `-qI` or `-qR` or `-qS` (V8.10 and above)
0	§20.8.2[3ed]	Turn off MX lookups for delivery agent (V8.8 and above)
1	§20.8.3[3ed]	Don't send null bytes (V8.10 and above)
2	§20.8.4[3ed]	Force SMTP even if ESMTP is offered (V8.12 and above)
3	§20.8.5[3ed]	Extend quoted-printable to EBCDIC (V8.7 and above)
5	§20.8.6[3ed]	Use the `localaddr` rule set 5 after local aliasing (V8.7 and above)
6	§20.8.7[3ed]	Always strip headers to 7 bits (V8.10 and above)
7	§20.8.8[3ed]	Strip the high bit when delivering (V8.6 and above)
8	§20.8.9[3ed]	Force `EightBitMode=p` MIME encoding (V8.7 and above)
9	§20.8.10[3ed]	Convert 7- to 8-bit if appropriate (V8.8 and above)
:	§20.8.11[3ed]	Check for `:include:` files (V8.7 and above)
|	§20.8.12[3ed]	Check for *|program* addresses (V8.7 and above)
/	§20.8.13[3ed]	Check for */file* addresses (V8.7 and above)
@	§20.8.14[3ed]	User can be User Database key (V8.7 and above)
a	§20.8.15[3ed]	Run extended SMTP protocol (V8.6 and above)
A	§20.8.16[3ed]	User can be to the LHS of an alias (V8.7 and above)
b	§20.8.17[3ed]	Add a blank line after message (V8.6 and above)
B	§20.1.1[V8.13]	Strips all leading backslashes (V8.13 and above)
c	§20.8.18[3ed]	Exclude comment from `$g` in headers (V8.6 and above)
C	§20.8.19[3ed]	Add *@domain* to recipient
d	§20.8.20[3ed]	Never enclose route addresses in <> (V8.7 and above)
D	§20.8.21[3ed]	Need `Date:` in header
e	§20.8.22[3ed]	Mark expensive delivery agents
E	§20.8.23[3ed]	Change extra `From` into `>From`
f	§20.8.24[3ed]	Delivery agent adds `-f` to *`argv`*
F	§20.8.25[3ed]	Need `From:` in header
g	§20.8.26[3ed]	Suppress `From:<>` (V8.6 and above)
h	§20.8.27[3ed]	Preserve uppercase in hostname
H		Reserved for Mail11v3 (preview headers)
i	§20.8.28[3ed]	User Database sender rewrite of envelope (V8.7 and above)
I	§20.8.29[3ed]	Send SMTP VERB to other site (deprecated)
j	§20.8.30[3ed]	User Database rewrite of header recipient addresses (V8.7 and above)

Table 20-3. Delivery agent F= flags (continued)

Flag	sendmail text reference	Meaning
`k`	§20.8.31[3ed]	Don't check for loops in EHLO command (V8.7 and above)
`l`	§20.8.32[3ed]	Agent performs local (final) delivery
`L`	§20.8.33[3ed]	Specify SMTP line limits (obsolete)
`m`	§20.8.34[3ed]	Multiple recipients possible
`M`	§20.8.35[3ed]	Need `Message-ID:` in header
`n`	§20.8.36[3ed]	Don't use Unix-style `From` in header
`N`		Reserved for Mail11v3 (returns multistatus)
`o`	§20.8.37[3ed]	Always run delivery agent as recipient (V8.7 and above)
`p`	§20.8.38[3ed]	Process return path per RFC821 (deprecated)
`P`	§20.8.39[3ed]	Need `Return-Path:` in header
`q`	§20.8.40[3ed]	250 versus 252 return for SMTP VRFY (V8.8 and above)
`r`	§20.8.41[3ed]	Delivery agent adds `-r` to *argv*
`R`	§20.8.42[3ed]	Use a reserved TCP port (V8.6 and above)
`s`	§20.8.43[3ed]	Strip quotation marks
`S`	§20.8.44[3ed]	Assume specified *user-id* and *group-id* (Revised for V8.7)
`u`	§20.8.45[3ed]	Preserve uppercase for username
`U`	§20.8.46[3ed]	Use UUCP-style `From` line
`v`		Reserved for SysVR4
`V`		Reserved for UIUC
`w`	§20.8.47[3ed]	Check for valid user identity (V8.7 and above)
`W`	§20.1.3[V8.13]	Ignore host status for this delivery agent (V8.13 and above)
`x`	§20.8.48[3ed]	Need `Full-Name:` in header
`X`	§20.8.49[3ed]	Delivery agent needs RFC2821 hidden dot
`z`	§20.8.50[3ed]	Deliver with LMTP (V8.9 and above)
`Z`	§20.8.51[3ed]	Apply `DialDelay` option's sleep (V8.12 and above)
`~`		Reserved for SGI (check for valid home directory)

CHAPTER 21

The D (Define a Macro) Configuration Command

Defined macros allow strings of text to be represented symbolically inside a *sendmail* configuration file.

21.1 What's New with V8.13

The behavior and use of most defined macros has not changed in V8.13. However, the values in two have changed, and eight new macros have been added:

- Two existing macros, `${auth_author}` and `${auth_authen}`, now have their values stored in xtext format (§21.1.1[V8.13]).
- The new macro `${client_connections}` holds the current number of connections to the listening server (§21.1.2[V8.13]).
- The new macro `${client_ptr}` holds the result of a PTR lookup of the connecting hosts IP address (§21.1.3[V8.13]).
- The new macro `${client_rate}` holds the number of inbound connections to the listening server over a specified interval (§21.1.4[V8.13]).
- The new macro `${msg_id}` holds the value of the current `Message-Id:` header (§21.1.5[V8.13]).
- The new macro `${nbadrcpts}` holds the number of envelope recipients for the current envelope that were not accepted (§21.1.6[V8.13]).
- The new macro `${quarantine}` holds the reason an envelope has been quarantined (§21.1.7[V8.13]).
- The new macro `${time}` holds the current time in seconds (§21.1.8[V8.13]).
- The new macro `${total_rate}` holds the total number of inbound connections to the listening server over a specified interval (§21.1.9[V8.13]).

21.1.1 The ${auth_author} and ${auth_authen} Macros

Some macros are assigned values from text that is supplied by outside connecting hosts, but such text cannot necessarily be trusted for use in rule sets or as keys in database-map lookups.

To protect itself, *sendmail* modifies this text by replacing each whitespace character (space or tab), nonprintable character (such as a newline or control character), and any of the following special characters with its corresponding hexadecimal value (based on US ASCII), where each new hexadecimal value is prefixed with a plus character.

```
< > ( ) " +
```

This is called `xtext` encoding (defined in RFC1891).

Beginning with V8.13, the values for the `${auth_author}` and `${auth_authen}` macros are also `xtext` encoded before being placed into those macros.

21.1.2 The ${client_connections} Macro

When a host connects to the listening *sendmail* server, that server forks a child copy of itself to handle the new connection. Before forking, the server increments the connection count associated with the IP number of the connecting client. When the forked child finishes and exits, the server decrements that count.

Beginning with V8.13 *sendmail*, the `${client_connections}` macro holds that count as its value, making it available for you to use in rule sets.

With V8.13, if you declare the `conncontrol` feature (§4.1.8[V8.13]), a rule set called `ConnControl` that looks up the current IP address in the *access* database will be added to your configuration file. The source text file for the *access* database may contain that address with a literal `ClientConn:` prefix—for example:

```
ClientConn:123.45.67.89         12
```

Note that the literal prefix is followed by the IP number to look up, tabs or spaces,* and lastly the limit to impose for the maximum number of connections for that IP number.

If the number of connections (as stored in this `${client_connections}` macro) exceed the limit imposed inside the *access* database, the new connection is rejected with the following error:

```
452 4.3.2 Too many open connections.
```

* Unless the `-t` command-line argument is used with *makemap* to change the separator.

21.1.3 The ${client_ptr} Macro

When a client host connects to the listening *sendmail* server, that server knows the IP number of the connecting client but not its hostname. To find the hostname, *sendmail* performs a reverse-lookup to find a PTR record that contains the host's name. Beginning with V8.13, the result of that lookup (the hostname) is stored in the `${client_ptr}` macro.

Note that if (and only if) the `${client_resolve}` macro (§21.9.22[3ed]) contains a literal `OK`, this `${client_ptr}` macro will hold the same value as the `${client_name}` macro (§21.9.20[3ed]).

21.1.4 The ${client_rate} Macro

When a host connects to the listening *sendmail* server, the server forks a child to handle the new connection. Before forking, the server increments the connection count associated with the IP number of the connecting client. The rate of connections is then updated inside a window of time defined by the `ConnectionRateWindowSize` option (see §24.1.13[V8.13]), which defaults to 60 seconds.

Beginning with V8.13 *sendmail*, the `${client_rate}` macro holds that count as its value, making it available for you to use in rule sets.

With V8.13, if you declare the `ratecontrol` feature (§4.1.7[V8.13]), a rule set called `RateControl` will be added to your configuration file, which looks up the current IP address in the *access* database. The source text file for the access database may contain that address with a literal `ClientRate:` prefix—for example:

```
ClientRate:123.45.67.89          4
```

Note that the literal prefix is followed by the IP number to look up, tabs or spaces,* and lastly by the limit to impose for the maximum connection rate for that IP number.

If the current rate (as stored in this `${client_rate}` macro) exceeds the limit imposed inside the *access* database, the new connection is rejected with the following error:

```
452 4.3.2 Connection rate limit exceeded.
```

If you are interested in knowing the total rate of connections for all clients, see the `${total_rate}` macro (§21.1.9[V8.13]).

21.1.5 The ${msg_id} Macro

The `Message-Id:` header (§25.12.23[3ed]) is used to uniquely identify each mail message. It must be declared in the configuration file. Its field must be an expression in the syntax of a legal address enclosed in angle brackets (< and >), and it must be composed of elements that create an identifier that is truly unique worldwide.

* Unless the `-t` command-line argument is used with *makemap* to change the separator.

Beginning with V8.13, when *sendmail* finds a `Message-Id:` header in the current message, it assigns the value for that header to this `${msg_id}` macro. If *sendmail* finds no `Message-Id:` header, it creates one and assigns that new value to this `${msg_id}` macro.

If a `Message-Id:` header appears in the original inbound message, its value can be made available to rule sets by using the `H` configuration command (§25.5[3ed]) and to Milters using an `xxfi_header()` routine. But if *sendmail* creates the `Message-Id:` header, its value can only be made available by using this `${msg_id}` macro.

21.1.6 The ${nbadrcpts} Macro

When *sendmail* receives an SMTP RCPT TO: command, it examines the recipient address contained in that command, accepts known local recipients, and rejects other recipients. If relaying is enabled for selected hosts, envelope recipients addressed to those hosts are also allowed. If the address is disallowed, it is rejected by *sendmail* and neither rule sets nor Milters ever see it.

Beginning with V8.13 *sendmail*, if knowing the number of rejected recipients for a given envelope is important to you, you may access that number using this `${nbadrcpts}` macro.

If used in rule sets, the `${nbadrcpts}` macro will only contain a true total after all envelope recipients have been processed. Thus, a good place to use it might be in the `check_data` rule set (§19.9.1[3ed]), because it is called just after the SMTP DATA command is received, but before that command is acknowledged (after all recipients have been processed):

```
LOCAL_RULESETS
Scheck_data
R $*                    $: $&{nbadrcpts}
R $+                    $: $(arith l $@ $1 $@ 25 $)
R FALSE                 $# error $@ 5.1.2 $: "553 Too many bad recipients"
```

Here, under the `LOCAL_RULESETS` portion of your *mc* configuration file, you first declare the `check_data` rule set, which contains three rules. The first rule simply matches anything on the LHS (the `$*`) and places the value of this `${nbadrcpts}` macro into the workspace. The second rule compares that value (using the `arith` database-map; see §23.7.1[3ed]) to the literal value 25. If the test fails (if there are 25 or more bad envelope recipients causing the second rule to return `FALSE` in the workspace), the message is rejected using the third rule.

This `${nbadrcpts}` macro can also be used by Milters, but it is only reliable if you fetch its value after all envelope recipients have been processed. You may add this macro to those passed to your Milter with a line such as the following in your *mc* configuration file:

```
define(`confMILTER_MACROS_EOM', confMILTER_MACROS_EOM``, {nbadrcpts}'')
```

Note that the double half quotes are necessary because the second argument to the `define` command contains a comma. This line in your *mc* configuration file makes the `${nbadrcpts}` macro available to your Milters after the entire envelope has been processed, but before the final dot has been acknowledged.

21.1.7 The ${quarantine} Macro

V8.13 introduced queue quarantining (§11.1.2[V8.13]), the process by which envelopes in the queue are marked as being ineligible for delivery. Such quarantined envelopes may then be reviewed manually or automatically.

When a message is quarantined, the reason it was quarantined is stored as the value of this `${quarantine}` macro. When it is later read from the queue, the value of the queue file's `q` line (§11.1.5[V8.13]) is again copied into this `${quarantine}` macro.

The `${quarantine}` macro can be used to detect whether a message has been quarantined.

21.1.8 The ${time} Macro

The C-language *time*(3) routine returns an integer value (type `time_t`) that represents the current time as the number of seconds since the start (00:00:00) of January 1, 1970. This current time is instantiated at three different moments as *sendmail* processes envelopes:

- Just after a connection to the server has been accepted, but before the SMTP conversation begins
- Just as the queue's *qf* file is being read
- Just as a new envelope is being created to handle bounced email

At these moments, an ASCII representation of the current number of seconds is placed into the `${time}` macro. At the same moment, the following other macros are also given the current time but in different formats:

- `$b` holds the current time in RFC2822 format
- `$d` holds the current time in Unix *ctime*(3) format
- `$t` holds the current time to the minute in the format *YYYYMMDDhhmm*

Although the `${time}` macro is not used in the standard configuration file, it is available for your use in rule sets of your own design. It can, for example, be useful to enforce a timeout on entries when using POP before relay.

21.1.9 The ${total_rate} Macro

When a host connects to the listening *sendmail* server, that server forks a child copy of itself to handle the connection. Before forking, the server increments the connection count associated with all connections. That count is then used to update the total rate of all connections.

The rate is measured over an interval defined by the ConnectionRateWindowSize option (see §24.1.13[V8.13]), which defaults to 60 seconds. This total rate differs from the client rate in that it is the rate for *all* connections rather than the rate for a particular client address.

The ${total_rate} macro is not used in the standard configuration file but is available for your use in rule sets of your own design.

If you are interested in knowing the rate of connections from individual clients, see the ${client_rate} macro (§21.1.4[V8.13]).

21.2 A Useful Table

The *sendmail* program reserves all lowercase letters, punctuation characters, and digits for its own use. For multi-character names, it reserves all those that begin with an underscore or a lowercase letter. Table 21-1 lists all the macro names that have special internal meaning to *sendmail*. Included in this list are macros that are used by the *mc* configuration technique.*

Table 21-1. Reserved macros

Macro	sendmail text reference	Description
$_	§21.9.1[3ed]	RFC1413-validation and IP source route
$a	§21.9.2[3ed]	The origin date in RFC822 format
${addr_type}	§21.9.3[3ed]	Is address recipient/sender or header/envelope?
${alg_bits}	§21.9.4[3ed]	The number of bits in the TLS cipher
${auth_authen}	§21.9.5[3ed]	RFC2554 SASL AUTH credentials
${auth_author}	§21.9.6[3ed]	RFC2554 SASL AUTH= parameter
${auth_ssf}	§21.9.7[3ed]	SASL AUTH encryption key length
${auth_type}	§21.9.8[3ed]	SASL Authentication mechanism used
$b	§21.9.9[3ed]	The current date in RFC2822 format
${bodytype}	§21.9.10[3ed]	The ESMTP (Extended SMTP) BODY parameter
$B	§21.9.11[3ed]	The BITNET relay (*mc* configuration, deprecated)
$c	§21.9.12[3ed]	The hop count
${cert_issuer}	§21.9.13[3ed]	Distinguished name of certificate signer

* Note that these are the exception to the usual rule in that they are all uppercase letters. This makes sense because these macros are being used by the configuration file, rather than the internals of the *sendmail* program.

Table 21-1. Reserved macros (continued)

Macro	sendmail text reference	Description
${cert_md5}	§21.9.14[3ed]	MD5 of cert certificate
${cert_subject}	§21.9.15[3ed]	The cert subject
${cipher}	§21.9.16[3ed]	Cipher suite used for connection
${cipher_bits}	§21.9.17[3ed]	TLS encryption key length
${client_addr}	§21.9.18[3ed]	The connecting host's IP address
${client_connections}	§21.1.2[V8.13]	Current count of client connections
${client_flags}	§21.9.19[3ed]	Flags for tuning the outgoing connection
${client_name}	§21.9.20[3ed]	The connecting host's canonical name
${client_port}	§21.9.21[3ed]	The connecting host's port number
${client_ptr}	§21.1.3[V8.13]	Result of looking up the connecting host's IP number
${client_rate}	§21.1.4[V8.13]	The current client connection rate
${client_resolve}	§21.9.22[3ed]	Result of lookup of ${client_name}
${cn_issuer}	§21.9.23[3ed]	Common name of certificate signer
${cn_subject}	§21.9.24[3ed]	Common name of certificate
${currHeader}	§21.9.25[3ed]	Current header's value
$C	§21.9.26[3ed]	The DECnet relay (*mc* configuration)
$d	§21.9.27[3ed]	The current date in Unix *ctime*(3) format
${daemon_addr}	§21.9.28[3ed]	Listening daemon's address
${daemon_family}	§21.9.29[3ed]	Listening daemon's family
${daemon_flags}	§21.9.30[3ed]	Listening daemon's flags
${daemon_info}	§21.9.31[3ed]	Listening daemon's syslog information
${daemon_name}	§21.9.32[3ed]	Listening daemon's name
${daemon_port}	§21.9.33[3ed]	Listening daemon's port
${deliveryMode}	§21.9.34[3ed]	The current delivery mode
${dsn_envid}	§21.9.35[3ed]	The DSN ENVID= value
${dsn_notify}	§21.9.36[3ed]	The DSN NOTIFY= value
${dsn_ret}	§21.9.37[3ed]	The DSN RET= value
$e	§24.9.105[3ed]	The SMTP greeting message
${envid}	§21.9.40[3ed]	The original DSN envelope ID
$E	§21.9.41[3ed]	The X.400 relay (unused) (*mc* configuration)
$f	§21.9.42[3ed]	The sender's address
$F	§21.9.43[3ed]	The fax relay (*mc* configuration)
$g	§21.9.44[3ed]	The sender's address relative to recipient
$h	§21.9.45[3ed]	Host part of the delivery agent triple
${hdr_name}	§21.9.46[3ed]	The current header's name

Table 21-1. Reserved macros (continued)

Macro	sendmail text reference	Description
`${hdrlen}`	§21.9.47[3ed]	The length of `${currHeader}`
`$H`	§21.9.48[3ed]	The mail hub (*mc* configuration)
`$i`	§21.9.49[3ed]	The queue identifier
`${if_addr}`	§21.9.50[3ed]	The IP address of the receive interface
`${if_addr_out}`	§21.9.51[3ed]	The IP address of the send interface
`${if_family}`	§21.9.52[3ed]	The network family of the receive interface
`${if_family_out}`	§21.9.53[3ed]	The network family of the send interface
`${if_name}`	§21.9.54[3ed]	The name of the receive interface
`${if_name_out}`	§21.9.55[3ed]	The name of the send interface
`$j`	§21.9.56[3ed]	Official canonical name
`$k`	§21.9.57[3ed]	UUCP node name
`$l`	§24.9.114[3ed]	The Unix From format
`${load_avg}`	§21.9.59[3ed]	The current load average
`$L`	§21.9.60[3ed]	The unknown local user relay (*mc* configuration)
`$m`	§21.9.61[3ed]	The DNS domain name
`${mail_addr}`	§21.9.62[3ed]	Saved `$:` value for MAIL FROM: triple
`${mail_host}`	§21.9.63[3ed]	Saved $@ value for MAIL FROM: triple
`${mail_mailer}`	§21.9.64[3ed]	Saved $# value for MAIL FROM: triple
`${msg_id}`	§21.1.5[V8.13]	Value of the `Message-Id:` header
`${msg_size}`	§21.9.65[3ed]	Size of the current message
`$M`	§21.9.66[3ed]	Whom we are masquerading as (*mc* configuration)
`${MTAHost}`	§21.9.67[3ed]	Host for the `msp` feature
`$n`	§21.9.68[3ed]	Error message sender
`${nbadrcpts}`	§21.1.6[V8.13]	Count of the bad recipients in the current envelope
`${nrcpts}`	§21.9.69[3ed]	Number of envelope recipients
`${ntries}`	§21.9.70[3ed]	Number of delivery attempts
`$o`	§24.9.77[3ed]	Token separation operators
`${opMode}`	§21.9.72[3ed]	The start-up operating mode
`$p`	§21.9.73[3ed]	The *sendmail* process ID
`$q`	§21.9.74[3ed]	The default format of the sender's address (obsolete)
`${quarantine}`	§21.1.7[V8.13]	The reason the envelope was quarantined
`${queue_interval}`	§21.9.75[3ed]	The interval specified by `-q` command-line switch
`$r`	§21.9.76[3ed]	The protocol used
`${rcpt_addr}`	§21.9.77[3ed]	Saved `$:` value for RCPT TO: triple
`${rcpt_host}`	§21.9.78[3ed]	Saved $@ value for RCPT TO: triple

Table 21-1. Reserved macros (continued)

Macro	sendmail text reference	Description
`${rcpt_mailer}`	§21.9.79[3ed]	Saved $# value for RCPT TO: triple
`$R`	§21.9.80[3ed]	The relay for unqualified names (*mc* configuration, deprecated)
`$s`	§21.9.81[3ed]	The sender host's name
`${sendmailMTACluster}`	§21.9.82[3ed]	The LDAP cluster to use
`${server_addr}`	§21.9.83[3ed]	The address of the connected-to machine
`${server_name}`	§21.9.84[3ed]	The hostname of the connected-to machine
`$S`	§21.9.85[3ed]	The smart host (*mc* configuration)
`$t`	§21.9.86[3ed]	The current time to the minute in the format *YYYYMMDDhhmm*
`${time}`	§21.1.8[V8.13]	The current time in *time*(3) seconds
`${total_rate}`	§21.1.9[V8.13]	Total connections over the specified interval
`${tls_version}`	§21.9.87[3ed]	TLS/Secure Sockets Layer (SSL) version
`$u`	§21.9.88[3ed]	Address part of a delivery agent triple
`$U`	§21.9.89[3ed]	The UUCP name to override `$k` (*mc* configuration)
`$v`	§21.9.90[3ed]	Version of the *sendmail*
`${verify}`	§21.9.91[3ed]	Result of cert verification
`$V`	§21.9.92[3ed]	The UUCP relay for class `$=V` (*mc* configuration)
`$w`	§21.9.93[3ed]	The short name of this host
`$W`	§21.9.94[3ed]	The UUCP relay for class `$=W` (*mc* configuration)
`$x`	§21.9.95[3ed]	The full name of the sender
`$X`	§21.9.96[3ed]	The UUCP relay for class `$=X` (*mc* configuration)
`$y`	§21.9.97[3ed]	Name of the controlling TTY
`$Y`	§21.9.98[3ed]	The UUCP relay for unclassified hosts (*mc* configuration)
`$z`	§21.9.99[3ed]	The recipient's home directory
`$Z`	§21.9.100[3ed]	Version of the *mc* configuration (*mc* configuration)

CHAPTER 22

The C and F (Class Macro) Configuration Commands

The configuration `C` and `F` class commands allow you to compare individual tokens to multiple strings when determining a match in the LHS of rules.

22.1 What's New with V8.13

Under V8.13 *sendmail*, one of these classes has been modified, and two have been renamed:

- The class `$=w` no longer is automatically filled with all domain prefixes.
- Two existing class macros, `$={tls}` and `$={src}`, have been renamed (the first letter is now capitalized) to become `$={Tls}` and `$={Src}`.

22.1.1 The $=w Class Is Less Auto-Filled

Prior to V8.13, *sendmail* would automatically fill the class `$=w` (§22.6.16[3ed]) with every possible form of domain address that it could find. Specifically, it would:

1. Find your machine's canonical hostname and add it to `$=w`—for example, *mail.bob.example.gov*.
2. Add each leading component of the canonical hostname to `$=w`—for example, *mail* and *mail.bob*.
3. Look up additional hostnames associated with each network interface and add each to `$=w`—for example, *internal.example.gov*.
4. Look up the IP addresses associated with each found name and add each found address (inside square braces) to `$=w`—for example, [192.168.1.5].
5. Reverse lookup each address and add the hostnames found for each (if not duplicated) to the class `$=w`—for example, *dsl.your.phone.company*.

Beginning with V8.13, *sendmail* eliminates the second and fifth step and no longer automatically stores that information for you. If you needed *sendmail* to store that information in class $=w for you, you will henceforth need to add it yourself—usually by placing it into your */etc/mail/local-host-names* file (§4.8.48[3ed]).

22.2 Useful Tables

This chapter contains three useful tables:

- Table 22-1 lists the *mc* macros used to fill class macros with values.
- Table 22-2 lists all the class macros that use the *mc* technique.
- Table 22-3 lists all the class macros defined internally by *sendmail*.

22.2.1 Use mc Macros to Fill Class Macros

Several *mc* macros are used to fill class macros with values based on a test file. These are listed in Table 22-1, along with the class macros they fill. Note that the classes shown should not be used directly because there is no guarantee that they will continue to be available in the future. To be safe, always use the *mc* macro instead. To reinforce this precaution, we use the *mc* name for the class (as the EXPOSED_USER class) instead of the class macro name (as the $=E class), as the leading items in the table.

Table 22-1. mc macros used to fill class macros

mc macro	sendmail text reference	Class macro
CANONIFY_DOMAIN_FILE	§4.8.28[3ed]	$={Canonify}
confCT_FILE	§4.8.47[3ed]	$=t
EXPOSED_USER_FILE	§4.4.1[3ed]	$=E
GENERICS_DOMAIN_FILE	§4.8.15[3ed]	$=G
LDAPROUTE_DOMAIN_FILE	§23.7.11.18[3ed]	$={LDAPRoute}
LDAPROUTE_EQUIVALENT_FILE	§23.7.11.18[3ed]	$={LDAPRouteEquiv}
LOCAL_USER_FILE	§4.5.5[3ed]	$=L
MASQUERADE_DOMAIN_FILE	§4.4.3[3ed]	$=M
MASQUERADE_EXCEPTION_FILE	§4.4.6[3ed]	$=N
RELAY_DOMAIN_FILE	§7.4.1.2[3ed]	$=R
VIRTUSER_DOMAIN_FILE	§4.8.50[3ed]	$={VirtHost}

22.2.2 Classes with mc Configuration

In configuring with the *mc* technique, many classes are defined for your convenience. You need to be aware of these, not only to take advantage of them, but also to avoid reusing their names by mistake. Table 22-2 lists all the class macros that the *mc* technique uses as of Version 8.13.

Table 22-2. Class macros used with the mc configuration technique

Class	sendmail text reference	Description
`$={Accept}`	§7.5.1[3ed]	With the `access_db` feature, the possible acceptance strings from the access database (V8.10 and later)
`$=B`	§4.8.7[3ed]	With the `bestmx_is_local` feature, the domains to look up in bestmx in place of `$=w`
`$={Canonify}`	§4.8.28[3ed]	With CANONIFY_DOMAIN or CANONIFY_DOMAIN_FILE, canonify these domains (V8.10 and later)
`$=E`	§4.4.1[3ed]	With EXPOSED_USER or EXPOSED_USER_FILE, the list of exposed users
`$=G`	§4.8.16.1[3ed]	With GENERICS_DOMAIN or GENERICS_DOMAIN_FILE, list of domains to look up in generics table
`$=L`	§4.5.5[3ed]	With LOCAL_USER or LOCAL_USER_FILE, the list of local users
`$={LDAPRoute}`	§23.7.11.18[3ed]	With LDAPROUTE_DOMAIN or LDAPROUTE_DOMAIN_FILE, route only LDAP hosts in this class (V8.10 and later)
`$={LDAPRouteEquiv}`	§23.7.11.19[3ed]	With LDAPROUTE_EQUIVALENT or LDAPROUTE_EQUIVALENT_FILE, the host to treat as equivalent to `$M` for LDAP routing lookups (V8.12 and later)
`$=M`	§4.4.3[3ed]	With MASQUERADE_DOMAIN or MASQUERADE_DOMAIN_FILE, the list of hosts to masquerade
`$=N`	§4.4.5[3ed]	With MASQUERADE_EXCEPTION or MASQUERADE_EXCEPTION_FILE, the hosts excepted from masquerading
`$=O`	§22.3[3ed]	The list of nonusername characters that can cause forwarding (@, %, and possibly !)
`$=P`	§22.3[3ed]	The list of pseudo top-level domains (e.g., `.uucp` and `.fax`)
`$={ResOk}`	§22.6.11[3ed]	Mark a successful DNS lookup (V8.12 and later)
`$=R`	§7.4.1.1[3ed]	With RELAY_DOMAIN or RELAY_DOMAIN_FILE, the list of domains and hosts for which to relay
`$={SpamTag}`	§7.5.6[3ed]	With the `delay_checks` feature, holds the strings SPAMFRIEND and SPAMHATER (V8.10 and later)
`$={src}`	§22.3[3ed]	List of rule sets to call for searching the *access* database-map (V8.11 and V8.12)
`$={Src}`	§22.3[3ed]	Same as above, but V8.13 and later
`$={tls}`	§22.6.13[3ed]	Possible values for TLS policy in the *access* database-map (V8.11 and V8.12)
`$={Tls}`	§22.6.13[3ed]	Same as above, but V8.13 and later

Table 22-2. Class macros used with the mc configuration technique (continued)

Class	sendmail text reference	Description
`$={TrustAuthMech}`	§10.9.3[3ed]	With TRUST_AUTH_MECH, the mechanisms used to allow relaying (V8.10 and later)
`$=U`	§4.6[3ed]	With MAILER(uucp), the locally connected UUCP hosts
`$=V`	§4.6[3ed]	With MAILER(uucp), the hosts connected to UUCP relay $V
`$={VirtHost}`	§4.8.50[3ed]	With VIRTUSER_DOMAIN or VIRTUSER_DOMAIN_FILE, the list of additional domains to look up in `virtuser` beyond `$=w` (V8.10 and later)
`$=W`	§4.6[3ed]	With MAILER(uucp), the hosts connected to UUCP relay $W
`$=X`	§4.6[3ed]	With MAILER(uucp), the hosts connected to UUCP relay $X
`$=Y`	§4.6[3ed]	With MAILER(uucp), the locally connected smart UUCP hosts
`$=Z`	§4.6[3ed]	With MAILER(uucp), the locally connected domain-ized UUCP hosts

22.2.3 Internal Class Macros

Prior to V8 *sendmail*, only the class `$=w` was used internally and only a small handful of classes were used in the configuration file. Recently, more and more classes have been added to that list. Table 22-3 lists all the class macros defined internally by *sendmail* as of V8.13.

Table 22-3. All the class macros defined internally by sendmail

Class	sendmail text reference	Description
`$=b`	§22.6.1[3ed]	MIME types for no NL-to-CRLF translation
`$={checkMIMEFieldHeaders}`	§22.6.2[3ed]	MIME headers for maximum parameter length checking
`$={checkMIMEHeaders}`	§22.6.3[3ed]	MIME headers for maximum legal length checking
`$={checkMIMETextHeaders}`	§22.6.4[3ed]	MIME headers for maximum arbitrary length checking
`$=e`	§22.6.5[3ed]	Encode this `Content-Transfer-Encoding:`
`$=k`	§22.6.6[3ed]	The local UUCP name
`$=m`	§22.6.7[3ed]	List of local domains
`$=n`	§22.6.8[3ed]	Don't encode these Content-Types
`$={persistentMacros}`	§22.6.9[3ed]	Macros preserved in the *qf* file

Table 22-3. All the class macros defined internally by sendmail (continued)

Class	sendmail text reference	Description
`$=q`	§22.6.10[3ed]	Always quoted-printable encode `Content-Type:`
`$=s`	§22.6.14[3ed]	Presume an RFC2822 7-bit body
`$=t`	§22.6.15[3ed]	List trusted users
`$=w`	§22.6.16[3ed]	List of our other names

Note that these classes really are used internally by *sendmail*, so don't try to redefine their use in the configuration file. Such an attempt will be doomed to failure.

CHAPTER 23

The K (Database-Map) Configuration Command

Database-maps can be used to look up information in databases, to perform transformations (such as dequoting), to perform computations, and to store values into macros.

23.1 What's New with V8.13

V8.13 *sendmail* has expanded the roles of database-maps in the following ways:

- Two new `ldap` database-map switches have been added: `-w` (§23.1.1.1[V8.13]) allows you to specify the LDAP API/protocol version to use; `-H` (§23.1.1.2[V8.13]) allows you to specify an LDAP URI instead of specifying the LDAP server with both the `-h` host (§23.7.11.4[3ed]) and `-p` port (§23.7.11.9[3ed]).*
- LDAP Recursion has been added (§23.1.2[V8.13]) with support for the `AliasFile` option (§24.9.1[3ed]) and class macros.
- The `ldap_routing` feature's third argument may now be a literal `sendertoo` to reject nonexistent envelope sender addresses. (§23.1.3[V8.13])
- The `ldap_routing` feature has had its arguments expanded from four to six. Support has been added to suppress an extra lookup of part of an unmatched address and to specify how to handle connection errors to and temporary failures from the LDAP server (§23.1.4[V8.13]).
- The `dnsbl` feature (§7.2.1[3ed]) no longer uses the `host` database-map type to look up addresses. Instead, it now uses the `dns` database-map type (§9.1.1[V8.13]). The `DNSBL_MAP_OPT` *mc* macro (§9.1.1[V8.13]) has been added to help tune the use of the `dns` database-map type with the `dnsbl` feature. (These new items are described in Chapter 9.)

* These new *ldap* switches allow the use of *ldapi* and *ldaps* (if supported by the underlying LDAP libraries).

- The new socket database-map type (§23.1.5[V8.13]) allows queries to be made over Unix-domain and TCP/IP sockets.
- The ph database-map type (§23.7.18[3ed]) -v switch (formerly deprecated) has been removed. Use the -k switch, instead, which is (and has been) the official replacement switch.

23.1.1 New LDAP Database-Map Switches

V8.13 *sendmail* has added two new switches to the ldap database-map type: -w and -H.

23.1.1.1 New LDAP -w database-map switch

When you build *sendmail*, you can include support for the ldap database-map type by adding -DLDAPMAP to confMAPDEF in your *Build m4* file:

```
APPENDDEF(`confMAPDEF´, `-DLDAPMAP´)
```

If your LDAP library returns one API version, but your LDAP server uses a different one, you can insist that *sendmail* use the version on the server by supplying this new -w switch with your ldap database-type declaration. For example, to look up a login name in an LDAP database and have the official email address for that user returned, you might use a declaration like this:

```
Kgetname ldap -k"uid=%s" -v"mail" -hhost -b"o=Organization, c=US" -w3
```

Note that the trailing argument to this K configuration line is the new -w switch, which specifies your wish to use LDAP API Version 3 with the server running on *host*.

If your system's *<ldap.h>* include file defines a maximum API version, and you exceed that maximum with -w, the following error will print:

```
LDAP version specified exceeds max of max in map name
```

If your system's *<ldap.h>* include file defines a minimum API version, and you specify too low a minimum with -w, the following error will print:

```
LDAP version specified is lower than min in map name
```

Either error will cause the API version specified with -w to be ignored. For example, on Solaris 9, with Sun supplied LDAP, the minimum and maximum are both set to 3.

23.1.1.2 New LDAP -H database-match switch

Modern versions of LDAP allow you to specify Universal Resource Identifiers (URI) in place of host and port combinations when specifying an LDAP server. Beginning with V8.13 *sendmail*, you may specify an LDAP URI by utilizing the new -H database-map switch. For example, prior to V8.13 *sendmail*, you might have used an *mc* configuration statement like this:

```
define(`confLDAP_DEFAULT_SPEC´, `-h ldap.example.gov -p 8389´)
```

Here, -h specifies the LDAP server host and -p specifies the nonstandard port 8389. Beginning with V8.13, you can simplify this declaration by using the new -H database-map switch:

```
define(`confLDAP_DEFAULT_SPEC', `-H ldap://ldap.example.gov:8389')
```

One advantage to using -H is that it allows you to fetch the URI from a secure server by using `ldaps://` instead of `ldap://`—for example:

```
define(`confLDAP_DEFAULT_SPEC', `-H ldaps://ldap.example.gov -b dc=example,dc=gov')
```

Here, the -b LDAP database-map switch (§23.7.11.2[3ed]) specifies the base from which to begin the search. If, rather than reading from a TCP/IP socket, your LDAP server uses a Unix-domain socket, you may use `ldapi://` instead of `ldap://`, to access that Unix-domain socket:*

```
define(`confLDAP_DEFAULT_SPEC', `-H ldapi:// -b dc=example,dc=gov')
```

Note that, when you build *sendmail* with LDAP support, the *sendmail* source determines whether you have a working `ldap_init()` function in your LDAP library. If you do (and all modern versions of LDAP do), you will be allowed to use the new -H database-map switch. If not, you will see the following warning when you attempt to use it:

```
Must compile with -DUSE_LDAP_INIT to use LDAP URIs (-H) in map name
```

If you believe *sendmail* interpreted your LDAP setup wrongly, you may define `USE_LDAP_INIT` when building to correct the error.

23.1.2 LDAP Recursion

Prior to V8.13, LDAP lookups could only return the actual data sought, rather than information that would automatically result in another lookup. Beginning with V8.13, lookups are allowed to be recursive. LDAP recursion allows a query to return either: a new query; a Distinguished Name (DN); or an LDAP URL. When any of these are returned, they result in another lookup.

LDAP recursion is requested with the -v `ldap` database-map switch (§23.7.11.14[3ed]), which specifies the list of attributes to return. Recursion is caused by specifying attributes like this:

```
-v attribute:type:objectclass|objectclass|...
```

Here, the *type* can be one of four literal values: `NORMAL`, `DN`, `FILTER`, or `URL`.

The `NORMAL` type says that the *attribute* will be added to the result of the lookup if the record found is a member of the *objectclass* specified. This is the default type if *type* is omitted.

* Note, however, in order to use Unix domain sockets, your underlying LDAP library must support Unix-domain sockets.

The DN type expects that any matches of the *attribute* have a fully qualified distinguished name. The *sendmail* program will perform a second lookup of the *attribute* using the returned DN record.

The FILTER type requires that any matches of the *attribute* have the value of an LDAP search filter. The *sendmail* program will perform the same lookup again but will replace the original search filter with the new filter returned.

The URL type expects that the lookup will return a URL. The *sendmail* program will perform a lookup using the returned URL and will then use the resulting attributes returned.

The *objectclass* list is optional and, if present, contains the object-class values for which the *attribute* applies. If there is more than one object-class value, each must be separated from the next by a vertical bar character (|). If object-class values are listed, the *attribute* will only be used if the LDAP record returned by a lookup is a member of any of the object-class values listed.

Note that recursion is liberal. It is not an error if recursion ultimately fails to lead to an LDAP record. The lookup will simply fail in the same manner as it would if a record does not exist.

To illustrate, consider the following *mc* configuration file lines.

```
define(`confLDAP_DEFAULT_SPEC´, `-H ldaps://ldap.example.gov -b dc=example,dc=gov´)

LOCAL_CONFIG
Kgetname ldap
-k (&(objectClass=sendmailMTAAliasObject)(sendmailMTAKey=%0))
-v sendmailMTAAliasValue,
   mail:NORMAL:inetOrgPerson,
   uniqueMember:DN:groupOfUniqueNames,
   sendmailMTAAliasSearch:FILTER:sendmailMTAAliasObject,
   sendmailMTAAliasURL:URL:sendmailMTAAliasObject
```

First, we use -H when defining confLDAP_DEFAULT_SPEC. The use of ldaps://, instead of ldap://, allows us to connect to the secure server, *ldap.example.gov*.

Second, under the LOCAL_CONFIG part of our *mc* configuration file, we define a database map using the K configuration command. We give the database-map the name getname and the type ldap. The -k LDAP database-map switch specifies the LDAP search query to use.

The -v *ldap* database-map switch illustrates LDAP recursion. There are five statements following -v, each on its own line for clarity and each separated from the next by a comma. The first statement is a lone attribute named sendmailMTAAliasValue. Because it lacks a colon-keyword type, it is presumed to be type NORMAL. Here, any value in the sendmailMTAAliasValue attribute will be added to any result-string regardless of any object-classes (because the attribute has no object-classes).

The second statement shows an attribute named mail, defined to be the type NORMAL, with a single object-class called inetOrgPerson. The value in the attribute mail will be added to the result string only if the LDAP record that is looked up is a member of the inetOrgPerson object-class. The type NORMAL is not recursive. Only a single lookup is performed and only a single result is added to the string.

The third statement shows an attribute named uniqueMember, defined to be the type DN, with a single object-class called groupOfUniqueNames. The type DN makes the action associated with the attribute uniqueMember recursive. When uniqueMember is looked up, the return value may contain zero or more DN records that belong to the object-class groupOfUniqueNames. Each of those returned DN records will again be searched to find any of the attributes listed in the -v line.

The forth statement shows an attribute named sendmailMTAAliasSearch, defined to be the type FILTER, with an object-class sendmailMTAAliasObject. The type FILTER makes the attribute sendmailMTAAliasSearch recursive. A lookup is made using the initial search (the -k line) to find any new filters that are in the object-class sendmailMTAAliasObject. For any that are found, a second lookup is performed using each new filter, to return any records that contain any of the attributes listed in the -v line.

The fifth statement shows an attribute named sendmailMTAAliasURL, defined to be the type URL, with an object-class called sendmailMTAAliasObject. The type URL makes the attribute sendmailMTAAliasURL recursive. A lookup is made using the default URL to find any new URLs that are in the object-class sendmailMTAAliasObject. For any that are found, a second lookup is performed using each new URL to return records that contain the attributes requested in the original search.

23.1.2.1 LDAP default schema for aliases includes recursion

As of V8.13, the default schema for alias lookups using LDAP has been changed to include LDAP recursion support. Recall that you declare alias lookups with LDAP like this:

```
define('ALIAS_FILE´, `ldap:´)
```

This causes aliases to be looked up using LDAP and the following default schema:

```
ldap -k (&(objectClass=sendmailMTAAliasObject)
        (sendmailMTAAliasGrouping=aliases)
        (|(sendmailMTACluster=${sendmailMTACluster})
        (sendmailMTAHost=$j))
        (sendmailMTAKey=%0))
     -v sendmailMTAAliasValue,
        sendmailMTAAliasSearch:FILTER:sendmailMTAAliasObject,
        sendmailMTAAliasURL:URL:sendmailMTAAliasObject
```

See §23.1.2[V8.13] for a description of this schema.

Note that *sendmail* macros (such as `$j` just shown) are not expanded when the default schema is first defined. Rather, they are expanded each time an LDAP lookup is performed.

In the event you wish to use your own schema rather than the default, you may do so by appending it to the `ldap:` when defining `ALIAS_FILE`:

```
define(`ALIAS_FILE´, `ldap:-k (&objectClass=mg)(mail=%0) -v mmember´)
```

Here, we replaced the long, recursive default schema above with a much shorter and nonrecursive schema of our own design.

See *cf/README* in the *sendmail* source distribution for an additional discussion of the default schema and how to use it.

23.1.2.2 LDAP default schema for classes includes recursion

As of V8.13, the default schema for class macro assignments using LDAP has been changed to include LDAP recursion support. Recall (§22.1.3.2[3ed]) that you declare classes with LDAP, for example, like this:

```
RELAY_DOMAIN_FILE(`@LDAP´)
```

This causes the class `$=R` (see §7.4.1.2[3ed]) to be filled with values that match a `sendmailMTAClassName` with the value `R`. More generally, for any class `X`, the following default schema will be used:

```
F{X}@ldap:-k (&(objectClass=sendmailMTAClass)
        (sendmailMTAClassName=X)
        (|(sendmailMTACluster=${sendmailMTACluster})
        (sendmailMTAHost=$j)))
    -v sendmailMTAClassValue,
        sendmailMTAClassSearch:FILTER:sendmailMTAclass,
        sendmailMTAClassURL:URL:sendmailMTAClass
```

Note that *sendmail* macros (such as `$j` shown earlier) are not expanded when the default schema is first defined. Rather, they are expanded each time an LDAP lookup is performed.

See §7.4.1.2[3ed] for a discussion of how to define you own default schema when declaring a class. Also, see *cf/README* in the *sendmail* source distribution for additional discussion of this default schema and how to use it.

23.1.3 ldap_routing Reviews Envelope Sender

Recall that the `ldap_routing` feature (§23.7.11.17[3ed]) is used like this:

```
FEATURE(`ldap_routing´, `newldapmh´, ` newldapmra´, `bounce´, `detail´)
```

Prior to V8.13, the third argument (*bounce*) could only be one of two literal words: `bounce` or `passthru`. If the third argument was present and was neither an empty string nor the literal string `passthru`, failed lookups would bounce.

Beginning with V8.13, a new literal word, `sendertoo`, may be used in place of either `bounce` or `passthru`. When you specify `sendertoo`, you cause the envelope sender to also be rejected if that address is not found in LDAP. Thus, `sendertoo` acts as if `bounce` was also specified (that is, both not-found recipients and senders will be rejected).

23.1.4 The ldap_routing Feature Offers More

Recall that the `ldap_routing` feature (§23.7.11.17[3ed]) is used like this:

```
FEATURE(`ldap_routing', `newldapmh', ` newldapmra', `bounce', `detail')
```

Beginning with V8.13, two more arguments are now available for your use:

```
FEATURE(`ldap_routing', `newldapmh', ` newldapmra', `bounce', `detail', ` nodomain',
`tempfail')
```

The new fifth argument, *nodomain*, is an argument with no special word required (`nodomain`, `no`, and `UncleBob`, for example, will all work). Without this new argument, a failed lookup of an address (*user@host.domain*) will cause the *@host.doman* part of the address to also be looked up in LDAP. Now, the presence of a *nodomain* argument prevents that secondary lookup.

The new sixth argument, *tempfail*, can be one of two possible literal expressions: `tempfail` or `queue`. These tell *sendmail* what do if *sendmail* cannot connect to the LDAP server, and what to do if the LDAP lookup fails because of a temporary LDAP failure. If the sixth argument is missing or if it is the `queue` literal, the message will be queued for a later attempt. If the sixth argument is the `tempfail` literal, the message will be temporarily rejected with a 4yz reply code. We recommend you use `queue` rather than omitting the sixth argument (relying on the default) to make your intent clear.

23.1.5 The socket Database-Map Type

Beginning with V8.13 *sendmail*, a new database-map type called `socket` is available for your use.* Declare an socket database-map type like this:

```
Kname socket type:port@host
```

Here, *name* is the identifier that you will later use in rule sets. The *type:port@host* is declared in the same fashion as a Milter is declared, by using the `X` configuration command (§7.6.2[3ed]). For example:

```
Ktrustedip socket inet:8020@db5.example.gov
```

* The *sendmail* program needs to be built with SOCKETMAP defined (§3.1.1[V8.13]) in order to use this new database-map type. NETUNIX is required to use Unix-domain sockets but is generally defined by default.

Here, lookups can be made in rule sets using the database-map `trustedip`. The *sendmail* program will make an IPv4 connection (the `inet`) to port `8020` on the host *db5.example.gov*. Once the connection has been made, lookups are performed using a simple dialogue that looks like this:

```
sendmail sends:      database_map_name key
sendmail receives:   status datum
```

Note that neither what is sent nor received may end in a carriage-return/linefeed pair, or in a carriage-return only, or in a linefeed only. Also note that the two parts of each dialogue are separated by a single space character.

Both the sent request and the received reply begin and end with characters that denote their length and termination.* The length is an ASCII representation of the number of characters sent or received, stated as a prefix and a colon. The entire sent or received message is terminated by a comma. The length prefix does not include the comma. For example:

```
sendmail sends:      17:trustedip 1.2.3.4,
sendmail receives:   14:OK VERYTRUSTED,
```

The *sendmail* program sends the database-map name declared earlier using a `K` configuration command. In our example, this is the database-map named `trustedip`. That name is followed by a single space and then the key to look up in the database. Again, the entire request is prefixed with the length and a colon and terminated with a comma (and excludes any terminating newline or carriage-return characters).

The connected-to host replies with one of the keywords shown in Table 23-1. Each must be completely uppercase. The keyword is followed by a single space, then information appropriate to the keyword (for `OK`, this is the sought datum). The entire reply is prefixed with a length and a colon and terminated with a comma.

Table 23-1. The socket database-map reply keywords

Keyword	Description
`OK`	The key was found in the database, and the datum is the value sought.
`NOTFOUND`	The key was not found in the database, and the datum is empty.
`TEMP`	A temporary failure occurred while performing the lookup. The datum may contain an explanatory message.
`TIMEOUT`	The lookup timed out. The datum may contain an explanatory message.
`PERM`	A permanent failure occurred while performing the lookup. The datum may contain an explanatory message.

To illustrate, consider the need to look up the name of the central mail server for your department. If such a database-map were called `mailservers`, you could use the following configuration file line to look up your domain in that database-map:

* The protocol for `socketmap` uses the "netstring" format invented by D.J. Bernstein. This format is described at *http://cr.yp.to/proto/netstrings.txt*.

```
Kmailservers socket -o inet:8020@db4.example.gov
...
R $* <@ $+ > $*           $: $1<@$2>$3 <$(mailservers $2 $)>
R $* <@ $+ > $* <$+>      $#smtp $@ $4 $: $1 < @ $2 > $3
...
```

Here, we look up the host part of an address (`$2`) in the `mailservers` database on the host *db4.example.gov*. The `-o` makes the existence of the database-map optional. If the host part is found, it is rewritten to be the name of the mail server for that host. In the last rule, we forward the original address to that server.

Only a few database switches are available with this socket database-map type. They are shown in Table 23-2.

Table 23-2. The socket database-map type K command switches

Switch	sendmail text reference	Description
`-a`	§23.3.2[3ed]	Append tag on successful match
`-D`	§23.3.3[3ed]	Don't use this database map if `DeliveryMode=defer`
`-f`	§23.3.4[3ed]	Don't fold keys to lowercase
`-m`	§23.3.7[3ed]	Suppress replacement on match
`-N`	§23.3.8[3ed]	Append a null byte to all keys
`-O`	§23.3.9[3ed]	Never add a null byte
`-o`	§23.3.10[3ed]	This database map is optional
`-q`	§23.3.11[3ed]	Don't strip quotes from key
`-S`	§23.3.12[3ed]	Space replacement character
`-T`	§23.3.13[3ed]	Suffix to return on temporary failure
`-t`	§23.3.14[3ed]	Ignore temporary errors

Note that the `socket` database-map type is available only if *sendmail* is compiled with the `SOCKETMAP` compile-time macro (§3.1.1[V8.13]) defined when you build *sendmail* (which is normally *not* done by default).

For examples of how to use this new socket database-map type, see the files *contrib/socketmapServer.pl* and *contrib/socketmapClient.pl*.

23.2 Useful Tables

This chapter contains three useful tables:

- Table 23-3 shows the possible compile-time definitions for `confMAPDEF`.
- Table 23-4 lists the possible `K` configuration command types.
- Table 23-5 lists the possible `K` configuration command switches.

23.2.1 Definitions for confMAPDEF

Possible compile-time switches are shown in Table 23-3.

Table 23-3. m4 definitions for confMAPDEF

Switch	sendmail text reference	Database support included
-DDNSMAP	§23.7.6[3ed]	*dns* lookups (V8.12 and above)
-DHESIOD	§23.7.8[3ed]	*hesiod*(3) aliases and *userdb*
-DLDAPMAP	§23.7.11[3ed]	*ldap*(3) support
-DMAP_NSD	§23.7.16[3ed]	Irix `nsd`
-DMAP_REGEX	§23.7.20[3ed]	Regular expression support
-DNDBM	§23.7.4[3ed]	*ndbm*(3) database files (dbm)
-DNAMED_BIND	§23.7.3[3ed]	*bestmx*(3) DNS lookups
-DNETINFO	§23.7.13[3ed]	NeXT *netinfo*(3) aliases only
-DNEWDB	§23.7.2[3ed]	*db*(3) *hash* and *btree* databases and *userdb*
-DNIS	§23.7.14[3ed]	Sun NIS network database-maps
-DNISPLUS	§23.7.15[3ed]	Sun NIS+ network database-maps
-DPH_MAP	§23.7.18[3ed]	PH database-maps
-DSOCKETMAP	§3.1.1[V8.13]	Socket database-maps

For example, the default *Build m4* file for Ultrix (in *devtools/OS/ULTRIX*) might include this line:

```
define(`confMAPDEF´, `-DNDBM -DNIS´)
```

which includes support for *ndbm*(3) and *nis*(3) database-maps. The *m4* file for SunOS 5.5 might include the following:

```
define(`confMAPDEF´, `-DNDBM -DNIS -DNISPLUS -DMAP_REGEX´)
```

which also includes support for the `nisplus` database-map and regular expressions.

23.2.2 Possible K Command Types

Recall that the *type** portion of the `K` configuration command follows the *name*:

```
Kname type args
```

Note that, in a joined indented line, the *name* and the *type* allows the addition of comments and improves readability:

```
          Kname         # Why this name
             type       # Why this type
             args       # and so on
```

* The *sendmail* source calls this `class`, but we chose *type* to make it clear that this is different from class macros.

The *type* declares which sort of database-map to use. It must be one of the types listed in Table 23-4.

Table 23-4. Possible K command types

Type	sendmail text reference	Version	Description
arith	§23.7.1[3ed]	V8.10 and above	Perform arithmetic computations
btree	§23.7.2[3ed]	V8.1 and above	A *db*(3) form of database
bestmx	§23.7.3[3ed]	V8.7 and above	Look up the best MX record for a host
dbm	§23.7.4[3ed]	V8.1 and above	Really ndbm supplied with most versions of Unix
dequote	§23.7.5[3ed]	V8.6 and above	Remove quotation marks
dns	§23.7.6[3ed]	V8.12 and above	Look up information using DNS
hash	§23.7.7[3ed]	V8.1 and above	A *db*(3) form of database
hesiod	§23.7.8[3ed]	V8.7 and above	MIT network user authentication services
host	§23.7.9[3ed]	V8.1 and above	Internal table to store and look up hostnames
implicit	§23.7.10[3ed]	V8.1 and above	Search for an aliases database entry
ldap	§23.7.11[3ed]	V8.10 and above	The Lightweight Directory Access Protocol (LDAP)
ldapx	§23.7.11[3ed]	V8.9 and earlier	Replaced by ldap
macro	§23.7.12[3ed]	V8.10 and above	Store a value into a macro using a rule
netinfo	§23.7.13[3ed]	V8.7 and above	NeXT, Darwin, and Mac OS X network information services
nis	§23.7.14[3ed]	V8.1 and above	Sun's Network Information Services (NIS)
nisplus	§23.7.15[3ed]	V8.7 and above	Sun's newer version of NIS (NIS+)
nsd	§23.7.16[3ed]	V8.10 and above	Irix nsd database-maps
null	§23.7.17[3ed]	V8.7 and above	Provide a never found service
ph	§23.7.18[3ed]	V8.10 and above	CCSO Nameserver (ph) lookups
program	§23.7.19[3ed]	V8.7 and above	Run an external program to look up the key
regex	§23.7.20[3ed]	V8.9 and above	Use regular expressions
sequence	§23.7.21[3ed]	V8.7 and above	Search a series of database-maps
socket	§23.1.5[V8.13]	V8.13 and above	Search over a TCP/IP connection
stab	§23.7.22[3ed]	V8.10 and above	Internally load aliases into the symbol table
switch	§23.7.23[3ed]	V8.7 and above	Build sequences based on service switch
syslog	§23.7.24[3ed]	V8.10 and above	Log information using *syslog*(3) using rule sets
text	§23.7.25[3ed]	V8.7 and above	Look up in flat text files
userdb	§23.7.26[3ed]	V8.7 and above	Look up in the User Database
user	§23.7.27[3ed]	V8.7 and above	Look up local *passwd* information

23.2.3 The K Command Switches

The *switches* must follow the *type* and precede the *file_or_map*:

```
Kname type switches file_or_map
```

If any *switches* follow *file_or_map*, they will be silently ignored.* All *switches* begin with a – character and are listed in Table 23-5. Note that some database-map types utilize only a small subset of all switches (e.g., dequote uses only -a, -D, -s, and -S, and sequence doesn't use any).

Table 23-5. K command switches

Switch	sendmail text reference	Description
-1	§23.7.11.1[3ed]	Consider successful only if exactly one key is matched (ldap only)
-A	§23.3.1[3ed]	Append values for duplicate keys
-a	§23.3.2[3ed]	Append tag on successful match
-b	§23.7.11.2[3ed]	Base from which to begin the search (ldap only)
-b	§23.7.20.1[3ed]	Use basic, not extended, regular expression matching (regex only)
-D	§23.3.3[3ed]	Don't use this database map if DeliveryMode=defer
-d	§23.7.11.3[3ed]	DN to bind to server as (ldap only)
-d	§23.7.20.2[3ed]	The delimiting string (regex only)
-d	§24.9.109.22[3ed]	The res_search() _res.retry interval (dns and host only)
-f	§23.3.4[3ed]	Preserve case
-H	§23.1.1.2[V8.13]	Specify an LDAP URI in place of a host and port (ldap only)
-h	§23.7.11.4[3ed]	Hosts that serve this network database (ldap only)
-h	§23.7.18.1[3ed]	Hosts that serve this network database (ph only)
-k	§23.3.5[3ed]	Specify column for key
-k	§23.7.11.5[3ed]	The search query (ldap only)
-k	§23.7.13[3ed]	The property that is searched (netinfo only)
-k	§23.7.18.2[3ed]	Specify a list of fields to query (ph only)
-L	§23.7.24[3ed]	The logging level at which to log (syslog only)
-l	§23.3.6[3ed]	Time limit to timeout connection (ldap and ph only)
-M	§23.7.11.6[3ed]	The method to use for binding (ldap only)
-m	§23.3.7[3ed]	Suppress replacement on match
-N	§23.3.8[3ed]	Append a null byte to all keys
-n	§23.7.11.7[3ed]	Retrieve attribute names only, not values (ldap only)
-n	§23.7.20.3[3ed]	NOT, that is, invert the test (regex only)
-O	§23.3.9[3ed]	Never add a null byte

* This is true as of V8.13. Future versions might change the semantics of the K line such that switches can follow.

Table 23-5. K command switches (continued)

Switch	sendmail text reference	Description
-o	§23.3.10[3ed]	The database-map is optional
-P	§23.7.11.8[3ed]	The secret password to use for binding (ldap only)
-p	§23.7.11.9[3ed]	Port to use when connecting to host (ldap only)
-q	§23.3.11[3ed]	Don't strip quotes from key
-R	§23.7.11.10[3ed]	Don't auto-chase referrals (ldap only)
-R	§23.7.6[3ed]	Record type to look up (dns only)
-r	§23.7.11.11[3ed]	Allow dereferencing of aliases (ldap only)
-r	§24.9.109.22[3ed]	The res_search() _res.retries limit (dns and host only)
-S	§23.3.12[3ed]	Space replacement character for database-map
-s	§23.7.11.12[3ed]	Search scope of "base," "one," or "sub" (ldap only)
-s	§23.7.20.4[3ed]	Substring to match and return (regex only)
-T	§23.3.13[3ed]	Suffix to append on temporary failure
-t	§23.3.14[3ed]	Ignore temporary errors
-V	§23.7.11.13[3ed]	Specify return attribute list separator (ldap only)
-v	§23.3.15[3ed]	Specify the value's column
-v	§23.7.13[3ed]	The property to return (netinfo only)
-v	§23.7.18[3ed]	Specify a list of fields to return (ph only, V8.10–V8.12)
-v	§23.7.11.14[3ed]	Specify the list of attributes to return (ldap only)
-w	§23.1.1.1[V8.13]	Specify the LDAP API version to use (ldap only)
-Z	§23.7.11.16[3ed]	Limit the number of matches to return (ldap only)
-z	§23.3.16[3ed]	Specify the column delimiter

If a switch other than those listed is specified, either an error is reported or the switch is silently ignored, depending on the version of *sendmail* and the particular map *type*.

CHAPTER 24

The O (Options) Configuration Command

Options affect the operation of the *sendmail* program. Options can be specified in the command line, in the *sendmail.cf* file, and in the *mc* configuration file.

Most options are preset in your *sendmail.cf* file in a way that is likely to be appropriate for your site. But some sites, especially those that have high mail loads or are connected to many different networks, will need to tune options for their unique needs.

24.1 What's New with V8.13

V8.13 *sendmail* has modified 12 existing options and introduced 6 new ones.

- The existing `AuthOption` option (§24.9.6[3ed]) now has a new `m` flag (§24.1.1[V8.13]) that requires *sendmail* to use mechanisms that support mutual authentication.
- The existing `ConnectionCacheSize` and `ConnectionCacheTimeout` options now affect delivery agents that use `P=[LPC]` for delivery (§24.1.2[V8.13]).
- The existing `CheckpointInterval` option (§24.9.13[3ed]) can no longer have its value raised on the command line by nontrusted users (§24.1.3[V8.13]).
- The existing `DaemonPortOptions` (§24.9.24[3ed]) option's new `InputMailFilters=` equate allows you to specify which Milters should processes arriving mail on each listening port (§24.1.4[V8.13]).
- The existing `DaemonPortOptions` (§24.9.24[3ed]) option's existing `Modifiers=` equate offers a new modifier `s` that tells *sendmail* to use SMTP over SSL (§24.1.5[V8.13]).
- The existing `ErrorMode` (§24.9.44[3ed]) option's `write` mode has been deprecated and removed (§24.1.14[V8.13]).
- The existing `Timeout.queuereturn` (§24.9.109.18[3ed]) option's `dsn` addition specifies when to return bounce notifications (§24.1.15[V8.13]).
- The existing `Timeout.queuewarn` (§24.9.109.19[3ed]) option's `dsn` addition specifies when to send time-out bounce notifications (§24.1.16[V8.13]).

- The existing Milter.macros (§24.9.70[3ed]) option's eom addition specifies the macros to pass to the Milter's end-of-message handling routine (§24.1.17[V8.13]).
- The existing PidFile option (§24.9.78[3ed]) now works with all persistent daemons (such as queue runners), is locked to prevent overwrites, and is removed when *sendmail* exits (§24.1.6[V8.13]).
- The existing SuperSafe option (§24.9.107[3ed]) now accepts a new PostMilter setting that delays fsync()ing the *df* file until after all Milters have reviewed the message. This improves performance when a great deal of email is rejected by Milters that review the message body.
- The existing QueueSortOrder option (§24.9.86[3ed]) now accepts a new n setting for "none," which turns off all presorting of the queue (§24.1.7[V8.13]).
- The new AuthRealm option (§24.1.8[V8.13]) defines the authentication realm that is passed to the Cyrus SASL library.
- The new CRLFile option (§24.1.9[V8.13]) defines the name and location of the file that contains the OpenSSL certificate revocation list.
- The new FallbackSmartHost option (§24.1.10[V8.13]) defines the fallback host of absolute last resort.
- The new RejectLogInterval option (§24.1.11[V8.13]) specifies how often an additional message notifying of refusing connections should be logged.
- The new RequiresDirfsync option (§24.1.12[V8.13]) overrides the setting of the REQUIRES_DIR_FSYNC compile-time macro (§3.4.47[3ed]).
- Then new ConnectionRateWindowSize option (§24.1.13[V8.13]) specifies the window size for the conncontrol (§4.1.8[V8.13]) and ratecontrol (§4.1.7[V8.13]) features.

24.1.1 New =m Flag for the AuthOption option

The AuthOptions option (§24.9.6[3ed]) provides a list of general tuning parameters that affect authentication. It is declared like this:

```
O AuthOptions=string                      ← configuration file (V8.10 and later)
-OAuthOptions=string                      ← command-line file (V8.10 and later)
define(`confAUTH_OPTIONS´, `string´)      ← mc configuration (V8.10 and later)
```

The argument, of type *string*, is a list of characters selected from those shown in Table 24-1, where each character sets a particular tuning parameter. If more than one character is listed, each must be separated from the next by either a comma or a space. As of V8.13, a new m parameter has been added.

Table 24-1. AuthOptions character settings

Character	Meaning
A	Use the `AUTH=` parameter from the `MAIL FROM:` command only when authentication succeeds. This character can be specified as a workaround for broken MTAs that do not correctly implement RFC2554 (client only).
a	Provide protection from active (nondictionary) attacks during the authentication exchange (server only).
c	Allow only selected mechanisms (those that can pass client credentials) to be used with client credentials (server only).
d	Don't permit use of mechanisms that are susceptible to passive dictionary attacks (server only).
f	Require forward-secrecy between sessions (where breaking one won't help break the next) (server only).
m	Require the use of mechanisms that support mutual authentication (server only) (V8.13 and above).
p	Don't permit mechanisms to be used if they are susceptible to simple passive attacks (that is, disallow use of PLAIN and LOGIN) unless a security layer is already active (for example, provided by STARTTLS) (server only).
T	The opposite of A (pre-V8.12 only, client only).
y	Don't permit the use of any mechanism that allows anonymous login (server only).

24.1.2 ConnectionCacheSize and ConnectionCacheTimeout with P=[LPC]

Some sites have developed delivery agents that receive messages using SMTP over the standard input/output. They have done so by making use of the `P=[LPC]` equate (§20.5.11[3ed]).

Beginning with V8.13, *sendmail* enables connection caching (§24.7.5[3ed]) for such delivery agents, thereby increasing delivery performance. If your site has a delivery agent that uses the `P=[LPC]` equate, note that the `ConnectionCacheSize` option (§24.9.19[3ed]) and the `ConnectionCacheTimeout` option (§24.9.20[3ed]) will now affect the performance of that delivery agent.

24.1.3 The CheckpointInterval Option

When a single email message is sent to many recipients (those on a mailing list, for example), a single *sendmail* process handles all the recipients—but should that *sendmail* process die or be killed halfway through processing, for example, there will be no record that the first half of the mailing list was delivered. As a result, when the queue is later reprocessed, the recipients in that first half will receive the message a second time.

The `FastSplit` option (§24.9.46[3ed]) and this `CheckpointInterval` option (§24.9.13[3ed]) can limit that duplication. The `CheckpointInterval` option tells *sendmail* to rewrite (checkpoint) its *qf* file (which contains the list of recipients; see §11.2.5[3ed]) after each group of a specified number of recipients has been delivered. Recipients who have already received mail are deleted from the list, and that list is rewritten to the *qf* file.

Prior to V8.13, the CheckpointInterval option could have its value raised by anyone using the command line. But beginning with V8.13, only the trusted user, as defined by the TrustedUser option (§24.9.112[3ed]), may raise this value on the command line.

24.1.4 DaemonPortOptions=InputFilter=

The *sendmail* program can run in two connection modes: as a daemon, accepting connections; or as a client, making connections. Each mode can connect to a port to do its work. The tuning for the client port is set by the ClientPortOptions option (§24.9.17[3ed]). The tuning for the daemon is set by the DaemonPortOptions option (§24.9.24[3ed]). The format for declaring the DaemonPortOptions option in the *mc* configuration file looks like this:

```
DAEMON_OPTIONS(``pair,pair,pair´´)
```

The list of *pair* items must be enclosed in double half-quote pairs because the list contains commas. Each *pair* is an equate of the form:

```
item=value
```

The new InputMailFilters= equate is used to list the Milters that should be called, and the order in which they must be called. This list overrides the setting of the InputMailFilters option (§24.9.54[3ed]) and, indeed, may contain Milters not declared in that option. This InputMailFilters= equate lists one or more Milters each separated from the next by a colon (not a comma):

```
DAEMON_OPTIONS(``N=inMTA, I=milterA:milterB´´)
```

Note, as with all DaemonPortOptions option items, only the first character of each is needed. That is, both of the following produce the same effect:

```
I=milterA:milterB
InputMailFilters=milterA:milterB
```

This item can be useful when you have multiple network interfaces. One interface, for example, might be connected only to the internal network where a Milter records all outbound email. Another might be connected to the external network where a Milter can screen for viruses and spam email.

24.1.5 DaemonPortOptions new Modify=s

Beginning with V8.10 *sendmail*, you can modify selected characteristics of the port. Modification is done by listing selected letters from Table 24-2 following the Modify=. Note that the letters are case-sensitive (X is different from x). As of V8.13, a new s modifier has been added which tells *sendmail* to speak SMTP over SSL.

Table 24-2. Modify= port option letters

Letter	Meaning
a	Require authentication with the AUTH ESMTP keyword before continuing with the connection. Do not use this setting on a public MTA that listens on port 25.
b	Only send mail out on the interface address through which mail has been received. This is most useful on a host that is known by many hostnames, such as an ISP supporting multiple company domains on a single server, although it is also useful on smaller machines that restrict inbound connections to particular addresses.
c	Always perform hostname canonification. Determined via the `${daemon_flags}` macro (§21.9.30[3ed]) and the `${client_flags}` macro (§21.9.19[3ed]).
f	Require fully qualified hostnames. Whether a hostname is fully qualified is determined via configuration file rules that employ the `${daemon_flags}` macro (§21.9.30[3ed]) and the `${client_flags}` macro (§21.9.19[3ed]). See also the `accept_unqualified_senders` FEATURE (§4.8.1[3ed]).
h	Ignored by the daemon.
r	Request fully qualified recipient address. Uses `${daemon_flags}` (§21.9.30[3ed]) and `${client_flags}` (§21.9.19[3ed]).
s	Use SMTP over SSL (V8.13 and later).
u	Allow unqualified addresses. Determined via the `${daemon_flags}` macro (§21.9.30[3ed]), the `${client_flags}` macro (§21.9.19[3ed]), and configuration file rules. See also the `accept_unqualified_senders` FEATURE (§4.8.1[3ed]).
A	Disable authentication—overrides the a modifier above. (V8.12 and later)
C	Don't perform hostname canonification.
E	Disallow use of the ETRN command (§11.8.2.6[3ed]), as per RFC2476. Used for the MSA port 587.
O	If opening a socket fails, ignore the failure. (V8.12 and later)
S	Don't offer STARTTLS at session beginning. (V8.12 and later)

24.1.6 The PID File Is Removed on Exit

One problem with scripts that start and stop *sendmail* is that they are difficult to write in a manner that allows them to be rerun benignly a second time after *sendmail* stops. For example, the following script abstract will stop *sendmail* once:

```
SERVER_PID_FILE="/var/run/sendmail.pid"
[ -f $SERVER_PID_FILE ] && kill `head -1 $SERVER_PID_FILE`
```

But if this script is run a second time after *sendmail* stops, an error such as the following will be reported:

```
4591: No such process
```

To prevent this sort of error, V8.13 *sendmail* removes its PID file when it exits. Once the file is gone, the above script fragment can be run a second time without producing an error.

However, be aware that existing scripts of your design, or those included with your operating system, may break under this new scheme. Consider, for example, the following script whose purpose is to restart *sendmail*:

```
SERVER_PID_FILE="/var/run/sendmail.pid"
kill `head -1 $SERVER_PID_FILE`
`tail -1 $SERVER_PID_FILE`
```

Recall (§24.9.78[3ed]) that the first line of *sendmail*'s PID file contains the process-ID of the currently running *sendmail*, and that the second and last line of the PID file contains the command line originally used to run *sendmail*. Here, the `head -1` captures the process-ID needed to kill *sendmail*, and the `tail -1` captures the command line needed to re-execute *sendmail*. This has worked fine until now, but, beginning with V8.13 *sendmail*, the second script command (the `tail -1`) will fail because *sendmail* has removed the PID file.

One correct way to rewrite such a script might look like this:

```
SERVER_PID_FILE="/var/run/sendmail.pid"
PID_NUM=`head -1 $SERVER_PID_FILE`
CMD_LINE=`tail -1 $SERVER_PID_FILE`
kill $PID_NUM
$CMD_LINE
```

The idea here is to capture and save the `head -1` and `tail -1` information from the PID file before killing *sendmail*, thereby avoiding the error of trying to read the file after it is removed. Naturally, such a simple script should not be used in production. With full error detection, a much more careful script might look like the following:

```
SERVER_PID_FILE="/var/run/sendmail.pid"
if [ -f /etc/mail/sendmail.cf ]; then
        SERVER_PID_FILE=`grep "^O PidFile" /etc/mail/sendmail.cf | \
                sed -e ´s/O PidFile=//´`
        if [ $? != 0 -o "$SERVER_PID_FILE" = "" ]; then
                SERVER_PID_FILE="/var/run/sendmail.pid"
        fi
fi

if [ -f $SERVER_PID_FILE ]; then
        PID_NUM=`head -1 $SERVER_PID_FILE`
        if [ $? != 0 -o "$PID_NUM" = "" ]; then
                echo "Could not read PID in $SERVER_PID_FILE"
                exit 1
        fi
        CMD_LINE=`tail -1 $SERVER_PID_FILE`
        if [ $? != 0 -o "$CMD_LINE" = "" ]; then
                echo "Could not read command in $SERVER_PID_FILE"
                exit 1
        fi
        if [ "$PID_NUM" = "$CMD_LINE" ]; then
                # Only one line in the file
                echo "$SERVER_PID_FILE is malformed"
                exit 1
        fi
        kill $PID_NUM
        $CMD_LINE
fi
```

24.1.7 The New QueueSortOrder None Setting

Prior to V8.7 *sendmail*, mail messages in the queue were sorted by priority when the queue was processed. Under V8.7, an enhanced sort can be implemented with the QueueSortOrder option, the forms of which are as follows:

```
O QueueSortOrder=how                     ← configuration file (V8.7 and later)
-OQueueSortOrder=how                     ← command line (V8.7 and later)
define(`confQUEUE_SORT_ORDER´, `how´)    ← mc configuration (V8.7 and later)
```

The argument *how* is of type character.* It can be a P or p (for priority), which causes *sendmail* to emulate its old (sort by priority) behavior. It can be an H or h (for host), which causes *sendmail* to perform an enhanced sort. Beginning with V8.8 *sendmail*, it can be T or t (for time), which sorts by submission time; beginning with V8.10 *sendmail*, it can be F or f (for file), which sorts by filename; beginning with V8.12 *sendmail*, it can be R or r (for random), which randomizes the list of hosts, or M or m, which sorts based on file modification time; and beginning with V8.13 sendmail, it can be N or n (for none), which skips the sort altogether.

24.1.8 The New AuthRealm Option

Prior to V8.13, the authentication realm passed to the Cyrus SASL library was always the value of the $j macro. Beginning with V8.13, the new AuthRealm option allows you to specify a different authentication realm:

```
O AuthRealm=realm                        ← configuration file (V8.13 and later)
-OAuthRealm=realm                        ← command-line (V8.13 and later)
define(`confAUTH_REALM´,`realm´)         ← mc configuration (V8.13 and later)
```

Here, *realm* is of type string and specifies the authentication realm to use in place of the $j macro's value. If *realm* is missing, the effect is the same as if the entire option was omitted—that is, the value of $j is used.

The AuthRealm option is not safe. If specified from the command line, it can cause *sendmail* to relinquish its special privileges.

24.1.9 The New CRLFile Option

Beginning with V8.13, *sendmail* now supports use of the certificate revocation lists available with OpenSSL† Version 0.9.7 and above. The new CRLFile option allows you to declare the location and name of a certificate revocation list file.

When *sendmail* receives an inbound connection, and when the connecting host requests a secure session by giving the STARTTLS command, the local *sendmail* (by

* Of course, we recommend using full words for clarity.

† Secure Socket Layer (SSLv2/v3) available from *http://www.openssl.org*.

way of the OpenSSL library) uses the information in CRLFile to determine whether the connecting host's certificate should be accepted or rejected.

The file specified by the CRLFile option is created using the *openssl*(1) command. After the file has been created, you need to declare its location like this:

```
O CRLFile=/path/file                    ← configuration file (V8.13 and later)
-OCRLFile=/path/file                    ← command-line (V8.13 and later)
define(`confCRL´,`/path/file´)          ← mc configuration (V8.13 and later)
```

Here, */path/file* is of type string and specifies the full-path location of the certificate revocation list file. If the file is declared with this CRLFile option, but does not exist, is unreadable, or has bad permissions, all STARTTLS commands are disallowed by *sendmail*. The */path/file* may contain *sendmail* macros, and those macros will be expanded as the configuration file is read. By default, the CRLFile option is not declared.

If your version of OpenSSL is too old, the following warning will print when you try to declare the CRLFile option, and that option will be ignored:

```
Warning: Option: CRLFile requires at least OpenSSL 0.9.7
```

The file referenced by the CRLFile option is created using the *openssl*(1) command. For example, if you are using your own CA, the following can be used to create a file named */etc/ssl/crl.pem*:*

```
openssl ca -revoke certificate-file   ← first revoke the certificate
openssl ca -gencrl -out crl.pem       ← then create the revocation list
```

If you need DER format in your revocation list file, you can use the following command after the second line above:

```
openssl crl -in crl.pem -outform der -out crl.der
```

Note that these examples are an over-simplification for illustrative purposes only. See the OpenSSL documentation for more details.

The CRLFile option is not safe. If specified from the command line, it can cause *sendmail* to relinquish its special privileges.

24.1.10 The New FallbackSmartHost Option

At sites with poor (connect-on-demand) or unreliable network connections, SMTP connections can often fail. In such situations, it might not be desirable for each workstation to queue the mail locally for a later attempt. Prior to V8.13 *sendmail*, the FallbackMXhost option (§24.9.45[3ed]) was used to provide a final, alternative method for getting a message out the door by specifying the name of a mail exchanger machine (MX record) of last resort.

* The directory that contains certificate revocation lists is found in your *openssl.cnf* configuration file and is generally defined as <ssl-base-dir>/crl/.

The trouble with this strategy is that the FallbackMXhost option works only if the recipient's hostname can be looked up in the first place. If the hostname cannot be found, not even the FallbackMXhost is tried.

For most well-managed sites, this is not a problem. Machines can still look up hosts on the Internet, even if they are on an internal business LAN or behind a firewall. But not all sites are well managed, and some sites disallow external lookups as a matter of policy. For such sites, the FallbackMXhost option will not do.

Beginning with V8.13, the FallbackSmartHost option has been added to solve this particular problem. Even if the recipient's host cannot be found, the fallback host specified with this new option will still be tried.

The FallbackSmartHost option is declared like this:

```
O FallbackSmartHost=host.domain                          ← config file (V8.13 and later)
-OFallbackSmartHost=host.domain                          ← command-line (V8.13 and later)
define(`confFALLBACK_SMARTHOST´, `host.domain´)          ← mc config (V8.13 and later)
```

Here, *host.domain* is the canonical name to which the host will fallback. If this option is entirely omitted (the default), no fallback smart-host is defined. If the hostname is an empty string or is the name of a nonexistent host, mail forwarded to that host fails. The *host.domain* may contain *sendmail* macros; if so, those macros will be expanded just before the attempt is made to connect to the host.

Note that the hostname specified for this FallbackSmartHost option must not exist in the class $=w (§22.6.16[3ed]). If it does, it will be silently ignored.

Another use for this new FallbackSmartHost option presents itself at sites that have unreliable FallbackMXhost servers. When that FallbackMXhost goes down, this FallBackSmartHost is tried, thus allowing outbound mail to still flow.

The FallbackSmartHost option is not safe. If specified from the command line, it can cause *sendmail* to relinquish its special privileges.

24.1.11 The New RejectLogInterval Option

Prior to V8.13, whenever the load level on a machine became greater than the setting for the RefuseLA option (§24.9.90[3ed]), further inbound connections would be refused, and the following warning message would be logged:

```
rejecting connections on daemon name: load average=load
```

Beginning with V8.13 *sendmail*, you may specify how often additional warnings should be logged. Note that the same message is logged when refusing begins—but if connections continue to be refused, you will be notified with a different message, to aid you in taking corrective actions.

The RejectLogInterval option tells *sendmail* how often (at what intervals) it should log a message saying that connections are still being refused. The RejectLogInterval option is declared like this:

```
O RejectLogInterval=interval                         ← configuration file (V8.13 and later)
-ORejectLogInterval=interval                         ← command-line (V8.13 and later)
define(`confREJECT_LOG_INTERVAL´, `interval´) ← mc configuration (V8.13 and later)
```

Here, *interval* is of type time. The default (if this option is omitted) is three hours. The default units are hours. For example, both of following set the periodic logging interval to one hour:

```
define(`confREJECT_LOG_INTERVAL´, `60m´)
define(`confREJECT_LOG_INTERVAL´, `1´)
```

When connections are first refused because the load level is too high, the following warning is logged, as before:

```
rejecting connections on daemon name: load average=load
```

Thereafter, for as long as the load continues to be too high, the following warning message is logged once per RejectLogInterval interval:

```
have been rejecting connections on daemon name for duration
```

Here, *name* is the name of the listening daemon (e.g., MTA-v4), and *duration* is the total amount of time that has elapsed since connections were first refused.

The RejectLogInterval option is not safe. If specified from the command line, it can cause *sendmail* to relinquish its special privileges.

24.1.12 The New RequiresDirfsync Option

Some versions of Unix (or implementations of disk I/O) do not support immediate updates of directories when their data changes. For these versions, the REQUIRES_DIR_FSYNC compile-time macro (§3.4.47[3ed]) must set to true, causing *sendmail* to *fsync*(2) the directory every time it is updated.

If your operating system is one of these, and if you need to avoid the overhead of this forced directory updating,* you may do so by defining the RequiresDirfsync option. It is declared like this:

```
O RequiresDirfsync=bool                          ← configuration file (V8.13 and later)
-O RequiresDirfsync=bool                         ← command-line (V8.13 and later)
define(`confREQUIRES_DIR_FSYNC´, `bool´)         ← mc configuration (V8.13 and later)
```

Here, *bool* is of type boolean. If this option is omitted, the default is true (that is directory *fsync*(2) is required if REQUIRES_DIR_FSYNC was defined at compile time). If this option is defined as false, however, directory *fsync*(2) is disabled even if REQUIRES_DIR_FSYNC was defined at compile time.

The RequiresDirfsync option is not safe. If specified from the command line, it can cause *sendmail* to relinquish its special privileges.

* You risk lost mail should the machine crash without this updating.

24.1.13 The New ConnectionRateWindowSize Option

Under V8.13, two new *sendmail* macros, called `${client_rate}` (§21.1.4[V8.13]) and `${total_rate}` (§21.1.9[V8.13]), are available to control the number of simultaneous connections allowed. They are used by the new `conncontrol` (§4.1.8[V8.13]) and `ratecontrol` (§4.1.7[V8.13]) features, which perform the same service via the *access* database. This new `ConnectionRateWindowSize` option sets the size of the window of time that is used to measure these rates. It is declare like this:

```
O ConnectionRateWindowSize=secs                      ← configuration file (V8.13 and later)
-O ConnectionRateWindowSize=secs                     ← command line (V8.13 and later)
define(`confCONNECTION_RATE_WINDOW_SIZE', `secs')    ← mc configuration (V8.13 and later)
```

Here, *secs* is of type `time`. If this option is omitted, the default for the window of time is 60 seconds. If this option is defined, but the time units are omitted, the default units are seconds.

We recommend you only change the default if you have not already made connection limiting entries in your *access* database. If you make those entries first, then later change this setting, you will inadvertently change the meaning of those *access* database entries.

The `ConnectionRateWindowSize` option is not safe. If specified from the command line, it can cause *sendmail* to relinquish its special privileges.

24.1.14 ErrorMode=write Deprecated

The *sendmail* program is flexible in its handling of delivery errors. By selecting from five possible modes with the `ErrorMode` option, you can tailor notification of delivery errors to suit many needs.

The possible settings are listed in Table 24-3. As of V8.13, the `w` (for write) setting has been deprecated and removed. If you have used this mode in the past and still need to use it, you may still do so under V8.13 by building *sendmail* with `-DUSE_TTYPATH=1` defined in your *Build* configuration file.

Table 24-3. ErrorMode option modes

Mode	sendmail text reference	Meaning
e	§24.9.44.1[3ed]	Acts like m, but always exits with a zero exit status.
m	§24.9.44.2[3ed]	Mail error notification to the sender no matter what.
p	§24.9.44.3[3ed]	Print error messages (the default).
q	§24.9.44.4[3ed]	Remain silent about all delivery errors.
w	§24.9.44.5[3ed]	Write errors to the sender's terminal screen (deprecated and removed as of V8.13).

24.1.15 The Timeout.queuereturn.dsn Addition

This queuereturn keyword (§24.9.109.18[3ed]) to the Timeout option is used to set the amount of time a message must wait in the queue before it is bounced as nondeliverable. It comes in three basic forms:

```
O Timeout.queuereturn=timeout                    ← configuration file (V8.7 and later)
-OTimeout.queuereturn=timeout                    ← command line (V8.7 and later)
define(`confTO_QUEUERETURN', `timeout')          ← mc configuration (V8.7 and later)
```

Going further, the Queuereturn keyword can tune on the basis of three possible levels of priority that a mail message can have. The above forms set all three levels at once, whereas the following forms tune each level independently:

```
O Timeout.queuereturn.urgent=timeout                   ← configuration file (V8.7 and later)
O Timeout.queuereturn.normal=timeout                   ← configuration file (V8.7 and later)
O Timeout.queuereturn.non-urgent=timeout               ← configuration file (V8.7 and later)
-OTimeout.queuereturn.urgent=timeout                   ← command line (V8.7 and later)
-OTimeout.queuereturn.normal=timeout                   ← command line (V8.7 and later)
-OTimeout.queuereturn.non-urgent=timeout               ← command line (V8.7 and later)
define(`confTO_QUEUERETURN_URGENT',`timeout')          ← mc config (V8.7 and later)
define(`confTO_QUEUERETURN_NORMAL',`timeout')          ← mc config (V8.7 and later)
define(`confTO_QUEUERETURN_NONURGENT',`timeout')       ← mc config (V8.7 and later)
```

The default for the *mc* configuration technique is to bounce all messages that remain in the queue for more than five days.

The keywords urgent, normal, and non-urgent correspond to the levels of priority indicated in the Precedence: header of the mail message. When the numeric equivalent of the Precedence: header (as translated from the P line of the configuration file; see §25.10[3ed]) is negative, the message is classified as non-urgent. When it is greater than zero, the message is classified as urgent. Otherwise, it is normal.

As of V8.7, a Priority: header is also available (see §25.12.28[3ed]) to directly specify the message priority and thereby bypass the need to set the value using the Precedence: header.

Beginning with V8.10, in addition to an interval specification, you can use the literal term now to force an immediate bounce.

Beginning with V8.13, a new keyword, dsn, has been added to the priorities of urgent, normal, and non-urgent. If the precedence of the message is normal (zero), and if the message is a return DSN message, the timeout defined by this new keyword is used:

```
O Timeout.queuereturn.dsn=timeout                ← configuration file (V8.13 and later)
-OTimeout.queuereturn.dsn=timeout                ← command line (V8.13 and later)
define(`confTO_QUEUERETURN_DSN',`timeout')       ← mc config (V8.13 and later)
```

One handy use for this new keyword is to return DSN messages sooner than normal mail. But note that when you return a bounce message, you create a double-bounce that is sent to the address specified by the DoubleBounceAddress option (§24.9.41[3ed]).

24.1.16 The Timeout.queuewarn.dsn Addition

When an email message is queued for longer than a predetermined time, *sendmail* sends a message to the sender explaining that, although the original message could not be delivered right away, *sendmail* will keep trying. The amount of time to wait before sending this message is set by the `Timeout.Queuewarn` option (§24.9.109.19[3ed]).

Beginning with V8.13, it is possible to set a separate wait for DSN messages. This wait is set with the `dsn` keyword:

```
O Timeout.queuewarn.dsn=wait                  ← configuration file (V8.13 and later)
-OTimeout.queuewarn.dsn=wait                  ← command line (V8.13 and later)
define(`confTO_QUEUEWARN_DSN´,`wait´)         ← mc config (V8.13 and later)
```

One handy use for this `dsn` keyword would be to prevent warnings from being sent for DSN mail. You can do this by setting this warning timeout greater than the return timeout for regular mail:

```
define(`confTO_QUEUERETURN´,  `5d´)
define(`confTO_QUEUEWARN_DSN´, `7d´)
```

Here, normal mail will be returned (bounced) after five days, but because DSN mail won't issue a warning until after seven days, no warnings will be sent.

24.1.17 The Milter.macros.eom Addition

Beginning with V8.13, the new `Milter.macros.eom` option defines a list of macros to be passed to a Milter's end-of-message handling routine. It is declared like this:

```
O Milter.macros.eom=list                      ← configuration file (V8.13 and later)
-OMilter.macros.eom=list                      ← command line (V8.13 and later)
define(`confMILTER_MACROS_EOM´,`list´)        ← mc configuration (V8.13 and later)
```

The `Milter.macros.eom` option is of type `string`. The *`list`* is a sequence of macro names, each separated from the next with a comma and each stripped of its leading $ prefix—that is, `{nbadrcpts}`, not `${nbadrcpts}`.

The default macro passed to the Milter's end-of-message routine is the `${msg_id}` macro (§21.1.5[V8.13]). If you wish to add other macros to the default list, you may do so using your *mc* configuration file like this:

```
define(`confMILTER_MACROS_EOM´, confMILTER_MACROS_EOM``,{nbadrcpts}´´)
```

Here, we added the `${nbadrcpts}` macro (§21.1.6[V8.13]) to the default list of macros. Note the use of double half quotes. They are needed because the added macro contains a comma (recall that the list of macros must be delimited with commas).

The `Milter.macros.eom` option is not safe. If specified from the command line, it can cause *sendmail* to relinquish its special privileges.

24.2 Useful Tables

In this section, we present two tables that will help you with your use of options:

- Table 24-3 lists all the options that can be used in the *mc* configuration file.
- Table 24-4 lists all options in order of *cf* filename.

24.2.1 Options in the mc File

When you create a configuration file with the *mc* configuration technique, you can tune each option by including an appropriate statement in your *mc* configuration file:*

```
define(`option´,`value´)                 ← enclose in opposing single quotes
define(`confAUTO_REBUILD´,`True´)        ← for example
DAEMON_OPTIONS(`Port=1097´)              ← for example
```

The *option* is selected from one of the *mc* option names shown in the leftmost column of Table 24-4. The *value* is an appropriate value for that option. Note that the *option* and the *value* should each be enclosed in *opposing* single quotes to prevent *m4* from wrongly recognizing either as a keyword or macro. Note that the leftmost single quote is actually the reverse apostrophe, and the rightmost is a normal apostrophe.

Table 24-4. All option mc macros ordered by name

mc name	Option name	sendmail text reference
ALIAS_FILE	AliasFile	§24.9.1[3ed]
CLIENT_OPTIONS()	ClientPortOptions	§24.9.17[3ed]
confALIAS_WAIT	AliasWait	§24.9.2[3ed]
confALLOW_BOGUS_HELO	AllowBogusHELO	§24.9.3[3ed]
confAUTH_MAX_BITS	AuthMaxBits	§24.9.4[3ed]
confAUTH_MECHANISMS	AuthMechanisms	§24.9.5[3ed]
confAUTH_OPTIONS	AuthOptions	§24.9.6[3ed]
confAUTH_REALM	AuthRealm	§24.1.8[V8.13]
confAUTO_REBUILD	AutoRebuildAliases	§24.9.7[3ed]
confBAD_RCPT_THROTTLE	BadRcptThrottle	§24.9.8[3ed]
confBIND_OPTS	ResolverOptions	§24.9.91[3ed]
confBLANK_SUB	BlankSub	§24.9.9[3ed]
confCACERT	CACertFile	§24.9.10[3ed]
confCACERT_PATH	CACertPath	§24.9.11[3ed]

* Some *mc* macros use the `define` *m4* directive, while others don't require this. Those that don't are suffixed with parentheses in the table.

Table 24-4. All option mc macros ordered by name (continued)

mc name	Option name	sendmail text reference
confCHECKPOINT_INTERVAL	CheckpointInterval	§24.9.13[3ed]
confCHECK_ALIASES	CheckAliases	§24.9.12[3ed]
confCLIENT_CERT	ClientCertFile	§24.9.15[3ed]
confCLIENT_KEY	ClientKeyFile	§24.9.16[3ed]
confCLIENT_OPTIONS (deprecated)	ClientPortOptions	§24.9.17[3ed]
confCOLON_OK_IN_ADDR	ColonOkInAddr	§24.9.18[3ed]
confCONNECTION_RATE_THROTTLE	ConnectionRateThrottle	§24.9.21[3ed]
confCONNECTION_RATE_WINDOW_SIZE	ConnectionRateWindowSize	§24.1.13[V8.13]
confCONNECT_ONLY_TO	ConnectOnlyTo	§24.9.22[3ed]
confCONTROL_SOCKET_NAME	ControlSocketName	§24.9.23[3ed]
confCON_EXPENSIVE	HoldExpensive	§24.9.50[3ed]
confCOPY_ERRORS_TO	PostmasterCopy	§24.9.79[3ed]
confCRL	CRLFile	§24.1.9[V8.13]
confDAEMON_OPTIONS (deprecated)	DaemonPortOptions	§24.9.24[3ed]
confDEAD_LETTER_DROP	DeadLetterDrop	§24.9.26[3ed]
confDEF_AUTH_INFO	DefaultAuthInfo	§24.9.27[3ed]
confDEF_CHAR_SET	DefaultCharSet	§24.9.28[3ed]
confDEF_USER_ID	DefaultUser	§24.9.29[3ed]
confDELAY_LA	DelayLA	§24.9.30[3ed]
confDELIVERY_MODE	DeliveryMode	§24.9.32[3ed]
confDELIVER_BY_MIN	DeliverByMin	§24.9.31[3ed]
confDF_BUFFER_SIZE	DataFileBufferSize	§24.9.25[3ed]
confDH_PARAMETERS	DHParameters	§24.9.33[3ed]
confDIAL_DELAY	DialDelay	§24.9.34[3ed]
confDIRECT_SUBMISSION_MODIFIERS	DirectSubmissionModifiers	§24.9.35[3ed]
confDONT_BLAME_SENDMAIL	DontBlameSendmail	§24.9.36[3ed]
confDONT_EXPAND_CNAMES	DontExpandCnames	§24.9.37[3ed]
confDONT_INIT_GROUPS	DontInitGroups	§24.9.38[3ed]
confDONT_PROBE_INTERFACES	DontProbeInterfaces	§24.9.39[3ed]
confDONT_PRUNE_ROUTES	DontPruneRoutes	§24.9.40[3ed]
confDOUBLE_BOUNCE_ADDRESS	DoubleBounceAddress	§24.9.41[3ed]
confEIGHT_BIT_HANDLING	EightBitMode	§24.9.42[3ed]
confERROR_MESSAGE	ErrorHeader	§24.9.43[3ed]
confERROR_MODE	ErrorMode	§24.9.44[3ed]
confFALLBACK_MX	FallbackMXhost	§24.9.45[3ed]
confFALLBACK_SMARTHOST	FallbackSmartHost	§24.1.10[V8.13]

Table 24-4. All option mc macros ordered by name (continued)

mc name	Option name	sendmail text reference
confFAST_SPLIT	FastSplit	§24.9.46[3ed]
confFORWARD_PATH	ForwardPath	§24.9.48[3ed]
confFROM_LINE	UnixFromLine	§24.9.114[3ed]
confHOSTS_FILE	HostsFile	§24.9.51[3ed]
confHOST_STATUS_DIRECTORY	HostStatusDirectory	§24.9.52[3ed]
confIGNORE_DOTS	IgnoreDots	§24.9.53[3ed]
confINPUT_MAIL_FILTERS	InputMailFilters	§24.9.54[3ed]
confLDAP_DEFAULT_SPEC	LDAPDefaultSpec	§24.9.55[3ed]
confLOG_LEVEL	LogLevel	§24.9.56[3ed]
confMAILBOX_DATABASE	MailboxDatabase	§24.9.57[3ed]
confMATCH_GECOS	MatchGECOS	§24.9.58[3ed]
confMAX_ALIAS_RECURSION	MaxAliasRecursion	§24.9.59[3ed]
confMAX_DAEMON_CHILDREN	MaxDaemonChildren	§24.9.60[3ed]
confMAX_HEADERS_LENGTH	MaxHeadersLength	§24.9.61[3ed]
confMAX_HOP	MaxHopCount	§24.9.62[3ed]
confMAX_MESSAGE_SIZE	MaxMessageSize	§24.9.63[3ed]
confMAX_MIME_HEADER_LENGTH	MaxMimeHeaderLength	§24.9.64[3ed]
confMAX_QUEUE_CHILDREN	MaxQueueChildren	§24.9.65[3ed]
confMAX_QUEUE_RUN_SIZE	MaxQueueRunSize	§24.9.66[3ed]
confMAX_RCPTS_PER_MESSAGE	MaxRecipientsPerMessage	§24.9.67[3ed]
confMAX_RUNNERS_PER_QUEUE	MaxRunnersPerQueue	§24.9.68[3ed]
confMCI_CACHE_SIZE	ConnectionCacheSize	§24.9.19[3ed]
confMCI_CACHE_TIMEOUT	ConnectionCacheTimeout	§24.9.20[3ed]
confMESSAGE_TIMEOUT (deprecated)	QueueTimeout	§24.9.87[3ed]
confME_TOO	MeToo	§24.9.69[3ed]
confMILTER_LOG_LEVEL	Milter.LogLevel	§24.9.70[3ed]
confMILTER_MACROS_CONNECT	Milter.macros.connect	§24.9.70[3ed]
confMILTER_MACROS_ENVFROM	Milter.macros.envfrom	§24.9.70[3ed]
confMILTER_MACROS_ENVRCPT	Milter.macros.envrcpt	§24.9.70[3ed]
confMILTER_MACORS_EOM	Milter.macros.eom	§24.1.17[V8.13]
confMILTER_MACROS_HELO	Milter.macros.helo	§24.9.70[3ed]
confMIME_FORMAT_ERRORS	SendMimeErrors	§24.9.97[3ed]
confMIN_FREE_BLOCKS	MinFreeBlocks	§24.9.71[3ed]
confMIN_QUEUE_AGE	MinQueueAge	§24.9.72[3ed]
confMUST_QUOTE_CHARS	MustQuoteChars	§24.9.73[3ed]
confNICE_QUEUE_RUN	NiceQueueRun	§24.9.74[3ed]

Table 24-4. All option mc macros ordered by name (continued)

mc name	Option name	sendmail text reference
confNO_RCPT_ACTION	NoRecipientAction	§24.9.75[3ed]
confOLD_STYLE_HEADERS	OldStyleHeaders	§24.9.76[3ed]
confOPERATORS	OperatorChars	§24.9.77[3ed]
confPID_FILE	PidFile	§24.9.78[3ed]
confPRIVACY_FLAGS	PrivacyOptions	§24.9.80[3ed]
confPROCESS_TITLE_PREFIX	ProcessTitlePrefix	§24.9.81[3ed]
confQUEUE_FACTOR	QueueFactor	§24.9.83[3ed]
confQUEUE_FILE_MODE	QueueFileMode	§24.9.84[3ed]
confQUEUE_LA	QueueLA	§24.9.85[3ed]
confQUEUE_SORT_ORDER	QueueSortOrder	§24.9.86[3ed]
confRAND_FILE	RandFile	§24.9.88[3ed]
confREAD_TIMEOUT (deprecated)	Timeout	§24.9.109[3ed]
confREFUSE_LA	RefuseLA	§24.9.90[3ed]
confREJECT_LOG_INTERVAL	RejectLogInterval	§24.1.11[V8.13]
confREQUIRES_DIR_FSYNC	RequiresDirfsync	§24.1.12[V8.13]
confRRT_IMPLIES_DSN	RrtImpliesDsn	§24.9.93[3ed]
confRUN_AS_USER	RunAsUser	§24.9.94[3ed]
confSAFE_FILE_ENV	SafeFileEnvironment	§24.9.95[3ed]
confSAFE_QUEUE	SuperSafe	§24.9.107[3ed]
confSAVE_FROM_LINES	SaveFromLine	§24.9.96[3ed]
confSEPARATE_PROC	ForkEachJob	§24.9.47[3ed]
confSERVER_CERT	ServerCertFile	§24.9.98[3ed]
confSERVER_KEY	ServerKeyFile	§24.9.99[3ed]
confSERVICE_SWITCH_FILE	ServiceSwitchFile	§24.9.100[3ed]
confSEVEN_BIT_INPUT	SevenBitInput	§24.9.101[3ed]
confSHARED_MEMORY_KEY	SharedMemoryKey	§24.9.102[3ed]
confSINGLE_LINE_FROM_HEADER	SingleLineFromHeader	§24.9.103[3ed]
confSINGLE_THREAD_DELIVERY	SingleThreadDelivery	§24.9.104[3ed]
confSMTP_LOGIN_MSG	SmtpGreetingMessage	§24.9.105[3ed]
confTEMP_FILE_MODE	TempFileMode	§24.9.108[3ed]
confTIME_ZONE	TimeZoneSpec	§24.9.110[3ed]
confTLS_SRV_OPTIONS	TLSSrvOptions	§24.9.111[3ed]
confTO_ACONNECT	Timeout.aconnect	§24.9.109.1[3ed]
confTO_AUTH	Timeout.auth	§24.9.109.2[3ed]
confTO_COMMAND	Timeout.command	§24.9.109.3[3ed]
confTO_CONNECT	Timeout.connect	§24.9.109.4[3ed]

Table 24-4. All option mc macros ordered by name (continued)

mc name	Option name	sendmail text reference
confTO_CONTROL	Timeout.control	§24.9.109.5[3ed]
confTO_DATABLOCK	Timeout.datablock	§24.9.109.6[3ed]
confTO_DATAFINAL	Timeout.datafinal	§24.9.109.7[3ed]
confTO_DATAINIT	Timeout.datainit	§24.9.109.8[3ed]
confTO_FILEOPEN	Timeout.fileopen	§24.9.109.9[3ed]
confTO_HELO	Timeout.helo	§24.9.109.10[3ed]
confTO_HOSTSTATUS	Timeout.hoststatus	§24.9.109.11[3ed]
confTO_ICONNECT	Timeout.iconnect	§24.9.109.12[3ed]
confTO_IDENT	Timeout.ident	§24.9.109.13[3ed]
confTO_INITIAL	Timeout.initial	§24.9.109.14[3ed]
confTO_LHLO	Timeout.lhlo	§24.9.109.15[3ed]
confTO_MAIL	Timeout.mail	§24.9.109.16[3ed]
confTO_MISC	Timeout.misc	§24.9.109.17[3ed]
confTO_QUEUERETURN	Timeout.queuereturn	§24.9.109.18[3ed]
confTO_QUEUERETURN_DSN	Timeout.queuereturn.dsn	§24.1.15[V8.13]
confTO_QUEUERETURN_NONURGENT	Timeout.queuereturn.non-urgent	§24.9.109.18[3ed]
confTO_QUEUERETURN_NORMAL	Timeout.queuereturn.normal	§24.9.109.18[3ed]
confTO_QUEUERETURN_URGENT	Timeout.queuereturn.urgent	§24.9.109.18[3ed]
confTO_QUEUEWARN	Timeout.queuewarn	§24.9.109.19[3ed]
confTO_QUEUEWARN_DSN	Timeout.queuewarn.dsn	§24.1.16[V8.13]
confTO_QUEUEWARN_NONURGENT	Timeout.queuewarn.non-urgent	§24.9.109.19[3ed]
confTO_QUEUEWARN_NORMAL	Timeout.queuewarn.normal	§24.9.109.19[3ed]
confTO_QUEUEWARN_URGENT	Timeout.queuewarn.urgent	§24.9.109.19[3ed]
confTO_QUIT	Timeout.quit	§24.9.109.20[3ed]
confTO_RCPT	Timeout.rcpt	§24.9.109.21[3ed]
confTO_RESOLVER_RETRANS	Timeout.resolver.retrans	§24.9.109.22[3ed]
confTO_RESOLVER_RETRANS_FIRST	Timeout.resolver.retrans.first	§24.9.109.22[3ed]
confTO_RESOLVER_RETRANS_NORMAL	Timeout.resolver.retrans.normal	§24.9.109.22[3ed]
confTO_RESOLVER_RETRY	Timeout.resolver.retry	§24.9.109.22[3ed]
confTO_RESOLVER_RETRY_FIRST	Timeout.resolver.retry.first	§24.9.109.22[3ed]
confTO_RESOLVER_RETRY_NORMAL	Timeout.resolver.retry.normal	§24.9.109.22[3ed]
confTO_RSET	Timeout.rset	§24.9.109.23[3ed]
confTO_STARTTLS	Timeout.starttls	§24.9.109.24[3ed]
confTRUSTED_USER	TrustedUser	§24.9.112[3ed]

Table 24-4. All option mc macros ordered by name (continued)

mc name	Option name	sendmail text reference
confTRY_NULL_MX_LIST	TryNullMXList	§24.9.113[3ed]
confUNSAFE_GROUP_WRITES (deprecated)	UnsafeGroupWrites	§24.9.115[3ed]
confUSERDB_SPEC	UserDatabaseSpec	§24.9.118[3ed]
confUSE_ERRORS_TO	UseErrorsTo	§24.9.116[3ed]
confUSE_MSP	UseMSP	§24.9.117[3ed]
confWORK_CLASS_FACTOR	ClassFactor	§24.9.14[3ed]
confWORK_RECIPIENT_FACTOR	RecipientFactor	§24.9.89[3ed]
confWORK_TIME_FACTOR	RetryFactor	§24.9.92[3ed]
confXF_BUFFER_SIZE	XscriptFileBufferSize	§24.9.120[3ed]
DAEMON_OPTIONS( )	DaemonPortOptions	§24.9.24[3ed]
HELP_FILE	HelpFile	§24.9.49[3ed]
INPUT_MAIL_FILTER( )	InputMailFilters	§24.9.54[3ed]
QUEUE_DIR	QueueDirectory	§24.9.82[3ed]
STATUS_FILE	StatusFile	§24.9.106[3ed]

24.2.2 Alphabetical Table of All Options

In this section, we present a table of all options in alphabetical order. The leftmost column of Table 24-5 lists the option name. The second column shows the section where each is described.

Table 24-5. All options ordered by option name

Option name	sendmail text reference	Description
AliasFile	§24.9.1[3ed]	Define the locations of the *aliases* files
AliasWait	§24.9.2[3ed]	Wait for *aliases* file rebuild
AllowBogusHELO	§24.9.3[3ed]	Allow no host with HELO or EHLO SMTP command
AuthMaxBits	§24.9.4[3ed]	Limit max encryption strength for SASL and STARTTLS
AuthMechanisms	§24.9.5[3ed]	The AUTH mechanisms
AuthOptions	§24.9.6[3ed]	Tune authentication parameters
AuthRealm	§24.1.8[V8.13]	Cyrus SASL authentication realm to use
AutoRebuildAliases	§24.9.7[3ed]	Auto-rebuild the *aliases* database (V8.11 and earlier) (deprecated)
BadRcptThrottle	§24.9.8[3ed]	Slow excess bad RCPT TO: commands
BlankSub	§24.9.9[3ed]	Set unquoted space replacement character
CACertFile	§24.9.10[3ed]	File containing certificate authority certs
CACertPath	§24.9.11[3ed]	Directory with certificate authority certs
CheckAliases	§24.9.12[3ed]	Check RHS of *aliases*

Table 24-5. All options ordered by option name (continued)

Option name	sendmail text reference	Description
CheckpointInterval	§24.9.13[3ed]	Checkpoint the queue
ClassFactor	§24.9.14[3ed]	Multiplier for priority increments
ClientCertFile	§24.9.15[3ed]	File containing the client's public certificate
ClientKeyFile	§24.9.16[3ed]	File with the client certificate's private key
ClientPortOptions	§24.9.17[3ed]	Client port option settings
ColonOkInAddr	§24.9.18[3ed]	Allow colons in addresses
ConnectionCacheSize	§24.9.19[3ed]	SMTP connection cache size
ConnectionCacheTimeout	§24.9.20[3ed]	SMTP connection cache timeout
ConnectionRateThrottle	§24.9.21[3ed]	Incoming SMTP connection rate
ConnectionRateWindowSize	§24.1.13[V8.13]	Size of the window used to calculate connection rates (V8.13 and above)
ConnectOnlyTo	§24.9.22[3ed]	Connect only to one specified host
ControlSocketName	§24.9.23[3ed]	Path to control socket
CRLFile	§24.1.9[V8.13]	Certificate revocation list file (V8.13 and above)
DaemonPortOptions	§24.9.24[3ed]	Options for the daemon
DataFileBufferSize	§24.9.25[3ed]	Buffered I/O *df* size
DeadLetterDrop	§24.9.26[3ed]	Define *dead.letter* file location
DefaultAuthInfo	§24.9.27[3ed]	Source of AUTH information (deprecated)
DefaultCharSet	§24.9.28[3ed]	Define `Content-Type:` header's character set
DefaultUser	§24.9.29[3ed]	Default delivery agent identity
DefaultGroup	§24.9.29[3ed]	Default delivery agent group identity (deprecated)
DelayLA	§24.9.30[3ed]	Add one second SMTP sleep on high load
DeliverByMin	§24.9.31[3ed]	Set default DELIVERBY minimum
DeliveryMode	§24.9.32[3ed]	Set delivery mode
DHParameters	§24.9.33[3ed]	Parameters for DSA/DH cipher suite
DialDelay	§24.9.34[3ed]	Connect failure retry time
DirectSubmissionModifiers	§24.9.35[3ed]	Daemon direct submission flags
DontBlameSendmail	§24.9.36[3ed]	Relax security checks
DontExpandCnames	§24.9.37[3ed]	Prevent CNAME expansion
DontInitGroups	§24.9.38[3ed]	Don't use *initgroups*(3)
DontProbeInterfaces	§24.9.39[3ed]	Don't probe interfaces for `$=w`
DontPruneRoutes	§24.9.40[3ed]	Don't prune route addresses
DoubleBounceAddress	§24.9.41[3ed]	Errors when sending errors
EightBitMode	§24.9.42[3ed]	How to convert 8-bit input
ErrorHeader	§24.9.43[3ed]	Set error message header
ErrorMode	§24.9.44[3ed]	Specify mode of error handling

Table 24-5. All options ordered by option name (continued)

Option name	sendmail text reference	Description
FallbackMXhost	§24.9.45[3ed]	Fallback MX host
FallbackSmartHost	§24.1.10[V8.13]	Fallback host of last resort (V8.13 and above)
FastSplit	§24.9.46[3ed]	Suppress MX lookups on initial submission
ForkEachJob	§24.9.47[3ed]	Process queue files individually
ForwardPath	§24.9.48[3ed]	Set forward file search path
HelpFile	§24.9.49[3ed]	Specify location of the help file
HoldExpensive	§24.9.50[3ed]	Queue mail destined for expensive delivery agents
HostsFile	§24.9.51[3ed]	Specify alternate */etc/hosts* file
HostStatusDirectory	§24.9.52[3ed]	Location of persistent host status
IgnoreDots	§24.9.53[3ed]	Ignore leading dots in messages
InputMailFilters	§24.9.54[3ed]	Set the order of input filters
LDAPDefaultSpec	§24.9.55[3ed]	Default LDAP switches
LogLevel	§24.9.56[3ed]	Set (increase) the logging level
MailboxDatabase	§24.9.57[3ed]	Choose a mailbox database
MatchGECOS	§24.9.58[3ed]	Match recipient in GECOS field
MaxAliasRecursion	§24.9.59[3ed]	Maximum recursion of aliases
MaxDaemonChildren	§24.9.60[3ed]	Maximum forked daemon children
MaxHeadersLength	§24.9.61[3ed]	Set maximum header length
MaxHopCount	§24.9.62[3ed]	Set maximum hop count
MaxMessageSize	§24.9.63[3ed]	Maximum incoming message size
MaxMimeHeaderLength	§24.9.64[3ed]	Maximum MIME header length
MaxQueueChildren	§24.9.65[3ed]	Limit total concurrent queue processors
MaxQueueRunSize	§24.9.66[3ed]	Maximum queue messages processed
MaxRecipientsPerMessage	§24.9.67[3ed]	Maximum recipients per envelope
MaxRunnersPerQueue	§24.9.68[3ed]	Limit concurrent queue processors per queue group
MeToo	§24.9.69[3ed]	Send to me too (deprecated)
Milter	§24.9.70[3ed]	Tune interactions with the Milter filters
MinFreeBlocks	§24.9.71[3ed]	Define minimum free disk blocks
MinQueueAge	§24.9.72[3ed]	Skip queue file if too young
MustQuoteChars	§24.9.73[3ed]	Quote nonaddress characters
NiceQueueRun	§24.9.74[3ed]	Default *nice*(3) setting for queue processors
NoRecipientAction	§24.9.75[3ed]	How to handle no recipients in header
OldStyleHeaders	§24.9.76[3ed]	Allow spaces in recipient lists
OperatorChars	§24.9.77[3ed]	Set token separation operators
PidFile	§24.9.78[3ed]	Location of the *sendmail* pid file

Table 24-5. All options ordered by option name (continued)

Option name	sendmail text reference	Description
PostmasterCopy	§24.9.79[3ed]	Extra copies of bounce messages
PrivacyOptions	§24.9.80[3ed]	Increase privacy of the daemon
ProcessTitlePrefix	§24.9.81[3ed]	Process listing prefix
QueueDirectory	§24.9.82[3ed]	Location of queue directory
QueueFactor	§24.9.83[3ed]	Factor for high-load queuing
QueueFileMode	§24.9.84[3ed]	Default permissions for queue files
QueueLA	§24.9.85[3ed]	On high load, queue only
QueueSortOrder	§24.9.86[3ed]	How to presort the queue
QueueTimeout	§24.9.87[3ed]	Limit life of a message in the queue (deprecated)
RandFile	§24.9.88[3ed]	Source for random numbers
RecipientFactor	§24.9.89[3ed]	Penalize large recipient lists
RefuseLA	§24.9.90[3ed]	Refuse connections on high load
RejectLogInterval	§24.1.11[V8.13]	Interval to log that connections are still being rejected (V8.13 and above)
RequiresDirfsync	§24.1.12[V8.13]	Disable *fsync*(2) of directories
ResolverOptions	§24.9.91[3ed]	Tune DNS lookups
RetryFactor	§24.9.92[3ed]	Increment per job priority
RrtImpliesDsn	§24.9.93[3ed]	Return-Receipt-To: is DSN request
RunAsUser	§24.9.94[3ed]	Run as non-*root*
SafeFileEnvironment	§24.9.95[3ed]	Directory for safe file writes
SaveFromLine	§24.9.96[3ed]	Save Unix-style From lines
SendMimeErrors	§24.9.97[3ed]	Return MIME-format errors
ServerCertFile	§24.9.98[3ed]	File containing the server's certificate
ServerKeyFile	§24.9.99[3ed]	File with the server certificate's private key
ServiceSwitchFile	§24.9.100[3ed]	Switched services file
SevenBitInput	§24.9.101[3ed]	Force 7-bit input
SharedMemoryKey	§24.9.102[3ed]	Enable shared memory by setting the key
SingleLineFromHeader	§24.9.103[3ed]	Strip newlines from From: headers
SingleThreadDelivery	§24.9.104[3ed]	Set single-threaded delivery
SmtpGreetingMessage	§24.9.105[3ed]	The SMTP greeting message
StatusFile	§24.9.106[3ed]	Specify statistics file
SuperSafe	§24.9.107[3ed]	Queue everything just in case
TempFileMode	§24.9.108[3ed]	Permissions for temporary files
Timeout	§24.9.109[3ed]	Set timeouts
TimeZoneSpec	§24.9.110[3ed]	Set time zone
TLSSrvOptions	§24.9.111[3ed]	Tune the server TLS settings

Table 24-5. All options ordered by option name (continued)

Option name	sendmail text reference	Description
TrustedUser	§24.9.112[3ed]	Alternative to *root* administration
TryNullMXList	§24.9.113[3ed]	If no best MX record, use A or AAAA
UnixFromLine	§24.9.114[3ed]	Define the From format
UnsafeGroupWrites	§24.9.115[3ed]	Check unsafe group permissions (deprecated)
UseErrorsTo	§24.9.116[3ed]	Use Errors-To: for errors
UseMSP	§24.9.117[3ed]	Run as a mail submission program
UserDatabaseSpec	§24.9.118[3ed]	Specify user database
Verbose	§24.9.119[3ed]	Run in verbose mode
XscriptFileBufferSize	§24.9.120[3ed]	Set *xf* file buffered I/O limit

CHAPTER 25
The H (Headers) Configuration Command

The H (header) configuration file command specifies headers that are required for inclusion in the header portion of mail messages. Some headers, such as Date:, are added only if one is not already present. Others, such as Received: (§25.12.29[3ed]), are added even if one or more are already present.

25.1 What's New with V8.13

One major and three minor changes have been made regarding the handling of headers under V8.13:

- The $>+ operator no longer balances special characters (§25.1.1[V8.13]).
- The Message-Id: (§25.12.23[3ed]) header's value is now stored in the new ${msg_id} macro (§21.1.5[V8.13]).
- The Delivery-Receipt-To: header used by SIMS (Sun Internet Mail System), is treated the same as a Return-Receipt-To: header (§25.12.33[3ed]). That is, *sendmail* now converts it to a DSN reply.
- The confMESSAGEID_HEADER *mc* macro has been added, which allows you to define a different Message-Id: header value (§25.1.2[V8.13]).

25.1.1 No Balancing with $>+

Recall (§25.5[3ed]) that header values can be passed to rule sets using the $> and $>+ operators:

```
Hname: $> rule set
Hname: $>+ rule set        ← don't strip comments
```

Prior to V8.13, the $>+ operator caused a header's value to be passed to the specified rule set with RFC2882 comments intact:

```
text (comments)
<address> commment
```

Also, prior to V8.13, the `$>+` operator checked for special balancing characters and performed a correction when they were not found. For example, if a `Subject:` header's value arrived like this:

```
Subject: ----> test <----
```

The `$>+` operator would cause it to be corrected to the following:*

```
Subject: <----> test ----
```

The `$>+` operator would then cause the result to be passed to the appropriate rule set. But if a rule set was designed to detect the first form (the ---> test), it would fail because it would actually receive the second form.

Beginning with V8.13 *sendmail*, however, the `$>+` operator now no longer tries to balance special characters. And because header values are passed to rule sets as is, rule set header–checking is now more accurate, and useless warnings about unbalanced characters have been eliminated.

The characters that used to be special (and that needed to balanced) are shown in Table 25-1.

Table 25-1. Former $>+ balancing characters

Begin	End
"	"
(	)
[	]
<	>

See also (§18.1.1[V8.13]) for a discussion of rules and how they, too, no longer need to balance.

25.1.2 The confMESSAGEID_HEADER Macro

V8.13 has introduced a new *mc* macro that makes it possible to define a new value for the `Message-Id:` header:

```
define(`confMESSAGEID_HEADER´, `newvalue´)
```

The default for the `Message-Id:` header (§25.12.23[3ed]) looks like this:

```
<$t.$i@$j>
```

Here, the default provides an address of the form *`identifier@domain`*, which is enclosed in angle brackets. The `$t` macro (§21.9.86[3ed]) is an integer representation of the current time to the nearest minute, in the format *YYYYMMDDhhmm*. The `$i` macro

* Warnings complaining about unbalanced angle braces would also be *syslog*'d.

(§21.9.49[3ed]) is the unique queue identifier that is used to identify this message locally. The `$j` macro (§21.9.56[3ed]) is the fully qualified domain name of the local host.

We recommend that if you change `Message-Id:` header's value from this default, you maintain the format *identifier@domain* because that format is required by RFC2821, and because some sites will reject the message if it is not in that format.

25.2 Useful Tables

This chapter contains ten useful tables that cover headers and their use:

- Table 25-2 lists all the well-defined headers by name (§25.2.1[V8.13]).
- Table 25-3 lists header flags as used in *conf.c* (§25.2.2[V8.13]).
- Table 25-4 lists *mc* configuration commands that relate to headers (§25.2.3[V8.13]).
- Table 25-5 lists sender headers by name (§25.2.4[V8.13]).
- Table 25-6 lists recipient headers by name (§25.2.5[V8.13]).
- Table 25-7 lists identification and control headers by name (§25.2.6[V8.13]).
- Table 25-8 lists date and trace headers by name (§25.2.7[V8.13]).
- Table 25-9 lists other standard headers by name (§25.2.8[V8.13]).
- Table 25-10 lists MIME headers by name (§25.2.9[V8.13]).
- Table 25-11 lists `Resent-` headers by name (§25.2.10[V8.13]).

25.2.1 Header Names

The *name* portion of the `H` configuration command must be one of the names shown in Table 25-2. Other names do not produce an error but might confuse other programs that process them. Names marked with an asterisk are defined by RFC2822.

Table 25-2. Header names

apparently-to	bcc*	cc*	comments*
content-length	content-transfer-encoding	content-type	date*
delivery-receipt-to	disposition	encrypted	errors-to
from*	full-name	in-reply-to*	keywords*
mail-from	message	message-id*	notification-to
posted-date	precedence	received*	references*
reply-to*	resent-bcc*	resent-cc*	resent-date*
resent-from*	resent-message-id*	resent-reply-to	resent-sender*
resent-to*	return-path*	return-receipt-to	sender*
subject	text	to*	via
x400-received			

25.2.2 Header Behavior in conf.c

The *sendmail* program has a built-in understanding of many header names. How those names are used is determined by a set of flags in the source file that *conf.c* supplied with the source distribution. Site policy determines which flags are applied to which headers, but in general, *conf.c* applies them in the way that is best suited for almost all Internet sites.

If you desire to redefine the flags for a particular header name, look for the name's declaration in the C-language structure definition `HdrInfo` in *conf.c*. Be sure to read the comments in that file. Changes to header flags represent a permanent site policy change and should not be undertaken lightly.

The flags that determine header use are listed in Table 25-3. Note that each flag name is prefixed with an H_.

Table 25-3. Header flags in conf.c

Flag	sendmail text reference	Version	Description
H_ACHECK	§25.6.1[3ed]	V5 and above	Always process `?flags?`
H_BCC	§25.6.2[3ed]	V8.7 and above	Strip value from header
H_BINDLATE	§25.6.3[3ed]	V8.10 and above	Expand macros at time of delivery only
H_CHECK	§25.6.4[3ed]	V5 and above	Process `?flags?`
H_CTE	§25.6.5[3ed]	V8.7 and above	Is "content transfer encoding"
H_CTYPE	§25.6.6[3ed]	V8.7 and above	Is "content type"
H_DEFAULT	§25.6.7[3ed]	V5 and above	If already in headers, don't insert
H_ENCODABLE	§25.6.8[3ed]	V8.8 and above	Field can be RFC2047-encoded
H_EOH	§25.6.9[3ed]	V5 and above	Terminates all headers
H_ERRSTO	§25.6.10[3ed]	V8.1 to V8.6	An `Errors-to:` header
H_ERRORSTO	§25.6.10[3ed]	V8.7 and above	An `Errors-to:`-type header
H_FORCE	§25.6.11[3ed]	V5 and above	Insert header (allows duplicates)
H_FROM	§25.6.12[3ed]	V5 and above	Contains a sender address
H_RCPT	§25.6.13[3ed]	V5 and above	Contains a recipient address
H_RECEIPTTO	§25.6.14[3ed]	V8.7 and above	Header field has return-receipt information
H_RESENT	§25.6.15[3ed]	V5 and above	Is a `Resent-` header
H_STRIPCOMM	§25.6.16[3ed]	V8.10 and above	Strip comments for header checks
H_TRACE	§25.6.17[3ed]	V5 and above	Count these to get the hop count
H_USER	§25.6.18[3ed]	V8.11 and above	Came from a local user via SMTP
H_VALID	§25.6.19[3ed]	V5 and above	Has a validated field value

25.2.3 Headers and mc Configuration

Table 25-4 lists a number of *m4* macros that you may use in your *mc* configuration file. They deal directly with headers.

Table 25-4. Header-related mc macros

Macro	sendmail text reference	Sets What
confFROM_HEADER	§25.12.18[3ed]	Define the format for the From: header
confRECEIVED_HEADER	§25.12.29[3ed]	Define the format for the Received: header
confOLD_STYLE_HEADERS	§24.9.76[3ed]	Declare the OldStyleHeaders option
confMAX_HEADERS_LENGTH	§24.9.61[3ed]	Declare the MaxHeadersLength option
confMAX_MIME_HEADER_LENGTH	§24.9.64[3ed]	Declare the MaxMimeHeaderLength option
confSINGLE_LINE_FROM_HEADER	§24.9.103[3ed]	Declare the SingleLineFromHeader option
confUSE_ERRORS_TO	§24.9.116[3ed]	Declare the UseErrorsTo option, which affects the Errors-To: header
confNO_RCPT_ACTION	§24.9.75[3ed]	Declare the NoRecipientAction option, which affects the To:, Cc: and Bcc: headers
confRRT_IMPLIES_DSN	§24.9.93[3ed]	Declare the RrtImpliesDsn option, which affects the Return-Receipt-To: header
confMESSAGEID_HEADER	§25.1.2[V8.13]	Declares the Message-Id: header format

25.2.4 Sender Headers

Certain header *names* are assumed by *sendmail* to contain information about the various possible senders of a mail message. They are listed in Table 25-5 in descending order of significance. Addresses with the H_FROM flag (§25.6.12) are rewritten as sender addresses.

Table 25-5. Sender headers (most to least significant)

Header	sendmail text reference	Flags	Defined by
Resent-Sender:	§25.2.10[3ed]	H_FROM, H_RESENT	RFC2822
Resent-From:	§25.12.18[3ed]	H_FROM, H_RESENT	RFC2822
Resent-Reply-To:	§25.2.10[3ed]	H_FROM, H_RESENT	RFC2822
Return-Path:	§25.12.32[3ed]	H_FORCE, H_ACHECK, H_BINDLATE	RFC2822
Sender:	§25.12.34[3ed]	H_FROM	RFC2822
From:	§25.12.18[3ed]	H_FROM	RFC2822
Apparently-From:	§25.12.1[3ed]	n/a	Smail 3.0
Reply-To:	§25.12.31[3ed]	H_FROM	RFC2822
Disposition-Notification-To:	§25.12.15[3ed]	H_FROM	RFC2298

Table 25-5. Sender headers (most to least significant) (continued)

Header	sendmail text reference	Flags	Defined by
`Return-Receipt-To:`	§25.12.33[3ed]	H_RECEIPTTO	Obsolete
`Delivery-Receipt-To:`	§25.12.33[3ed]	H_RECEIPTTO	As of V8.13, a synonym for `Return-Receipt-To:`
`Errors-To:`	§25.12.17[3ed]	H_FROM, H_ERRORSTO	*sendmail* (deprecated)
`Full-Name:`	§25.12.19[3ed]	H_ACHECK	UUCP (obsolete)

Note that when returning bounced mail, *sendmail* always uses the envelope sender's address. If the special header `Errors-To:` appears in the message, and if the `UseErrorsTo` option (§24.9.116[3ed]) is set, a copy of the bounced mail is also sent to the address in that header.

25.2.5 Recipient Headers

Recipient headers are those from which one or more recipients can be parsed. Addresses in headers with the H_RCPT flag (§25.6.13) are rewritten as recipient addresses. When *sendmail* is invoked with the `-t` command-line switch, it gathers a list of recipients from all the headers marked with an H_RCPT flag and delivers a copy of the message to each.

The list of recipient headers used by *sendmail* is shown in Table 25-6.

Table 25-6. Recipient headers

Header	sendmail text reference	Flags	Defined by
`To:`	§25.12.37[3ed]	H_RCPT	RFC2822
`Resent-To:`	§25.2.10[3ed]	H_RCPT, H_RESENT	RFC2822
`Cc:`	§25.12.5[3ed]	H_RCPT	RFC2822
`Resent-Cc:`	§25.2.10[3ed]	H_RCPT, H_RESENT	RFC2822
`Bcc:`	§25.12.4[3ed]	H_RCPT, H_BCC	RFC2822
`Resent-Bcc:`	§25.2.10[3ed]	H_RCPT, H_BCC, H_RESENT	RFC2822
`Apparently-To:`	§25.12.2[3ed]	H_RCPT	Obsolete

25.2.6 Identification and Control Headers

Some headers serve to uniquely identify a mail message. Others affect the way *sendmail* processes a mail message. The complete list of all such identification and control headers is shown in Table 25-7.

Table 25-7. Identification and control headers

Header	sendmail text reference	Flags	Defined by
`Message-ID:`	§25.12.23[3ed]	none	RFC2822
`Resent-Message-Id:`	§25.2.10[3ed]	H_RESENT	RFC2822
`Message:`	§25.12.24[3ed]	H_EOH	Obsolete
`Text:`	§25.12.36[3ed]	H_EOH	Obsolete
`Precedence:`	§25.10[3ed]	n/a	All *sendmails*
`Priority:`	§25.12.28[3ed]	n/a	Many (maps to X.400)

Note that the `Precedence:` and `Posted-Date:` headers (discussed next) are hardcoded into *sendmail* rather than being declared in *conf.c*.

25.2.7 Date and Trace Headers

Date headers are used to document the date and time that a mail message was sent or forwarded. Trace headers (those with an H_TRACE header flag; §25.6.17[3ed]) are used to determine the hop count of a mail message and to document the message's travel from machine to machine. The list date and trace headers are shown in Table 25-8.

Table 25-8. Date and trace headers

Header	sendmail text reference	Flags	Defined by
`Date:`	§25.12.13[3ed]	none	RFC2822
`Posted-Date:`	§25.12.26[3ed]	n/a	Obsolete
`Resent-Date:`	§25.2.10[3ed]	H_RESENT	RFC2822
`Received:`	§25.12.29[3ed]	H_TRACE, H_FORCE	RFC2822
`Via:`	§25.12.38[3ed]	H_TRACE, H_FORCE	Obsolete
`Mail-From:`	§25.12.22[3ed]	H_TRACE, H_FORCE	Obsolete
`X-Authentication-Warning:`	§25.12.39[3ed]	H_FORCE	V8 *sendmail*
`X400-Received:`	§25.12.40[3ed]	H_TRACE, H_FORCE	IDA and V8 only

25.2.8 Other Headers

Some headers that you will see in mail messages are defined by the RFC2822 standard but are not otherwise internally defined by *sendmail*. A few of them, such as `Return-Path:`, should be declared in the configuration file. The others are usually inserted by MUAs. Table 25-9 lists these other headers.

Table 25-9. Other headers

Header	sendmail text reference	Flags	Defined by
`In-Reply-To:`	§25.12.20[3ed]	n/a	RFC2822
`References:`	§25.12.30[3ed]	n/a	RFC2822
`Keywords:`	§25.12.21[3ed]	n/a	RFC2822
`Subject:`	§25.12.35[3ed]	H_ENCODABLE	RFC2822
`Comments:`	§25.12.6[3ed]	H_FORCE, H_ENCODABLE	RFC2822
`Encrypted:`	§25.12.16[3ed]	n/a	RFC822
`Content-Length:`	§25.12.10[3ed]	H_ACHECK	SysV

25.2.9 MIME Headers

MIME is documented in RFC2045, RFC2046, RFC2047, RFC2048, and RFC2049. The *sendmail* program only cares about MIME when bouncing messages and when determining how to convert the message body between 7 and 8 bits. The MIME headers for which *sendmail* possesses special knowledge are shown in Table 25-10.

Table 25-10. MIME headers

Header	sendmail text reference	Flags	Defined by
`MIME-Version:`	§25.12.25[3ed]	n/a	RFC2045
`Content-Disposition:`	§25.12.8[3ed]	n/a	RFC2183
`Content-Id:`	§25.12.9[3ed]	n/a	RFC2045
`Content-Transfer-Encoding:`	§25.12.11[3ed]	H_CTE	RFC2045
`Content-Type:`	§25.12.11[3ed]	H_CTYPE	RFC2045

25.2.10 Forwarding with Resent Headers

Some MUAs allow users to forward (resend, bounce, or redirect) messages to other users. For example, the *mush*(1) MUA forwards the current message to the user named `fred` with the following command:

```
message 1 of 3> m -f fred
```

Messages can also be forwarded with *dist*(1) from *mh*(1) and from within other MUAs.

When messages are forwarded, header lines that describe the forwarding user must begin with the `Resent-` prefix. When a user receives such a message, that user sees two similar header lines:

```
From: original-sender
Resent-From: forwarding-sender
```

When both the original `From:` and the forwarded `Resent-From:` appear in the same header, the `Resent-` form is always considered the most recent.

If *sendmail* finds any header with a name beginning with `Resent-`, it marks that message as one that is being forwarded, preserves all `Resent-` headers, and creates any needed ones.

The few header names *sendmail* examines to see whether a mail message has been forwarded are listed in Table 25-11.

Table 25-11. Known resent headers

Resent- form of	Header
Resent-Bcc:	Bcc:
Resent-Cc:	Cc:
Resent-Date:	Date:
Resent-From:	From:
Resent-Message-ID:	Message-ID:
Resent-Reply-To:	Reply-To:
Resent-Sender:	Sender:
Resent-To:	To:

Index

Symbols

A

B

C

We'd like to hear your suggestions for improving our indexes. Send email to *index@oreilly.com*.

D

E

F

G

H

I

J

K

L

M

N

O

P

Q

R

S

T

U

V

W

About the Authors

Bryan Costales lives and works in California. He has been active in system administration for more than 20 years and has been writing articles and books about computer software for over 25 years. His most notable books are *C from A to Z* (Prentice Hall), *Unix Communications* (Howard Sams), and, of course, *sendmail* (O'Reilly). In his rare free time, he travels, writes fiction, and exercises with his dog.

George Jansen is a freelance writer who has worked with Bryan Costales on several of Bryan's books. His first novel, *The Jesse James Scrapbook* (Hilliard & Harris), was published in October. He lives in Mountain View, California, drives a 1983 Ford, and enjoys baseball, classic jazz, and taking long naps.

Gregory Neil Shapiro began his professional career as a systems administrator for Worcester Polytechnic Institute (WPI) after graduating from the institute in 1992. During his tenure as Senior Unix Systems Administrator, he became involved with beta testing the BIND name server, the sendmail mail transfer agent, and other Unix utilities such as emacs and screen. His involvement with sendmail grew until he became Lead Engineer at Sendmail, Inc., where he continued to support the open source version while working on Sendmail's commercial products. He later moved into the IT team at Sendmail, Inc. as the Senior Unix Network Systems Administrator. He is also a FreeBSD committer and has served as program committee member for BSDCon 2002 and program chair for BSDCon 2003. Greg lives in Emeryville, California and enjoys reading science fiction and fantasy books, traveling, and seeing movies and theater productions.

Claus Aßmann is a member of the Sendmail Consortium and works for Sendmail, Inc. He is the maintainer of sendmail 8 and currently designs and implements the next generation of sendmail. His main interests in computer technology are security and performance. He studied computer science at the University of Kiel in Germany, where he received his Ph.D. in 1992.

Colophon

Our look is the result of reader comments, our own experimentation, and feedback from distribution channels. Distinctive covers complement our distinctive approach to technical topics, breathing personality and life into potentially dry subjects.

The animal on the cover of *sendmail 8.13 Companion* is a leaf-nosed bat, also known as the "New World" or "California" leaf-nosed bat. These bats are native to North America (Southern California, Arizona, and Nevada), Central America, and South America, as well as to parts of the Caribbean. They are so named because of a distinctive, "leaf-shaped" triangle that projects upward from their noses.

The leaf-nosed bat is nocturnal, rising late in the evening. It leaves its home to search for food, returns home after eating, then goes out again in the very early morning hours to repeat the cycle. It feeds on such things as insects, fruit, pollen, frogs, and spiders. This particular type of bat does not hibernate in the winter, nor does it migrate. It tends to become a bit more lethargic in cold weather, however. It prefers dry, desert climates, choosing to live mostly in caves and old abandoned mines. It lives in one of two social settings: either one male and many females, or all males who seek out females only in mating season, which occurs in early fall.

Mary Brady was the production editor and copyeditor for *sendmail 8.13 Companion*. Sarah Sherman was the proofreader. Jamie Peppard and Claire Cloutier provided quality control. Johnna Van Hoose Dinse wrote the index. Mary Agner provided production support.

Ellie Volckhausen designed the cover of this book, based on a series design by Edie Freedman. The cover image is a 19th-century engraving from the Dover Pictorial Archive. Clay Fernald produced the cover layout with QuarkXPress 4.1 using Adobe's ITC Garamond font.

David Futato designed the interior layout. This book was converted by Julie Hawks to FrameMaker 5.5.6 with a format conversion tool created by Erik Ray, Jason McIntosh, Neil Walls, and Mike Sierra that uses Perl and XML technologies. The text font is Linotype Birka; the heading font is Adobe Myriad Condensed; and the code font is LucasFont's TheSans Mono Condensed. This colophon was written by Mary Brady.